WAITING FOR FIDEL

CHRISTOPHER HUNT

 WAITING FOR FIDEL

A MARINER ORIGINAL

HOUGHTON MIFFLIN COMPANY

BOSTON   NEW YORK   1998

For information about permission to reproduce selections from
this book, write to Permissions, Houghton Mifflin Company,
215 Park Avenue South, New York, New York 10003.

Library of Congress Cataloging-in-Publication Data
Hunt, Christopher, date.
  Waiting for Fidel / Christopher Hunt.
    p.   cm.
  "A Mariner original."
  ISBN 0-395-86886-6
  1. Cuba — Description and travel. 2. Hunt, Christopher, 1963–
— Journeys — Cuba.   I. Title.
  F1765.3.H86   1998
  972.9106'4 — DC21   97-42173   CIP

Printed in the United States of America

QUM 10 9 8 7 6 5 4 3 2 1

Book design and map by Melodie Wertelet

In memory of Mima,
who made all things possible

Straits of Florida

HAVANA ⊛
•Mariel   Matanzas Varadero

Santa
Clara

Playa Girón •
Bay of Pigs   Cienfuegos

Caribbean Sea

LEGEND
⊛ Capital
• City
- - Route

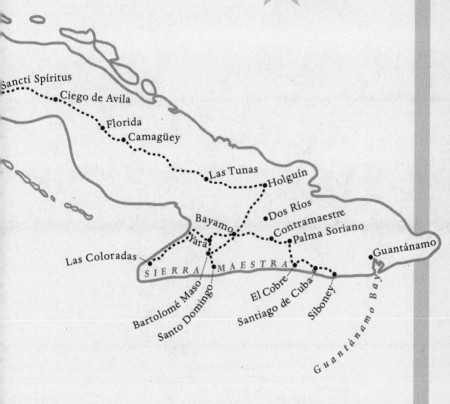

CUBA

Sancti Spíritus
Ciego de Avila
Florida
Camagüey
Las Tunas
Holguín
Dos Ríos
Bayamo
Contramaestre
Yara
Palma Soriano
Las Coloradas
Guantánamo
SIERRA   MAESTRA
Bartolomé Maso
Santo Domingo
El Cobre
Santiago de Cuba
Siboney
Guantánamo Bay

WAITING FOR FIDEL

1

RUM SPELLS TROUBLE. Cuba had taught me that much. Months on the island had also taught me how to handle the steady flow of people who, upon spotting a lone foreigner, sought anything from casual conversation to intricate favors. Distinguishing the good eggs from the bad became second nature; I knew which hands to shake and which to slap. But how my judgment lapsed long enough for Ricardo and his rum to vault into my life remains murky.

Clearer are the circumstances of our encounter. We met on the corner of Twenty-first and N Streets. Just a block away from the main drag in Havana's sleepy downtown district, the stoop where I squatted faced a hotel called the Capri, whose normally bustling entrance was dormant at three A.M. An hour had passed since the manager of the hotel's nightclub had extinguished the neon letters that spelled SALON ROJO.

That left only the street lamps to light our spot. High on weathered poles, the bulbs emanated a beige glow that tried and mostly failed to pierce the mix of warm air and ocean spray. The dimness transformed the intersection into a surreal stage where simple movements assumed unnatural heft. A man paused to check his wristwatch. A mongrel broke stride and nibbled its tattered fur before making a quick, self-conscious exit. A teenager gripping the tail of a fat, flat fish ambled by. Twice.

A lifeless cast peopled the ponderous scene. When not excavating her nostrils, a flabby woman scratched her ribs by sliding painted fingernails under a white halter. A husky teenager who had lost interest in me alternately sighed and adjusted the scarlet baseball cap on his head. The other five, maybe six, Cubans seated on the wedge of steps simply stared ahead like high schoolers on detention. Where did I fit in?

I didn't. My blue eyes and pink complexion made me a freak amid a brown-eyed crew whose colors ranged from caramel to cocoa. My jeans and T-shirt fit my physique. The Cubans, on the other hand, deferred to the tropical heat by wearing tops that hung from the shoulders and bottoms that ballooned below the waist. Switch on some salsa and every hip on that corner would break into a gentle, rhythmic grind. They were classic Cubans. I was undeniably American.

But we had two things in common. We all had problems. Theirs was a slow-burning fatigue. Cubans spent their lives treading to keep their heads above the surface. Spotting the next wave of change demanded constant vigilance. Mine, a more enviable quandary, related to a woman. Our other common ground was insomnia. Weary but not sleepy, awake but not alert, night crawlers sought and found company with whom to silently consider the state of their lives.

"*Aye, Cuba,*" sighed the teenager.

I rose from the steps. A few yards away a couple had turned a garage into a round-the-clock snack stand. Christmas lights strung above a counter illuminated the slim pickings. The menu was limited to pale hot dogs and single slices of ham suffocated by dry bread. The drink options were coffee and a powdered fruit punch. Neither I nor the local perusing the larder found reason to disturb the vendor's tinkering with his boombox.

We exchanged nods and names, his being Ricardo. The brown skin sagging from his face's bones and gray flecks in his thin mustache placed him close to forty. His T-shirt and slacks had also seen better days. Yet his accessories, tennis shoes and a Chicago White Sox baseball cap, were mint. Leaning two bony forearms on the counter, Ricardo moaned that he couldn't afford a sandwich, which was selling for ten pesos, less than fifty U.S. cents.

Still, the pauper had expensive tastes. Ricardo reached an arm behind the counter and grabbed a bottle. A broad label said Havana Club. A smaller sticker indicated that the booze had been aged for seven years. The mulatto twisted off the cap and tipped a half-inch of amber liquid into his mouth. After a hard swallow and a slight gasp he held out the bottle.

I took the handoff. The rum left a tingle on my tongue, a sign that Ricardo was drinking the good stuff rather than the acid swilled by most Cubans. Appreciative of a man willing to share the wealth, I dropped my doubts about the food's freshness and bought a ham sandwich for each of us. The friendship sealed, we began to chat. I asked why he kept such late hours.

"Working."

"At three o'clock in the morning?"

Ricardo listened to a digest of my story before spending a half-hour explaining his "work." The man was doing nothing different from any of his compatriots. He was scrambling to survive. True, he went further than most, breaking the spirit as well as the letter of the law. Equally true is that other Cubans wouldn't hesitate to mimic the latter-day pirate had they less fear and more cunning. I liked Ricardo. But he made me nervous.

Cubans were friendly. Ricardo was too friendly. Appreciative though I was for the late company, I recognized that mixing with foreigners was still officially discouraged. And he was too frank. Thrilled when people talked straight, I also knew that excessive candor, particularly excessive public candor, could lead to trouble. I should have gone home to bed. Instead I changed the subject.

"You have a family?"

"I live there," said Ricardo, pointing down the block. "I have a wife, two children. She complains that I'm not in her bed at night. She's humping other men. I know it. But what can I do? I have to feed my kids. Right?"

I nodded as if I knew.

"Rum?" asked Ricardo, extending the bottle.

I tilted another mouthful of Havana Club between my lips. My throat was still aglow when a woman in a cotton blouse and a flowing skirt sidled up to the spot where Ricardo and I had seated ourselves. She didn't speak. Nor did she show any expectation of being spoken to. I held out the bottle, which she accepted without hesitation.

"Beautiful girl," said Ricardo.

I nodded. The woman settled between us but still didn't speak. She spread her feet, rested her elbows on her knees, and joined the meditative stillness. The only sound was the distant pulse of salsa muffled by air thickened by sea spray and human sweat.

"*Aye, Cuba,*" sighed the teenager.

A sedan stopping at the curb broke the ensuing silence. Two of the passengers were European. Italian was my guess. With them were two unmistakably Cuban women: afros pinned back, lips painted red, they refused to let the confines of a car keep them from bouncing to the music blasting from the car's stereo. Brought to his feet by the sight of the party on wheels, Ricardo approached the driver. The exchange of words ended with Ricardo's sliding beside the couple in the back seat. As the car pulled away, he pointed to the bottle of rum he had left beside my leg.

"Christopher, it's yours," he called out.

"Is Ricardo a friend of yours?" I asked the woman.

Rosa hadn't known Ricardo for long. He was a Habanero, a Havana native. She had only just arrived from Niquero, a town on Cuba's southeast coast. The move to the capital was the brainchild of her teenage sister, who grew tired of being broke and bored in a provincial backwater. The sister persuaded a girlfriend to accompany her to the capital. With nothing holding her back — "no job, no boyfriend" — Rosa joined the expedition. The easterners rented a room, where they spent most of their days "resting."

"Where's your sister now?"

"With a man." Minutes passed before she spoke again. "You look tired."

"I am tired," I said.

"You should go to sleep."

"I should."

But I didn't. Havana's streets were an opiate. Whether tired, confused, or just plain overwhelmed, I relaxed by staring at Cuba's lugubrious pace. Self-hypnosis often fathered tiny revelations, moments when complications evaporated and left behind nuggets of truth. Other times a calm spell served as a prologue to the appearance of unimaginable people and unpredictable events. What followed fell squarely into the latter category.

A white police car sighed to a halt at the curb. The Cubans appeared not to notice the officers. I, on the other hand, felt my teeth clench while the officer in the passenger seat of the four-door Lada looked hard at the crew on the stoop. He beckoned for one of the Cubans to approach the vehicle. Nobody moved. Half of the group still hadn't noticed the cops. Clarifying his first gesture with a second, more precise movement, the policeman pointed a finger at the odd man out on the steps, at the only foreigner on the block, at me.

I pointed at myself in disbelief. Cuba's cops rarely bothered visitors. Not that I shouldn't have been nabbed months earlier. My activities had been at best naughty and at worst illegal. Had I declared my purpose upon arrival I would have been jailed, questioned, and sent packing with a baggage tag that said "Counterrevolutionary."

Flight was pointless. The Russian police car could certainly outrun me. If it didn't, an outsider had nowhere to run to, nowhere to hide on an island where citizens were expected to snoop for the state. My only option was to put on a brave face and show the locals that the *Yanqui* had dignity. Left hand gripping my notebook, right hand clutching the neck of the rum bottle, I walked the plank of pavement separating the stoop from the vehicle.

Neither the driver nor the cop who flagged me down spoke when I reached the car. The officer in the passenger seat jerked his thumb backward. Following the path of the gesture, I noticed a third man in the darkness of the back seat. A White Sox cap was the first thing to register as I peered in the rear window. Then I saw a familiar face.

"We want to take you somewhere," said Ricardo.

My belly turned to lead. Fairly certain of what was happening — by all appearances I had been duped by an undercover officer — I tugged open the back door and lowered myself onto the seat. I looked at Ricardo, who patted my knee without catching my eye.

"Let's go," he said to the officer at the wheel.

The Lada began to roll. Looking out the side window, I saw my stoopmates tracking my disappearance. As expressionless as witnesses to an execution, they must have known what I would learn. I would be out of Cuba within forty-eight hours.

2

ASK ANY SKYJACKER: moments after entering Castro's airspace is no time to reconsider a porous plan to winter in Cuba. Too many things could go wrong.

Take the crew. Each of the Cuban stewardesses looked capable of leveling a cream puff heading for the cockpit. The Soviet-trained pilots probably wouldn't think twice about the demands of an unarmed intruder. But say they did. What control tower would believe that an American wanted to reverse aviation history by diverting a Havana-bound aircraft to Miami?

Outlaw fantasies gave way to rational thought. My real worry was Cuba's immigration form. There was nothing unusual about the landing card. Address, nationality, and passport number were the name, rank, and serial number of overseas travel. Still, I balked at a standard question. Profession?

The truth could lead to trouble. That much I had gleaned from calls placed before leaving New York City. My search for travel tips began at the Cuban mission to the United Nations. The staff directed me to Washington, D.C. There, holed up in the Swiss Embassy, was a corps of Cuban officials who handled questions such as mine: how could an American travel to Cuba?

"What is your business?" asked the bureaucrat manning the lines.

"I'm a writer."

"That is not a business." Hearing no protest, he continued. "Writers must have a sponsor, an organization in Cuba."

"And without a sponsor?"

"You can visit as a tourist. No writing."

My urge to see Cuba was born during the fiftieth birthday of the U.N., a pageant that attracted a *Who's Who* of big shots. The list included Nelson Mandela, Boris Yeltsin, and whoever happened to be running Japan at the time. Saddam Hussein and Muammar Qaddafi stayed home. Other villains — Yasser Arafat, for one — and despots — China's Ziang Zemin comes to mind — would sooner have dropped their Uzis than miss the swirl of soirées attended by every leader.

Well, almost every leader. Of the two hundred–plus heavies, one was excluded from the fun. Welcome at tedious speeches and dreary events put on by the U.N., Fidel Castro was persona non grata on the private-party circuit. New York's mayor left him off the list for his fête. President Clinton barred the Cuban from a black-tie mixer. Why was Castro the blackest of the sheep?

Hard-liners cited economics. Castro remained a communist even though other Reds had swapped hammers and sickles for spreadsheets and stock options. Other critics said he was a menace even though more than three decades had passed since he helped Khrushchev aim missiles at America. More credible protesters charged him with murder, torture, and a fear of free elections.

The flap lured me to the scene of Castro's arrival. The Cuban mission in New York City looked like Hitler's bunker in Berlin.

Iron barricades kept the entrance clear. Other barriers restricted access to the sidewalks. Men in blue escorted the block's residents to their doors. Bomb-sniffing dogs, riot police, and detectives outnumbered the demonstrators and rubberneckers braving a chilly downpour.

I took shelter under the awning of a posh apartment building. So did an unshaven dogwalker named Merritt. He filled my Cuba file with a five-minute discourse that touched on Castro (only Jordan's King Hussein had ruled longer), the New York visit (the Cuban's first since 1979), and "the embargo" (Washington's long-standing ban on commerce with the island). A bleached blonde dripping with costume jewelry pitched in her thoughts. She asked her square-jawed escort to explain the commotion outside her home.

"The fiftieth anniversary of the U.N.," he said.

"Oh." Pause for thought. "Why are all these people in front of my building?"

"Fidel Castro is staying across the street."

"Oh." Pause for thought. "Is he the guy with the beard?"

"Right."

"It looks terrible." Pause for thought. "Somebody should tell him."

Two events completed the link between the rainy vigil and the Havana-bound Tupolev. The first was a televised interview with the Cuban president. Focused on the man for the first time, I was struck by the seventy-year-old's style. The infamous ragged beard looked oddly dignified above a blue suit, white shirt, and striped necktie. Pressing his fingers together while awaiting questions, he had the cool confidence of a king.

Castro was captivating. Asked a question, he paused. His answers, invariably deliberate and intelligent, began in soft, measured tones. An avuncular tenor gave way to the fervor of a Baptist minister. He stressed points by hammering an index finger or clenching his dark eyebrows. The gestures belied something remarkable, something I never saw in American leaders. Fidel Castro truly believed what he said.

I was hooked. He may well have been a murderer. A torturer? I couldn't say. But if the man was an outlaw, he was a magnetic one, like Pancho Villa. It was easy to imagine dropping all for the honor and adventure of riding with Castro.

The second circumstance was a call from Rick, a friend who hadn't let his U.S. passport keep him out of Cuba. Rick said that a mutual friend, Carolyn, had gone one step further. On holiday in Havana, she had met Castro. I wondered, Could I do the same?

"No problem," said Carolyn. "Fidel loves foreigners."

I was curious. Castro had spawned spitting rage during his stay in New York. One of his illegitimate daughters walked around the city with a placard that said, "My dad's a killer." Equally rabid fans applauded Cuba's president; hundreds of supporters jammed a Harlem church to hear him speak. The more I saw, the more I read, the more I wondered who had it right. Was Fidel Castro a devil or an angel?

There was little to keep me from seeking an answer. I wasn't working. I had neither a wife to please nor kids to feed. In other words, I could disappear for two weeks or two months, and nobody would know the difference. The worst-case scenario had me returning in midwinter with a tropical tan and a suitcase of cigars.

Oh. There was that federal law called the Cuban Assets Control Regulations. Designed during the Kennedy administration, the rules didn't actually forbid Americans from traveling to the island. The crime was to spend money once you got there. Those who did so were guilty of "trading with the enemy," an offense punishable by as much as $250,000 and as many as ten years in prison. Daunted by the tough talk, I was assured that Uncle Sam never nabbed sightseers.

What about the other side? How would Cuba feel about an American traveler?

The question monopolized my mind as the airplane dropped into Havana in the autumn of 1995. Having never fibbed to a bureaucrat senior to an Internal Revenue Service clerk, I wanted to come clean. I wanted to say that I was a writer. I wanted to say that I had come to Cuba to meet Fidel Castro. I also wanted to avoid expulsion and/or jail.

A coffee-colored woman welcomed me to Cuban tarmac. The rest of a female hospitality crew beckoned for me to enter the terminal, a concrete block painted in Spanish that said, "I'm what you're looking for." Even the peach-fuzzed immigration officer smiled until he looked at my arrival card. A frown crossed his face when he saw my profession: investor.

"What's an investor?"

Delivered in Spanish reeking from five years in mothballs, my explanation of compound interest and capital gains stupefied the officer. Judging from the O formed by his open mouth, the official thought he was looking at an alchemist.

He lifted his stamp and riffled through my passport in search of a spot to chop. Confused after two tours of my document, the teenager posed another question. "Visa?"

I pointed to my passport.

"No visa."

I handed him my air ticket.

"No visa."

With nothing left to hand over, I could only repeat what my inquisitor had been saying — "no visa" — and vow to seek-and-destroy the Bahamian who had neglected to clip the entry permit to my ticket during my stopover on the island, one of the back doors Americans used to enter Cuba. There was nothing left to do but wait and see how Cuba handled Americans trying to enter without permission.

The delay attracted a second officer, this one twice as old. Epaulets on his scrawny shoulders indicated bureaucratic muscle. The calculated stiffness in his step suggested that he liked to flex it. After a brief exchange with his subordinate and a critical glance at me, the immigration boss directed me to a row of plastic seats. There I pondered my fate for the twenty minutes it took for him to consider my case and prepare his interrogation.

"How much money have you got?" he asked.

"Enough."

"How much?"

I kept quiet. Not that I objected to bribing my way into Cuba. It simply seemed unwise to show my entire hand to a man with the power to clean me out and send me home. The delay tactic angered the little man. He puffed his pecs.

"It is my duty to know how much money you have," he said.

I admitted to a couple grand in traveler's checks.

"Give me twenty dollars."

I pulled two tens from my wallet.

"Enjoy yourself," he said, holding out a tourist visa.

I waited for the catch. None appeared. The official shuffled back to his post. I was free to enter Cuba.

3

SOLIDARIDAD CONTRA EL BLOQUEO
SOCIALISMO O MUERTE
¡REVOLUCION!

No space was safe from Cuban patriotism. Or so I thought as a taxi carried me through the viscous night. Low walls along the Havana-bound lanes bore giant letters that spelled out SOLIDARITY AGAINST THE BLOCKADE and SOCIALISM OR DEATH. A simpler exhortation — REVOLUTION! — was splayed on a billboard. IT'S TIME TO SCREAM REVOLUTION, THE REVOLUTION LIVES IN YOUR WORK, and other motivators had been painted, punctuated, and left for contemplation.

"Who paints the signs?" I asked the driver.

"Fidel."

The heavy cabbie didn't sound like the joking type. Our conversation never veered much beyond one word. Name? Alberto. Car? Toyota.

The quiet inside the auto exaggerated a dull thump on the outside. I looked at Alberto. He looked at the rearview mirror, crossed himself, and kissed the tips of his fingers. I twisted around and saw a mound of gray fur and scarlet flesh. Probably the remains of a dog, the carcass had been overrun several times. But by what?

Ours was the only vehicle on the road. Every few minutes Alberto passed the shadow of a cyclist slowly pedaling along the road's rim. Pairs and trios of pedestrians plodding on the road's dim shoulder showed no more lust for life. I hoped things would pick up nearer my destination, the Hotel Ambos Mundos, which my travel guide billed as the place Ernest Hemingway slept and wrote when not fishing or drinking.

Alberto didn't know the landmark. Nor was it easy to find somebody able to pinpoint the place. Narrower than they were dark, the streets of Havana's Old Quarter were empty at eleven P.M. A five-minute search turned up just two people. One knew of Hemingway but not the hotel. The other knew the hotel — "Closed for repairs until March," he said — but hadn't heard of its link to the author.

I landed at the Caribbean, a hotel rating a half-star above tenement. The lobby looked like a sleepy social club featuring a refrigerator and a wall-mounted television. Two western men in polyester shirts and three local women in cotton shorts turned to examine a newcomer.

A chunky clerk slid a registration form across the reception counter. In exchange for a key she took my passport, payment for two nights, and my ball-point pen. Nobody offered to show me my fourth-floor room. Nobody told me to mind the wires around the light switch. The chambermaid forgot to turn down my stained covers.

Propaganda recaptured my attention when, at daybreak, I stepped into the street. WE WILL NEVER RETURN TO CAPITALISM was painted in red on the wall of a ten-story block beside the hotel. Nearby, blue paint said, FIRM, DECISIVE AND CERTAIN OF VICTORY, WE WILL DEFEND THE GLORY OF AMERICA IN REVOLUTION. Years of sun had left the letters faded on the white background. The only sign of maintenance was to a slogan that said LONG LIVE THE 36TH ANNIVERSARY OF THE REVOLUTION! A slash through the "6" made a "7."

More than the paint had chipped along Paseo de Martí, a broad boulevard flanked by grandeur from another era. Designed in the Old World, the facades of buildings comprised an arsenal of moldings, columns, and terraces poised to drop and clobber passersby. Iron terraces not missing bars were riddled with rust. Shutters looked just a breeze away from coming unhinged.

The hot air wasn't shifting. Nor were the people. An old man in striped pajama bottoms and a white T-shirt leaned on the rail of his balcony and examined the steps up to the promenade bisecting the avenue. On another terrace a woman in curlers fixed her gaze on an indefinite spot above the canopy of trees over the raised walkway. Both heads turned when a blast of static shattered the meditative mood. The culprit was a congested loudspeaker, which ripped a second electronic fart. An explosion of horns and percussion followed. Three full seconds passed before the decibels fell to a roar recognizable as music, salsa. At nine A.M.?

The neighborhood welcomed the wake-up. Residents drifted to windows and terraces. Reactions ranged from pleasant surprise to tempered joy. Shirtless men began to sway. Women in housecoats grooved to the beat. Mothers bounced babies.

Down on the promenade, a mob was forming. Kids of every shade on the beige to brown spectrum poured from the doorways of the primary schools along Paseo. The boys wore scarlet slacks and white shirts. The uniform for girls was a pinafore over a blouse. Some of the children had red kerchiefs around their necks. All grappled for the hula hoops, jump ropes, and skateboards tossed out like chum by the teachers supervising the mayhem known as recess.

Only one group of girls minded the music. Gathered in a tight circle, they were split into two teams. One bunch practiced grinding unformed hips in taut circles. The others pumped pelvises at a pace common to nature films and porno flicks. The movements troubled their teacher. But the thick woman's attempts to break the dance fever only encouraged the students. Hips ground harder. Pelvises pumped faster. The schoolmarm shook her head and joined the fun.

"You like the girls?" The speaker's taut skin and soft, brown eyes were those of a man no older than twenty-five. His baggy shorts and battered T-shirt were a drop-kick away from the scrap heap. "Cuban girls? You like Cuban girls?"

"Yes. I mean, I think Cuban girls are very nice, very pretty," was the start of my fitful answer to a question I would be asked over and over in the months to come.

"I'm going to teach you something," said the young man, who told me that his name was Juan.

The scrawny Cuban steered me toward the sea. With every pace he spewed a fresh fact. Did I know that Cubans ate six pounds of rice per month? That the monument ahead of us honored a group of young doctors who died fighting for freedom? That foreigners often mispronounced Malecón, the boulevard that snaked around Havana's waterfront, turning it into *maricón,* Spanish for "fag"?

We passed a truck-size billboard whose tricolor letters said, CUBANS, LET'S GO FORWARD TOGETHER. How, I asked, did he feel about the propaganda? Juan flipped the back of his hand.

Other Cubans were equally insouciant. Beside the memorial we saw a corps of armed youths. Soldiers preparing for drill, was my first thought. My second impression was that the college-age men and women were unfit to fight. No two uniforms matched. Legs were covered with fatigues, khakis, or jeans. The women wore sandals. The men preferred battered sneakers and black shoes. There wasn't a combat boot in sight. Both sexes tugged at shirts and fussed with hair. Two coeds compared earrings.

The girls were under attack from a smooth-cheeked man trying to impress them by spinning his rifle like a pinwheel. He grimaced as the weapon slipped from his hands and clattered against the pavement. The girls tittered. They mocked their suitor's machismo by attempting the maneuver he botched. Another trainee straightened his posture, threw rifle over shoulder, and goose-stepped five paces before collapsing in a fit of giggles.

Standing tall among the motley crew was a model revolutionary. Hollywood handsome, the young man wore a blue work shirt that accented his V-shaped frame. Olive-green pants hugged his behind. The maroon beret draped over his head added an authoritative touch. Red high-top sneakers made him hip.

Two she-soldiers were tracking the stallion's every move. Squatting with their rifles erect, the shapely pair looked at each other, nodded, then continued to follow the object of their desire. One of the lustlorn girls whispered in her pal's ear. The next time he passed, two right hands began to slide, slowly, up and down the barrels of their weapons.

"Cuban girls," said Juan.

The unclouded sun made me squint as the scrawny Cuban led me across the Malecón's lanes. Steered left, I felt a drop slide down my temple. More sweat followed as we ambled along a walkway whose curve formed a giant sickle on the water's edge.

A waist-high stone wall blocked the view of the sea sloshing against Havana. On the opposite side of the Malecón, ocean spray had taken its toll on a row of buildings. Coats of pink, aqua, and yellow had faded into dull pastels. Boards replaced windows. Cracks in the faces of the low-rise homes were a prelude to falling plaster. Wooden beams supported elegant archways.

Juan's chatter diverted me from the decay. What was my job? Did I have brothers and sisters? A car? He rattled off more information, such as the fact that Madonna's (then) boyfriend was Cuban-born.

The withering enthusiasm melted my concern that Cubans would cold-shoulder a capitalist. Others joined the welcome wagon. Seated along the sea wall, clusters of three or more women nodded and smiled. Men waved and shouted greetings. Not even snuggling couples missed a chance to hail an outsider.

There was one exception, a teenager whose white tank top

exposed a set of granite shoulders. Pedaling on the Malecón's bicycle lane demanded just a fraction of his attention. The remainder was devoted to the girl seated on his handlebars. Facing her man, the mulatta had necklaced her arms around his neck and fixed her lips onto his. The pair rolled by, oblivious of all but their embrace.

"If you have heart surgery in the United States, how much do you pay?"

Twenty thousand dollars was my guess.

"In Cuba, heart surgery is free."

I countered that the surgery might cost less if you had insurance, if you had a couple thousand bucks to cover the premiums, and if your deductible weren't too high.

"Here it is free for everybody. How many unemployed people are there in the United States?"

"About five percent."

"Here everybody has a job. In the USA there are people without homes. True?"

"True."

"Here everybody has a home."

I changed the subject. Rising from the patch of green at the end of the Malecón's curve was a simple palace. Or was it a luxury prison? Capped with terra-cotta tiles, the roofs of twin towers at either end of a long midsection looked suited to armed guards. Did they keep intruders out or prisoners in? Either way, the eight-story edifice resembled a phoenix rising from the surrounding rot.

"The Hotel Nacional," said Juan.

The hotel was the site of Carolyn's encounter with Castro. Wandering through the lobby in search of diversion, she and a friend had ambled into a reception. Two stylish New Yorkers stuck out in a room filled with tribal wear from Africa and polyester from Eastern Europe. The president took note. He parted the sea of people and beckoned for the ladies to approach. What did Carolyn learn?

"The man is a fox" was her main impression.

Hope of gleaning further information drove me up a road

that bent around the rear of the hotel. Two dark men in light blazers stood by the entrance. Beyond the toughs lay an oval drive with a landscaped center. At the far end a red carpet spilled down the steps from a pair of swinging doors. These were manned by a pair of doormen whose white uniforms dripped with ropes of gold braid. I headed for the front door.

Juan stopped short.

"Let's have a look," I said.

"It's better if I wait here." He changed his mind. "I've got to go. I have something to do."

Fidel Castro wasn't in the hotel. Outside, a trio of preteens grinned as I wandered past their perch halfway down the hill from the hotel. My return smile was taken as an invitation.

"Where are you from?" asked the boldest boy. "Spain?"

I shook my head.

"Italy?"

A firmer no.

"France? Yes, of course you are French."

I wrinkled my nose like a child chewing liver.

My inquisitor's playmates joined the game. Germany and Canada were their best guesses. More denials bred more guesses. Holland. Sweden. Japan. Japan? The kids took one last stab. A solemn conference ended in collective disbelief of their earlier stupidity. "Soviet," said their spokesman. "You look like a Soviet." The guys turned gloomy when I shook my head. The mood shifted when I divulged the secret.

"America," squealed the slaphappy kids. "He's American."

The incline ended at a street called La Rampa. The main drag of the downtown district lacked the bustle of most capital cities. There wasn't a suit or a cell phone in sight. Nor was there anything that looked like an office building. The people who moved did so with deliberate ease. Most of the Cubans were simply idling in place.

The liveliest of the lot was a man whose matted hair reached the neckline of a tattered T-shirt. He grabbed me by the elbow and asked where I came from. I hesitated, in part because he looked dangerous, and in part because the kids' enthusiastic reaction hadn't erased my suspicion that locals might not take kindly to an American. Still, I wanted to know. More curious than fearful, I told him.

"United States?" he gasped. "Don't leave."

The grungy man disappeared into the shop behind him. Moments later he returned, followed by a muscular, crew-cut buddy carrying a dirty glass with two inches of murky liquid. He held out the drink and said, "This is for you."

I eyed the glass. The men eyed me.

"Rum," he said. "Cuban rum."

My tongue seized up the moment the stuff passed my lips. The alarm reached my throat, which tried to block the liquid. I choked. My ears rang and my eyes teared. The certainty that I had been poisoned evaporated only when the scraggly man laughed, grabbed the glass, and knocked back the rest of the drink.

The unkempt fellow couldn't do enough for an American visitor. He took me into the shop, a cafeteria selling disks of dough that, when brushed with tomato paste, posed as pizza. Was I hungry? If so, he could get me free food. How about rum? Would I like more? Did I have a bike? Paid to watch the bicycles of customers waiting in line, he would guard mine for free. Even if I didn't have wheels, I should come by. To talk. To drink.

The final respondent to the haphazard opinion poll was a fleshy man seated under a tree near the meeting of La Rampa and the Malecón. Well over sixty, minus most of his teeth, days away from his last shave, he looked as beaten as the neighborhood. Stretched in front of him were a crutch and a row of cassettes. When I stopped, he looked up.

"Salsa," he said matter-of-factly. "You like salsa?"

"I'm learning."

"Friend, where are you from?"

"America."

"*¡COÑO CARAJO!*"

Jammed together, two of the uglier words in the Spanish

language translated into something along the lines of "Holy shit!" The codger started to cackle. He rose, steadied himself, and threw his arms around me. He grabbed my shoulders and pulled back for a longer look before asking a nagging question: was New York a state as well as a city?

"That's confusing," he said when I confirmed the nagging rumor. "But you should know. You're an American. True?"

"True."

He hugged me again.

4

BORIS SEEMED AN ODD NAME for a mulatto tall enough to touch ceilings. It made more sense when he explained his father's infatuation with all things Soviet around the time of his birth in the mid-1960s. Since then he had sprouted a mustache thick enough to cover his upper lip. The growth garbled his speech. One phrase, however, stuck out: *"No hay problema."*

No problem. In our first half-hour Boris repeated it no less than a dozen times. Every iteration increased my concern that there was, in fact, a significant problem with our deal.

"Are you sure I can rent your apartment?"

"No problem."

"It's not against the law?"

"No problem."

"And the neighbors won't report me?"

Boris's answers probably would have differed little had I asked whether Castro killed Kennedy. The gangly giant had just wrapped his fingers around a wad of my dollars. In a country where monthly wages were averaging less than eight bucks, the prospect of returning several twenty-dollar bills could probably breed tales taller than Everest. "No problem" would be repeated until I was in trouble or out of twenties.

The look of my lodgings did little for my confidence. Years

had passed since paint touched the outside of the four-story block. Laundry hung from rusted balconies. Shutters dangled at unnatural angles. Moving to the front door, I found that plywood had replaced glass in the frame. Bulbs intended to light the spiral of stairs either didn't work or didn't exist.

A gate of iron bars guarded the fourth-floor apartment. The front door had two bolts. Both the door and the gate, warned Boris, were to be locked at all times. Before returning to his in-laws' home, where his family of three would bunk until my departure, Boris added a final thought.

"Don't let anybody in the door."

"Who's going to come to the door?"

"Nobody. But don't let him in."

Maybe the bogeymen *were* imaginary. The dangers inside the dank apartment were real. A trial of the television in the uncarpeted living room produced a blizzard of specks. In the kitchen, a coffin-size refrigerator alternately groaned to life and rattled to a halt. Running the water required twisting a faucet beyond the bars guarding the window.

The stove was no less idiosyncratic. Nothing happened when I turned on the gas. I remembered the taped rod hanging behind the stove. Boris had shown me how scraping the metal tip against a burner created a spark. He hadn't pointed out that the rod was attached to a wire inserted in a socket. Grabbing the exposed end of the homemade lighter shot a disconcerting ZZZTTT up my forearm.

The bathroom was no easier to operate. An attachment the shape of a can took the place of a standard shower head. A sliding lever allowed bathers to select cold, warm, or hot water, which Boris promised would gush. My test of the warm setting produced a dribble. Hopeful that less heat would mean more volume, I reached a wet hand up to the lever. ZZZTTT.

I lay on the bed and retraced the steps that had brought me from the Cuban mission in New York to the apartment in Havana. The backtracking lasted until the voice of a woman wafted in the windows, which opened onto an air shaft. She sounded strong, though not particularly young. I never learned her name or, in the weeks I spent a few feet above her window, saw her face. I did, however, know the name of her lover.

"Lázaro." Twenty or so seconds later she repeated the name. "Lázaro."

The woman reiterated the name in octaves high and low. The decibels also varied. Embarrassed by my sightless voyeurism, I wondered whether an awareness of her audience would alter the woman's course. And what about Lázaro? How would Lázaro feel about my tuning in to his lovemaking?

The woman increased her vocabulary. First came *"mi amor."* "My love" was joined by other sounds of Cuban passion, some intelligible, others not. Words devolved to grunts. These ended, leaving the three of us in a sweaty, midday silence.

For a time, meeting Fidel Castro took a back seat to another priority. I had found a home. What I hadn't found was a level of comfort. I felt strange in Cuba, like a man sleepwalking through somebody else's dream. To snap out of it, I forced myself out the door and into my new neighborhood.

The grid called Vedado was filled mostly by two-story homes. The original owners had decorated the faces of their homes with moldings, ledges, and other frills. Iron gates separated cramped yards from numbered streets and lettered avenues. Covered verandahs provided a place to unwind. Through doors left open for ventilation, I spied high-ceilinged parlors built in another era.

Remnants of high times contrasted with the streets' torpor. Vedado was dead. The roads were traffic-free. On the edges, parked cars had gathered weeks of dust. The heat kept most Cubans off of narrow sidewalks cracked beyond repair. Those who did venture outdoors moved slowly, their eyes cast down. The alternative was sitting in the shade and staring at the heavy air.

That was the choice of the rash of people who had set up tables at the end of their walkways. Hand-drawn signs advertised homemade sweets and savories. Scraps of cardboard attached to fences announced the availability of sofas, chairs, and kitchenware. A notice tacked to a tree in front of one colonial home said: "I'm selling a crib and children's clothing. Used but in good shape. Ring the bell."

The density of enterprise increased near the Hotel Nacional. A middle-age man spread battered books on wooden racks as well as the sidewalk. Titles included *An Interview with Fidel, Fidel and Religion,* and *On the March with Fidel.* Another vendor had stretched secondhand records on his patch of pavement. A family of four took advantage of their location opposite a row of state stores by roping off an area in which they guarded shoppers' bicycles.

The grass-roots capitalism supported Boris's lecture on Cuban economic reform. The shift, said my landlord, dated to the 1989 collapse of the Soviet Union. Overnight, Moscow cut annual subsidies worth about $5 billion. Trade with the Eastern bloc, which had accounted for nearly all of the island's commerce, evaporated. Cuba stuck to its communist guns — central planning over private enterprise, rationed goods instead of shopping sprees. Output dropped by a third over the next four years.

Then the Party's line wavered. Its coffers all but empty, the state permitted mechanics, plumbers, and other tradesmen to sell their services. Cubans were allowed to hold dollars for the first time in more than thirty years. Later, the government sanctioned farmers' markets. More liberalization, including the right to rent out apartments, followed as part of a policy known as "the Opening."

"Doesn't sound like communism," I said.

"Cuba is a confusing place," agreed Boris.

Proof came at a shaded food stand whose proprietors, a bony man and a fleshy woman, had nodded off. They awakened as I looked over the two plates on their table. Both featured potatoes that had been mashed, balled, and fried. While I chewed one of the pasty balls, the vendor, a retired librarian, filled me in on the birth of their business. State rations left them hungry. Inflation made their pensions meaningless. The pair had no choice but to set up shop. The results?

"There's a lot of competition," said the man.

"It's not easy," said his wife.

"*La Lucha,*" he sighed.

"The Struggle," mimicked his wife.

I asked the price of the potato ball.

"Three pesos."

That's when I realized I had no cash. Rather, no Cuban cash. I held out a dollar bill. Emptying his pocket, the vendor found just a few coins; their sum fell far short of the exchange rate, which I didn't know.

"You can pay me later. Or tomorrow. We are here every day, all day."

"The Struggle," sighed his wife.

I learned more about capitalism, Cuban style, near Old Havana. A cluster of men gathered in a tight circle in the plaza of Central Park. Judging from the boisterous shouts and shaking fists, they were watching a brawl. Closer, I saw that the crowd was focused on two men faced off like cocks in a pit.

A black man in a faded yellow tank top pushed his face to within inches of his opponent's nose. His brown eyes widened. Smooth features contorted. One palm extended outward, as if pleading for reason. The other hand flapped like a bronco. His point made, the aggressor planted his feet and folded his arms.

The adversary, a stocky man in a checked shirt, sprang to life. Arms spread, veins popping, he launched an oral bombardment that looked likely to end in fisticuffs or apoplexy. Communism versus capitalism? Is there a God? The chainsaw buzz of their Spanish made it impossible for me to tell the stakes.

I turned to a sturdy youth who was also watching the debate. Broad shoulders and a square jaw gave him the air of an athlete. A button-down shirt, khaki pants, and tasseled loafers were pure Brooks Brothers.

"What are they arguing about?"

"Baseball."

"This is about baseball?"

"Baseball is very serious for Cubans. Do you want to buy cigars?"

"No. Thanks."

"Cuban cigars are very good, very famous."

"I don't smoke."

"Maybe you have friends who smoke."

The dapper hustler, Luis, also told me to watch my step. Matching my slow strides across the park, he warned that the streets of Havana were filled with cigar dealers. Most sold phony stogies. He, on the other hand, insisted that he had the real deal: "My uncle works in a cigar factory. They give cigars to the workers. But my uncle needs money more than he needs cigars. So we sell them to tourists. Good quality."

When not hustling, the twenty-two-year-old worked at the airport. His dismal salary — the equivalent of six dollars a month — barely dented the cost of supporting his wife and infant son. So Luis became a "businessman." Cigars were his main line. His sideline was befriending foreigners in the hope of getting cash and clothes. That didn't make him a thief. Nor did he hurt people. Others were less scrupulous.

Luis took my notebook and asked for a pen. The young mulatto opened the back cover and began to scribble. Speaking as he wrote, he said that new words were entering the Cuban vocabulary. To understand the new lexicon was to understand Cuba. Luis finished writing and handed back the notebook, now filled with the local lingo.

Wanikiki meant money. *Fula* was a more specific way to refer to dollars. These were usually found in the possession of a *papirici*, a word that combined the words for "papa" and "rich." A *jinetero*, Spanish for "jockey," was a guy looking to separate a *papirici* from his *wanikiki*. The process of doing so was *el fuego*. "The fire," literally.

"So you're a *jinetero*," I said.

"These days, all Cubans are *jineteros*."

Luis asked if I needed a taxi to take me home. I did. The afternoon sun had drained my energy. What I didn't need was to pour more money into a state cab like the one that charged me twenty dollars — three times Luis's monthly pay — for a ride from the airport.

"No problem," said Luis. "I'll get you a taxi for Cubans."

Luis surveyed the vehicles stationed along the rim of Central Park. Cardboard signs hand-printed TAXI rested inside the windscreens of battered American classics and slightly less battered Soviet buckets. Luis approached a Lada idling in the shade. The seated driver listened hard as the hustler spoke. The chat ended with the Cubans shaking hands and beckoning me to board the front seat.

"He will take you home for three dollars," Luis announced.

Cooled by the breeze created by the Lada's movement along the Malecón, I looked at the driver. The sun had burnished an indelible tan as well as dozens of lines on his gaunt face. Scarred arms and rough hands identified the man as a manual laborer. I wondered how he could afford a car.

"I earned it by cutting sugarcane," he said.

"It must take a lot of cane to pay for a car."

"I was one of Cuba's best cane cutters."

The driver explained that the state motivated workers with promises of goods. Televisions were common rewards for top workers. The big prize was a car. The country's best cane cutter got one for free. Lesser standouts won the right to buy a vehicle. Named to his province's all-star team in 1981, he paid for the Lada by pooling his savings with loans from friends.

Havana's fleet of free-lance taxis was rife with similar success stories. The drivers of the Soviet bloc autos were men who had played and won the government's game. In the weeks that followed, crack factory workers drove me to Old Havana. Topnotch bureaucrats brought me back. So did military heroes. In other words, model communists were leading the capitalist charge.

"Three dollars is a lot," I noted at the end of the ride.

"Gas is very expensive in Cuba. Ninety cents, American cents, for one liter."

"How many liters did you just use?"

"One."

"So your profit is two dollars."

"Only one. I have to give one dollar to your friend."

My friend? The meeting in the park. The stuff about Cubans surfing the changing economy. Had any of the banter been genuine?

I handed over the fare. The cane cutter passed the notes from his right hand to his left. Raising the index finger on his free hand, he leaned across the seat. Rather than thank me, the driver offered a broader view on dollar-wielding outsiders: "In Cuba, you are Jesus."

5

"DO YOU HAVE A LIGHT?"

"What?"

"A light."

"No. Sorry."

The dark-skinned woman stayed put. Standing flush against the rim of my bar stool, she waited, as if I might remember a matchbook buried in my pocket's lint. Or maybe she expected chivalry. Fidel Castro had promised social, political, and economic equality for women. But did progress excuse a comrade from helping a lady?

Yes or no, this lady was a fire hazard. She nibbled thick lips painted scarlet. The swatch of color floated amid a stretch of chestnut skin that began at her forehead and ended at the neckline of a white leotard that hugged curves normally found in centerfolds. She held my stare for several elongated seconds before moving away, slowly, and casting a last look over her shoulder.

Physically, the second woman to approach my bar stool had little in common with the first. A brown mane spilled past the edges of green eyes and an inviting grin. The hair came to rest on toasted shoulders left bare by a cocktail dress. Silver sequins covered, though just barely, buttocks raised three inches by black spiked heels. She, like her predecessor, wanted a light from an American barfly.

"I don't smoke," I said.

"Do you like to dance?"

"I don't know how."

Dumb answer. The music blasting from linebacker-size speakers wasn't salsa. Born in the USA, the tunes called for nothing trickier than a wiggle and a bounce. What's more, the girl in the cocktail dress probably wasn't looking for Fred Astaire. She may not have even wanted a light. I would never know. Two clipped answers were enough to scare off one feline Cuban.

There were plenty more like her. I struggled not to stare at the mulatta wearing a black evening gown, the bleached blonde whose behind just about burst its Lycra casing, and the rest of the parade of head-turners populating the Hotel Comodoro's nightclub. Deconstructed, the women provided a catalogue of undulating hair, painted lips, and unhidable curves. Reassembled, they were a harem.

"Impressive, isn't it," said a voice behind me.

The slightest of accents told me that Peter had returned. Turning, I found his familiar blue eyes and dirty blond hair. The German's doughy face cracked a sinister smile that spread to my mouth.

"Unbelievable," I replied.

A resident of Havana, Peter was teaching me about living large in Cuba. He started by instructing me on eating in *paladares,* private restaurants in the homes of Cubans willing to let foreigners masticate in their living rooms and on their terraces. He also told me about the wave of European and Latino businessmen streaming into Havana. "Everybody can see that this should be a great place to do business. Their education system has produced a big pool of well-educated people." The German's true love, however, was cars.

No newcomer could miss the automobiles cruising the capital. Paint weathered, bodies dented, windshields cracked like spider webs, classic Fords and Chevrolets clattered along the Malecón every few minutes. Engines minted back when Americans liked Ike rumbled like outboard motors. Maneuverability? Sherman tanks sprung to mind. That the beasts from Detroit moved at all was nothing short of a miracle.

Not so the Buick convertible in which Peter had picked me up. A smooth layer of red coated the car's unblemished hide. The chrome grill caught and magnified the lights above the street. The convertible's soft top exposed shiny red seats. White-wall tires were the final touch to a flawless flashback. The German revved the engine and hit the car's mighty horn.

The cherubic entrepreneur blasted his klaxon again when the Buick passed a billboard on the Malecón. Painted in full view of the so-called U.S. Interests Section, America's unofficial embassy in Havana, the propaganda showed a hopping mad Uncle Sam reacting to the taunts of another cartoon figure. One hand gripping a rifle, the other cupped beside his mouth, a Cuban soldier was shouting, "Imperialists, we have absolutely no fear of you."

Resettled on the bar stool beside mine, Peter demonstrated his mastery of things Cuban. Standing halfway around the bar from our spot was a woman who, while not beautiful, dripped sexuality. An eruption of kinked brown hair and swollen painted lips took back seat to a figure that punished the seams of a skimpy sleeveless top cut from black leather. Swaying to the throbbing beat, she scanned the crowd with the concentration of a big-game hunter. Her eyes landed on two of the bar's smaller fry.

"Got a light?" said the slight lift of her unlit cigarette.

"Of course," replied Peter's cool nod.

The vamp swaggered her way around the bar. She placed the cigarette between her lips and waited for Peter, a nonsmoker, to produce a lighter and ignite its end. She closed her eyes to draw in the first breath and took pains to pucker her lips for the extended exhalation that followed. Only then did she introduce herself. And only to Peter.

Just as well. No small-talker in English, I saw no hope of learning the nonstop banter that came naturally to Cubans. Peter chattered like a native, leaving me to wonder what was going on. Had I died and gone to heaven? Or was there something else at work?

"Are these girls prostitutes?" I asked after the woman excused herself with a gentle stroke of Peter's thigh.

"No."

"Then why are they all so . . . friendly?"

"Cuban women know what they want," was the start of the answer.

The rest took more explaining. Cubans, he said, had just enough money to survive. Extras — clothing, for example — were beyond the means of most locals. Foreigners, on the other hand, came to Cuba flush with cash. They were met by small-time hustlers selling cigars or renting rooms. Long on desire but short on cash, the ladies prowled through the night for their slice of the pie. Known as *jineteras,* they sought sugar daddies to buy a drink tonight, dinner tomorrow, and perhaps new shoes and a dress in between.

Peter insisted that the Cubans in the nightclub were nice girls. Several were known to be the daughters of Party officials. The rest came from good families, the type that read books and said prayers. Virtually all had studied at a university. Breeding didn't mean they weren't (a) young and (b) restless.

"That girl who was just here, the one with the black . . ." Peter struggled to define the top, which covered more than a bra but less than a vest. "She has a master's degree in engineering."

I wasn't the only one marveling at the quantity of life in Cuba.

"The name's Karl" was how the man beside me on the inbound flight introduced himself. I had barely turned to register my neighbor's features — gray and thinning hair, a tummy that heaved with every breath, and a fleshy face given to avuncular grins — when he began filling me in on his life. British, he directed artsy films whose grit had caught the eye of Cuba's movie makers, who invited him to attend their annual film festival.

I next saw Karl in the polished lobby of the Hotel Nacional. The Brit raved about the cast of characters he had encountered in the bar. There was an Italian trader and a cameraman from a U.S. television network. The former was negotiating an import contract. The latter was spreading a rumor that Washington and Havana were about to normalize relations. Then there was Barnaby, an American who had come to Cuba to write about martinis.

More indigenous delights were on Barnaby's mind when we met that evening. Lean and balding, the fortyish man lifted his elbows from the oak bar and introduced himself. Then he introduced the bow-tied bartender as well as the *mojitos*, a blend of rum, sugar, seltzer, and a mintlike leaf called *hierba buena*. "Local specialty," informed the American. "Hemingway loved *mojitos*."

Entranced by mythical Cuba, Barnaby waxed nostalgic about vintage cars. Plymouths and DeSotos took him back to an era when men were called Mack and gas cost a nickel. He segued to the capital's colonial architecture. From there he moved on to the island's wondrous cigars, one of which he lifted from the pocket of his blazer. Preferring a light from the barman to his own book of matches, the man puffed his long stogie and asked, aloud, whether it was all a dream.

"Dreamy" described 1830, the place Barnaby wanted to dine. Carried by one of the gypsy cabs that hovered outside the Nacional, we arrived at the colonial mansion turned government restaurant. Decorative columns and an oversize doorway preceded an airy, ornate foyer. A broad staircase spiraled up to a second floor. Dead ahead lay the parquet floor of the main room.

A grand piano took center stage. At its keyboard sat a severe, dark-haired woman moonlighting from one of Havana's orchestras. Her soft, classical melodies warmed a room whose walls glowed with fresh white paint. A mammoth mirror framed in gold reflected a room with roughly twenty tables covered by white cloths.

The waiter matched the linen. Dressed in a jacket too broad for his bony shoulders, he couldn't hide his fatigue as he sagged to a stop beside our table. But the place wasn't about service; the waiter needed five minutes to find a corkscrew and another three to grasp its operation. Nor was it about food; high schools served better chicken than 1830. We were paying for ambiance; the room felt like a salon worthy of Gatsby.

After dinner Barnaby steered us to the Cohiba Hotel, a glassy tower overlooking the Caribbean swells. Breezing past a pair of hotel guards, he made a beeline for a lounge raised three steps above the lobby. The place was packed. Only a fraction, maybe a third, of the barflies were men, all foreign, mostly middle-age. Circled around them, like satellites to planets, were dozens and dozens of women. Few looked over twenty-five. None rated less than a double take.

Merciless scrutiny welcomed newcomers. Aggressive eye contact awaited men who made the grade. Heads turned quickly from males with the wrong plumage. The ocular rubdown made me squirm.

Not so Barnaby. Emboldened by a daiquiri ("Hemingway loved daiquiris") and a cigar called Cohiba ("Castro's brand"), the writer sidled up to two women at the bar. Karl joined them. Neither man tried to mask his lack of Spanish. Nor did they hide their interest in the superior view of four breasts, a brownish pair left exposed by the sunken neckline of a yellow sundress and a whiter set framed by the tight, square cut of a black velvet gown.

The women leaned back. They giggled at the men's attempts at communication via gesticulation. Barnaby bought a round of drinks. The girls giggled some more. Barnaby bought more drinks.

I found myself sandwiched by two teenagers. Each grabbed an arm. One asked, "Can we stand near you?" The pair stuck to my ribs as a hotel employee wearing a blazer and carrying a walkie-talkie passed within inches of us. The girls released me only once the coast was clear.

"If we are not with a tourist, he makes us leave," said a stocky girl with alabaster skin. Her svelte friend nodded.

"Is it worth the trouble to be near tourists?"

"Cuban men aren't interesting."

"They aren't?"

"They have no *wanikiki*."

Barnaby interrupted. Having reached a linguistic impasse, he needed help. Kati, the girl in the gown, seemed interested in dancing. Could I confirm?

Kati placed her hands around mine. She slid one leg over the other, a motion that pushed her dress to one side and exposed a stretch of black lace. When her face was just inches from mine, the woman moistened her painted lips and said, "Tell your friend seventy-five."

"Seventy-five?"

"Seventy-five dollars."

"For . . . ?"

Kati pulled back. She glared. Was I trying to humiliate her by forcing her to spell it out? Or did I really not know what she was proposing? She clarified her wishes by twirling her hair and arching her back. I hesitated to relay the message that dancing wasn't all that Kati had in mind.

Barnaby clearly relished his romantic vision of Cuba. Would the news that Kati admired his wallet, not his charm, shatter the illusion? On the other hand, who was I to interfere with a changing economy? I condoned Cubans selling cars and cigars. Shouldn't Kati get similar approval? Saddened to see flesh for hire, I wouldn't judge her choice.

"Ask your friend if he wants two," said Kati's sidekick.

"Two what?"

"Two girls."

I felt out of place among the gang of men banging around Havana. Autos didn't interest me. Salsa did, but I couldn't dance.

Try though I did to let the colonial setting carry me back in time, I failed. I wondered whether there were any alternatives to the neoimperialist fun.

Defunct streetlights outside the Cohiba meant that I had to head home in the dark. Frightened by what sounded like a scream, I spotted a lanky youth vomiting on the sidewalk. Doubled over, arms wrapped around his midriff, he moaned steadily until he heard my footsteps. He stood up, said "Rum," and bent over again for another purge.

Alcohol wasn't his only problem. Accompanying me along an avenue called Linea, Jorge said that he was a student. English was his major and, with a big exam coming up, he was worried about passing. Did he want my help? No, he had a tutor, a woman who had completed the course at the University of Havana. But she was part of the problem.

Three times a week Jorge lugged his books to the tutor's home. Three times a week he vowed to buckle down and study. Three times a week he failed to crack a book. The student found the teacher irresistibly sexy. She felt likewise. The pair spent their tutorials making love instead of learning English.

"Cuban men can make love five times in one night," said Jorge. "How about American men?"

"Something like that."

"Have you ever been with a Cuban girl?"

My answer shocked the boozed-up student. A determination to initiate me renewed his energy. Jorge strode down the street until we reached a sign that said Joker. "It's a discotheque," he said. "A Cuban discotheque." Forgetting the imminent exam as well as his rotted gut, he pulled me down a flight of stairs leading to a basement.

The wooden door closed behind us and I found myself in utter darkness. Jorge vanished. Heated by a mass of bodies I could sense but not see, the clammy air fogged my eyeglasses. I could just about make out silhouettes until flashes of strobe light blinded me. A minute passed before I felt safe enough to take a second step.

Left, I saw a corps of twenty Cubans — men in tank tops,

women in halters, everybody in a sweat — writhing to the thumping conga. Others did their thing against a wall. Three men in their late teens slouched and bumped their pelvises while three girls ground their rears into the thrusts. Moving toward the roomier, right side of the club, I knocked into a couple pressed face-to-face. Two men turned and smiled before resuming their mutual exploration.

The tender of a battered bar was conducting a probe of his own. Dressed in shorts and a T-shirt, the wiry youth couldn't see his customers. The reason? His eyes were closed. Had they been open, they would have seen no further than the face of the teenage girl whose grip on his neck improved her leverage on his lips. Trying to catch his eye and order two shots of rum, I found myself staring at hips rocking in time to the hands up her skirt.

"What's your name?" demanded a thin mulatta with a tattoo on her bare shoulders. "Why aren't you dancing?"

I said again, stupidly, that I couldn't dance.

"I'm going to Cubanize you."

Would Cubanization hurt? The girl yanked me into the sea of dancers. Faced off, my hands in hers, I was expected to lead. I froze. Stunned by the sight of the truth — I really couldn't dance — she reverted to remedial measures. Firm hands grabbed my hips. Pulling me into contact with her pelvis, the teenager began to rock gently, steadily, in time to the music. Self-consciousness doomed my earlier efforts to get in sync; gyrating with a girl I had known less than a minute felt queer.

"Move," she whispered. "Move."

I tried. Then I stopped trying. Then I tried to forget that I was an American in Cuba, that I was a stiff in the land of rhythm, that I was . . . I lost track of the reasons that I couldn't enjoy myself. Instead I focused on the rhythm of the teenager. And the sound of the salsa.

6

THERE WAS NO SNEAKING in or out of my building. A committee of no less than four noted my every move.

The pack's leader was a pudgy granny stationed opposite my front door. Up close, her face was a road map of tender lines. The crinkles multiplied when she smiled, which was often. But softness would be a perfect disguise, wouldn't it? So would the goodies she sold to neighbors beginning at seven A.M. every morning. Fruit puffs, sandwiches, coffee . . . Who would suspect that the vendor was a spy?

Not I. Thus my surprise at Mrs. Guerra's first words to me: "You're the American living in apartment 401." Impressed, and intimidated, I asked for a coffee, which came in a plastic demitasse dented by tooth marks.

The old lady volunteered that she had lived on the block for decades. She pointed to a third-floor window behind the umbrella-covered table that served as her shop. Painted large on the wall to the left of the ground-floor entrance was a crest shaped like a shield. Thick vertical stripes of blue and white formed the bottom section. The top half was a man raising a sword above his head. Fat red letters said CDR. Smaller print spelled out Comité por la Defensa de la Revolución.

The Committees for the Defense of the Revolution were a big reason for a foreigner to be edgy in Cuba. Every block, factory, and farm had a council to which Cubans reported anything out of the ordinary. Signs of excessive wealth rated a black mark. So did a neighbor caught bad-mouthing the government. Failing to inform was also a no-no. Irregularities were logged by the CDR. Serious infractions and strange people were reported to the security forces, who could turn a morning sighting into a midday arrest.

The CDR logo labeled Mrs. Guerra's building the nerve center of the block's intelligence operations. The buck stopped here for the collective vigilance that Fidel Castro said was necessary for the Revolution to survive. Did that make the old lady a spy?

"Do you have any laundry?" she asked.

"I just arrived."

"But you will have laundry."

"One day."

"Bring it to my apartment," she said. "Do you have any dollars to sell?"

Luis the hustler had suggested I save money by buying food with Cuban pesos, which he would gladly sell me at the official rate of five to a dollar. At the time, I appreciated the offer. Neither the airport's arrivals hall nor my hotel had an exchange desk; dollar-dependent tourists were more likely to spend money on goods and services sold by the government. Embarrassed by my inability to pay the potato seller, I bought fifty pesos for ten bucks. The money hadn't run out when Mrs. Guerra made her offer.

"But you can buy dollars yourself," I said.

"The state buys dollars for twenty-five pesos. It sells them to Cubans for thirty. If I can buy from you, I save five pesos."

"I thought the rate was five to one."

"No. Twenty-five."

Her illegal offer cleared the coffee lady of espionage charges. That left three young men as the better candidates for neighborhood watchdog. Every morning all three were stationed to the left of my doorway. Two had clear reasons to be there. The muscular men dispensed green tomatoes, green oranges, and other miscolored produce from a rusted trough. Coping with lines of as many as twenty shoppers, they raised their heads every time I passed. But they looked too busy to report my comings and goings.

What about the doe-eyed man who spent his days lingering beside the vendors? The guy never smiled. Nor did he work. He spent his time watching the labors of his buddies and adjusting the angle of his Florida Marlins baseball cap. My inclination was to avoid him. A stronger urge led me to approach a man with time on his hands. Who, I asked, owned the produce stand? Was it public or private?

"He owns it," replied the young man.

"Who is he?"

"*El caballo.*"

"The horse?"

He placed an index and middle finger side by side, reached across his chest, and tapped his shoulder. It was a gesture I would see hundreds of times in the coming months. On that day, however, I didn't know that the tapping indicated the shoulder boards of a military officer. So the young man tried another gesture. He spread his fingers on his chin and stroked down a long imaginary beard. I didn't get it. He sighed deeply and gave it one last try.

"The oranges belong to the king of this place."

"The king of Cuba?"

"Fidel."

Getting guidance to Fidel Castro should have been a snap. Or so I judged from the flow of unsolicited information. Taking note of an outsider ogling a school named Abraham Lincoln, a middle-age woman explained that humble beginnings and the liberation of slaves earned Honest Abe a place on Cuba's pedestal. A mechanic bent over the engine of a 1948 Plymouth let me know that his previous car, a 1955 Ford Fairlane, had been easier on the eye but tougher on the gas tank. Somebody else told me, again, that Madonna's boyfriend was Cuban.

The odd man out in a gabby city was Boris's father-in-law. Always dressed in cotton pajamas and high-top sneakers, fifty-year-old Ricardo rose to a half crouch to shake my hand. The rugged man always settled back down in his armchair and resumed gazing at the opposite wall or out the window. His participation in conversations was limited to nods, grunts, and the occasional smirk.

One day Ricardo excused his attire. Stricken with bone cancer, he lacked the energy to dress. Conversation drained him, so

I felt lucky when he felt fit enough to talk about his work on health studies. Recently, the focus had been on AIDS, a scourge Cuba hoped to keep off the island. Before that he studied birth control. "In Cuba, any woman can have an IUD for free," said Ricardo. "Condoms, diaphragms, and pills are cheap enough for everybody to afford."

"How about abortion?"

"Abortions are free. Of course, we would rather have a healthy baby. But an abortion is better than an unwanted child." I nodded. He continued. "Here very few women die from abortions. The reason is that we have good facilities and, above all, we Cubans accept responsibility. In other countries — like yours — women die because they have to go to hidden, dirty places to get abortions."

Maybe it was the open discussion of a touchy subject. Or was it the surgical tweaking of American health care? Whichever the case, I felt Ricardo would address my growing backlog of questions about Cuba. Indeed, he gladly confirmed that the official exchange rate was twenty-five pesos per dollar. He also told me that I had arrived during the baseball season. My next question met a colder front.

"Do you know how I can meet Fidel Castro?"

Ricardo's face lost its elasticity. His right leg folded over his left. He lowered his eyes, as if my question and I would vanish. He rubbed a hand back to front over a graying stubble of dark hair.

"Maybe I could just shake his hand?" I said.

Ricardo turned his face to the window. The talk was terminated.

Ricardo wasn't the first Cuban to stonewall my inquiry. When I returned to pay off my three-peso debt, the sidewalk vendor went rigid at the mention of the leader's name. His eyes shot left, then right, scanning for whoever might be within earshot. There was nobody in sight. Still, the retired librarian lowered his eyes and buttoned his lip.

Younger Cubans reacted differently to the sound of "Fidel."

A group gathered nightly opposite the Hotel Nacional. Some simply sought company and a breath of evening air. Others were trolling for tourists seeking cars, cigars, or other local specialties. Lined up like can-can dancers, eight men set aside commercial interests to grill the *Yanqui* taking a break along the low wall on which they sat.

"What do Americans think about Cuba?" asked a spokesman.

"Most Americans don't think about Cuba."

I said that the U.S. was a massive country with massive problems. We were obsessed with crime, education, and health care, issues their country appeared to have resolved. Most Americans, I said, probably hadn't noticed Cuba since rafters were last washing up on Florida's beaches.

"And the blockade?" asked a wiry guy with a droopy mustache.

I added that Americans didn't devote much brain power to foreign policy. At least not until disaster struck. Personally, I thought the economic embargo was an embarrassing anachronism that should have died long before the end of the Cold War.

"Clinton lifted the blockade on Vietnam," said one of the gang. "So why is there still a blockade on Cuba?"

"I don't know."

"Will Clinton lift the blockade?"

"I don't know."

"Are you a Democrat or a Republican?"

"Neither," I said. "Sometimes I don't vote."

"Like us."

The group chuckled. A comfortable quiet followed as everybody looked across the lifeless street. I felt as if our political and economic gaps were melting, as if we were just a bunch of guys hanging out on a street corner that could be anywhere. The camaraderie was confirmed by the passing of two girls. Lovely in their thin blouses and knee-length skirts, the teenage pair had yet to shed the last of their baby fat.

"*Oye, mami.*"

"*Que linda.*"

"*Un beso. Por favor, un besito.*"

The catcalls — "Hey mama," "How beautiful," "A kiss. Please, a little kiss" — were followed by an elbow in my ribs. Jerking his fist up and down, as if knocking on a horizontal door, the man to my right asked whether I had slept with a Cuban girl.

"I haven't even gotten a handshake."

Maybe worth a grin, the crack ignited a round of hysterics. Suddenly, the sidewalk crew couldn't do enough for me. One man pledged to introduce me to his neighbor's daughter, an aerobics teacher. Another insisted that I meet his family. A third asked how long I would be in Cuba.

"Until I meet Fidel."

Silence struck. A second passed. Then another two seconds. I feared I had killed the buzz until six men erupted into even greater hilarity. Knees were slapped. Ears teared. The Cubans couldn't stop repeating the funniest thing they had heard . . . ever?

"'Until he meets Fidel.'"

"That's funny."

"Let's go see Fidel."

Eduardo took me more seriously. An old friend of Boris's family, he was sitting across from Ricardo when I stopped by to ask for a map of Havana. A tanned face and loose-fitting clothes gave the sixtyish man a beachcomber's appearance. Thick spectacles and a tendency to speak only after a deliberate pause gave him the air of an academic. He was, in fact, a lifelong bureaucrat with a passion for books.

Eduardo defrosted the moment he learned I was a writer. Would I like to see his collection of books? I hesitated for the moment it took for him to add that he had a spare map at his house, just four blocks away. He lived with his sister, her daughter, and two cousins. None of them was home, so we passed quickly through a living room furnished with a table, four chairs, and a boxy television set. The walls were bare.

Not so the library. Books, hundreds of them, lined shelves that Eduardo had built by stacking boards on bricks. He showed me one of his favorites, a history of Cuba's indigenous population, which showed how explorers returning from the New World had imported words such as *cigarro* and *barbacoa,* "cigar" and "barbecue." Had I heard about Spain's treatment of the island's hundred thousand or so natives? The professorial man relished recounting how Cuba's natives were enslaved, murdered, or left to rot from European diseases. By the mid-1500s, just five thousand remained.

Pleased to have a pupil, Eduardo spread his map of the capital on the floor and noted some highlights. Must-sees included Plaza de Armas, which for roughly four hundred years had served as the center of Spanish power on the island; the palace formerly inhabited by U.S.-backed dictators; and Revolution Square, the monument to the end of foreign rule. The tour went east to a town called Cojimar, where Eduardo said one could find the pilot of Hemingway's fishing boat. In the opposite direction was a ritzy neighborhood called Miramar. Farther along the coast was Siboney, the suburb known as the home of government bigwigs.

"Does Fidel live in Siboney?" I asked.

Eduardo raised his head to take a brief but hard look at me. Once his eyes confirmed what his ears had heard, he looked down at the map. An electric hush invaded the room. I couldn't think of a way to break the silence. Eduardo could.

"Don't even mention his name," he hissed.

"Why?"

"Somebody might hear."

"But there's nobody home."

"In Cuba, you never know who is listening," said Eduardo. "If you want to stay out of trouble here in Cuba, don't talk about" — a stroke of the imaginary beard. "Don't even mention his name."

7

"I'VE LEARNED HOW to get in to see Fidel."

Desperate for an angle on Fidel Castro, I grew anxious during the gaps between the British reporter's sentences. His hushed tone forced me to lean in.

"You pay one of his friends to arrange a meeting," he said. "They pocket the money and recommend that Fidel see you."

The scheme made sense. Journalists pined to see the Cuban. Visiting reporters such as the Brit treated the leader like Godot. They waited days and weeks and even months for the interview that could turbocharge their career. Everybody wanted to be the first to hear Castro say, "This socialism thing just ain't working" or "Maybe I'll hold elections tomorrow." An ambitious hack might pay big bucks for such a scoop.

"How much?" I asked.

"I don't know."

"Who are the friends to bribe?"

"Well . . . his top two or three friends."

"Do you know their names?"

"No," said the Brit. "But he can't have that many."

I heard a sounder scenario from a French journalist who had spent more than two years in Havana; the idea rated attention. Experience would have taught the Frenchman to separate fact from fantasy. More important, he had met Fidel Castro. Twice.

"Fidel likes embassy parties," said the Frenchman. "When you see him there he's relaxed. There aren't bodyguards surrounding him. People come up to shake his hand, to say hello. They ask him to sign Cuban money. Or dollar bills. He loves it."

There was just one snag. Invitations to embassy events were limited to special guests and Cuba-based nationals. The Spaniards invited the Spaniards. The Mexicans invited their own. The Americans . . . the Americans had no embassy in Havana. There was the U.S. Interests Section, where diplomats handled issues such as immigration. But they had minimal contact with Cuban officials. And none with Castro.

The Frenchman knew another way to meet Cuba's president. As elsewhere, journalists called out questions after speeches or other events. The leader ignored drivel about tensions with America and the collapse of the Soviet Union. The trick, said the Frenchman, was to intrigue him. An interesting question always caught his attention.

"He might not speak to you right then," said the Frenchman. "But he finds out who you are. Then his people call you and take you to speak to him."

"How do you get close enough to ask that question?"

"It's easy to get through the security if you have a press credential."

"What if you don't have a credential?"

"You have to get lucky."

I got despondent. My Havana holiday wasn't panning out as planned. Yes, the sunny capital beat the alternative, icy temperatures back home in New York. On the other hand, I hadn't found anybody with whom I could drink or dance on a steady basis. Nor was finding Fidel simply a matter of waiting for him to show up at a bar. Seated on a sofa in the Hotel Nacional, I saw the possibility of going home empty-handed.

An old and pale man crash-landed beside me. Relieved to have reached the airy lobby, he fanned his face with a baseball cap before unzipping a vest decorated with pins and buttons. Next he opened the top of a track suit. The striptease ended with a giant sigh, which jiggled a jelly-belly covered but not disguised by a tennis shirt.

"Hot day," I said.

"Yes sir."

His New York accent triggered a memory. The face was also familiar. The hooked nose, the frizz of gray hair, the thin lips pursed around a well-chewed cigar . . . I had seen them somewhere. But the name printed on one of his buttons — Al Lewis — didn't ring a bell. Another button did.

The badge bore a photo of a vampire. Hair slicked back, shoulders caped, face powdered white, the character was a flashback to my childhood TV addiction. The batlike man was one of *The Munsters,* a family of Frankensteins settled in an all-American neighborhood.

"Are you Grandpa? Grandpa Munster?"

"Yes sir."

"What are you doing here?"

Grandpa said that he always came for Havana's annual film festival. The retired actor skipped the flicks and spent the days wandering the streets. When night fell there were parties. The biggest bash, he said, came at the end of the three-week festival, when the movie moguls took over the Palace of the Revolution, the headquarters of Cuba's Communist Party.

"Fidel Castro hosts the party," said Grandpa.

"He attends?"

"Of course."

"And you met him?"

"A few times."

I had laughed at Karl's offer to register me in the film festival. I knew little about film and had no particular interest in Latino film, the focus of the festival. And I expected to be too busy to waste my time at the movies. Karl persisted and enrolled me as a "producer." My status was proved by a photo ID, which I showed to the old man beside me.

"Will this get me into the party?"

Grandpa nodded.

"So at the end of the festival I can meet Fidel?"

Grandpa nodded. Then he nodded off.

Havana was an easy place to kill time. Cubans emerged early to stretch limbs and lungs; there were never fewer than three people lingering around Mrs. Guerra's sidewalk stand. The sun heated up and people took their chatter indoors until sunset, when the Malecón and other boulevards became open-air social clubs. Whatever the time, Cubans were happy to pass it with conversation.

A neighbor named Rosa showed extra enthusiasm. Green eyes and a freckled face gave the twenty-year-old an apple pie appearance. She smiled readily, always with a toss of the tangle of sandy hair on her head. The bubbly insouciance made her a magnet for my attention. So I jumped the morning she asked me to walk with her to the state store. She shifted her empty bag to the crook of her left arm, freeing her right to hook around my elbow. Joining the shopping spirit, I asked what we needed.

"Need!" cried Rosa with an exaggerated slap of her bare thigh. "You don't go to the bodega to get what you need. You go to see what they have."

She pulled a plastic-covered booklet from her back pocket. It was her ration book, the basis of the Cuban diet. The inside flap carried her photograph, her address, and the number assigned to her household. It also bore the number and address of the bodega where food and other basics cost just pennies.

Each of the following pages corresponded to a month. Down the left side of each page ran a list of staple foods: rice, beans, oil, lard, sugar, jam, and tomato paste. Coffee and salt were also essentials, as were soap, detergent, and toothpaste. Vices taxed by Uncle Sam — cigarettes, cigars, and rum — were deemed essentials and sold at a discount by Cuba.

A grid of boxes to the right served as a scorecard. Marked by employees of her bodega, the "6" in the box beside "rice" indicated that Rosa had already collected her six pounds for the month. The "10" in the row for beans meant she had her ten ounces. Swatches of unmarked boxes indicated that she had never received many of the groceries. The year had passed with no tomato paste. In January Rosa got cigarettes. Matches didn't show up until February and disappeared in March. Detergent arrived in April. There was no cooking oil or soap until May.

"It's not easy," she sighed.

The sight of a shop brought her back to life. "That's where we get fish." After a pause she added, "When there is fish." The shop's closed shutters suggested that fish weren't in stock. "It's also where we get eggs. Two per month. When there are eggs."

"Where do you get meat?"

"MEAT! I can't remember the last time I had meat."

The store was on the ground floor of a low-rise apartment building. There was no door; workers opened shop by rolling up a metal sheet. Inside the narrow cave, a long counter separated customers from bins of rice, beans, and sugar. Above, a single shelf displayed a packet of cigarettes, a can of evaporated milk, and a silver tube of toothpaste. Three rows of faded words painted on the wall said: TO COMBAT. WITH MORAL PRINCIPLES. CERTAIN OF VICTORY.

"Is there soap?" Rosa asked the woman behind the counter.

"No."

"Coffee?"

"No."

"Sugar?"

Sugar *was* in stock. But there wasn't much, so Rosa was entitled to only three pounds, or half her ration, in the first half of the month. Having bought three pounds the previous week, she would have to wait until the next shipment. She impassively accepted news of the shortage and turned to leave, her shopping bag empty.

The shortage of food meant I ate alone. Generous with time and talk, Habaneros couldn't share their rations. I, on the other hand, could afford to dine in the private restaurants cropping up all over the capital. The *paladares* served meals for three dollars, feasts for five.

Entertainment cost extra. Eating in Vedado, I listened to a chunky guitarist strum and sing a medley of local favorites. At the end of "Guantanamera," he asked whether I liked the music. Did I have any requests? He was fishing for a tip. I bought him a beer, which led the guitarist, Pedro, to invite me to a weekly songfest at a cultural center.

We agreed to meet at his home. The center wasn't too far, but the fuel shortage that had crippled the bus system meant we had to allow two hours of travel time. He said it would be worth the trip. He promised to introduce a girl — "Very beautiful. Very intelligent. She will like you" — who worked at the center.

I never met the girl. I barely found Pedro, who lived up an unlit staircase, in an unmarked alley, just five blocks from my place. Timidly pushing open the door, I found a pregnant woman sprawled on the floor of a small, square living room. Opposite her, his belly nearly as bloated, the musician was teaching his son to strum.

The father rose and outlined his plans for the battered home. The exposed metal rods on the living room ceiling were due for a layer of plaster and a coat of paint. A wall would divide the bedroom shared by this branch of his family. (Two other children lived with his first wife.) In the kitchen, the tangle of exposed wires ranked lower than the concrete counter, which needed tiles.

"Little by little I will improve my home," said Pedro. "But it's not easy. I need money. And I need at least twenty-five dollars to buy clothes for my boy."

"Where can you get that kind of money?"

"When I play, Cubans give what they can. A few pesos. Sometimes a dollar."

Despite his cash crunch, Pedro had decided to cancel his gig at the cultural center. Instead we walked to the Colón Cemetery, Cuba's most famous burial ground. The musician showed me how the graveyard's pathways mimicked Havana's grid of numbered and lettered streets. He showed me the tomb of the mother of José Martí, a patriot whose significance I had yet to appreciate. Then he raised "a delicate question."

"In four days it will be my wife's birthday," he said. "I'm going to have a party for her. You must come."

I thanked him.

"But I have a problem."

In Cuba . . .

"Maybe you can help me."

. . . I was learning . . .

"I want to get her something. A cake."

. . . there was always a problem.

"But a cake costs five dollars. I don't have the money. Can you help me?"

Pedro's poverty was indisputable. Birthday or no birthday, his wife was pregnant. Then there was his unbearably adorable son. Was there a wad tight enough to deny such a family a birthday cake? Or even a five-dollar donation?

Pedro hugged me when I forked over a fiver. His warmth stayed with me for hours. Then I wondered whether I was the world's biggest sucker.

The feeling of foolishness resurfaced at a mansion in Vedado. Like many of the buildings in the area, the place was a throwback to a grander era. Iron gates opened to a walkway leading to the sort of elegant entrance where a butler waited to announce his master's guests. Inside, the oversize dwelling was all stone floors and high ceilings. A broad staircase spiraled up to a second floor. But it was outside that I made my first contact with the members of UNEAC, Cuba's writers and artists union.

An actor named Reynaldo saw me ogling the mansion. He had filled me in on the organization within a minute of our meeting. Within two he was insisting I join his friends for a cabaret that evening. I hesitated, but the thirty-year-old was too pretty to be dangerous. The darkest of browns, his skin hugged his fine features. He wore a vest with no shirt underneath.

We reconvened on the mansion's flank. He brought two friends, a singer and an actress. Twenty pesos bought us seats at one of the metal tables squeezed onto the tree-shrouded patio, a bottle of clear rum, four cans of Tropicola, the same number of glasses. Ice wasn't included. Or available. None of the dozens of well-groomed Cubans facing the microphones and amplifiers on the verandah seemed to mind. Songs sung by a middle-age diva and boleros strummed by a leather-faced man carried us far away.

The next evening I found the actor back in the garden of UNEAC. Gone were the schmaltzy singers and weepy listeners.

Present was Roberto, a photographer. So was Susanna, a small woman who wore an immense grin and a mane of kinked hair. Roxana, a big-boned gal with bedroom eyes, wrote for a magazine. José wrote children's books. Diego made movies.

An apprehensive quiet followed the introductions. Feet tapped. Eyes roved. Fingers drummed the table. More about distraction than boredom, the lull suggested that they were missing somebody. Or something.

"We need some alcohol," said Roberto.

"Rum," agreed Susanna.

A round of nods dissolved into further idling. I asked why we didn't get some rum. UNEAC's open-air bar was just twenty feet away.

"No money," said Roberto.

The statement was only partly true. Roberto had ten pesos. Susanna had five, as did Diego. That left the group twenty pesos short of the cost of a bottle. The group was out of luck unless . . . All eyes turned to me.

The Cubans knew I had money: I was a foreigner. They also knew that twenty pesos was meaningless to me. The unspoken expectation that I treat the group made me squirm. My uneasiness multiplied when Reynaldo enunciated the obvious: "If you pay twenty pesos we can all have rum."

"And Tropicola," added Susanna.

Would I mind covering the pitifully small shortfall to the cost of a bottle of rum? Of course not. Would I mind being treated like a chump? Definitely. The possibility that Reynaldo & Co. viewed me as a wallet on wheels made me pause. The table waited.

"In Cuba, when you have money, you treat your friends," said the author of children's books. "Another day, when you have nothing, they take care of you. That's how we survive. We share."

To reject what was characterized as the Cuban spirit would have been churlish. Embarrassing too. Refusing to pay my share would have been the same as rejecting their company. Besides, exploited benefactors had more fun than cynical misers. Reynaldo took my money and ran.

Banter burst out. Diego had heard that Los Van Van, Cuba's biggest salsa stars, were going to play at UNEAC. Roxana chattered about her new job. Susanna asked me to model for her portfolio. A television director arrived and insisted we sing a duet of "New York, New York."

Reynaldo returned. One hand held a bottle of cheap rum, the other, two cans of Tropicola. Expectations rose. The actor announced that the bar had no glasses. Faces fell. A collective sigh was followed by silence.

"This is a bar with no glasses?" I said.

"This is Cuba," said Diego.

"You will get used to it," added Susanna.

"What about plastic cups?"

Susanna touched the back of my hand. Speaking with sympathy for my ignorance, she said that Cubans had learned when to expend and when to conserve their energy. Some battles just couldn't be won. This one was a loser. Plastic cups were hard to find and expensive when available. Agreeing to save the rum for another night, the group prepared to disperse. Just as well. The lights went out.

"A blackout," sighed Diego.

I asked how long it would last.

"All night."

"So this happens a lot?"

"Cubans learn to accept."

8

"I'm going to meet Fidel."

Boris shook his head.

"You don't understand," I protested.

"No, *you* don't understand."

Boris grabbed a handful of newspapers stacked beside the telephone and extracted a recent edition of the government's tabloid-size daily, *Granma*. A bold headline said, FIDEL LEAVES

FOR CHINA. The giant mulatto salted my wound by showing me a picture of Castro hugging China's president. The president was out of town.

The text mollified my concern that he was far from Havana. It said that the leader planned to visit model farms and factories and, in Shanghai, the first stock exchange in a socialist country. Most important, the stay would last just eight days. A quick calculation told me that Fidel would be back for the party.

I tried to buy my own copy of *Granma*, which dubbed itself "the Official Organ of the Central Committee of the Cuban Communist Party." Easier said than done. Cost wasn't the issue; the Official Organ cost just twenty centavos, less than an American penny. The problem was availability. "Sold out" was the answer I got from every vendor I could find.

The kiosk keepers always posted a copy of the paper. I became a regular at my neighborhood stand. *Granma* taught me that Cubans referred to Castro as *"El Máximo,"* the big one; *"El Último,"* the ultimate one; and *El Líder,* the leader. *El Líder Último* combined both honorifics. Banner headlines let me track the man:

FIDEL VISITS THE GREAT WALL.

FIDEL AT CHINA'S HISTORIC MONUMENTS.

FIDEL VISITS IMPORTANT DEVELOPMENT SIGHTS IN SHANG-HAI.

FIDEL ENDS HIS VISIT TO SHENZHEN.

It would be a stretch to call *Granma* a newspaper, for it was virtually free of news. Articles resembled monologues by officials fleshing out truisms, such as "The quality of education is important for our society." Raw statistics were another staple. One morning the editors devoted a half page to a table showing province-by-province infant mortality rates for the past six years.

International coverage came in three flavors. One was good things happening in socialist countries. China's record harvest of cereals rated a glowing report. So did the North Korean leader's reiteration of the importance of socialism. The PLO and the IRA got good reviews.

Type-two stories described bad things happening to lapsed socialists. Moscow had three hundred thousand homeless people. East Germans were burning the homes of Turks. What had once been Yugoslavia was now utter chaos.

But *Granma* saved its fiercest spin for events in the U.S. Texas legalizes carrying arms. Alarming rise in violent adolescents. Miami is the seat of the Cali cartel. A banner year for the deportation of illegal immigrants. Record cold kills six.

The distorted truths* didn't keep me from trying to acquire a hard copy of *Granma*. One morning I joined a ragged line of more than thirty Cubans. Pointing to the kiosk ahead, I asked a stocky, gray-haired man whether this was the line for the paper. He looked up, examined me, and nodded.

"When does it come?"

He shrugged.

Another man pulled to a stop behind me. *"¿El último?"* he asked.

The ultimate? I didn't understand.

"¿El último?"

The man in front intervened. Jerking a thumb back at me, he said, *"Es el último."* I fixed my gaze forward to avoid catching the eye of the newcomer, who assumed the position behind me, *el último*, the last in line.

Vacant gazes were the norm among the torpid bunch waiting for *Granma*. Bodies hung limp. Feet shuffled and necks rolled. Nobody wondered, at least not aloud, why, with the clock preparing to strike ten, the paper hadn't arrived. Twenty more minutes passed before the vendors interrupted their own reading and plopped a pile of papers on the counter of the kiosk. The air buzzed. The line straightened as people assumed places behind one another.

A minute later I had barely moved forward. Meanwhile, order was turning to chaos. Like pigeons to bread crumbs, Cu-

---

*A Cuban joke had Fidel Castro and Napoleon meeting in the afterlife. "If you had my Soviet missiles, you would have never lost at Waterloo," says Fidel. Napoleon replies, "If I had your press, nobody would have found out."

bans were flocking to the kiosk. Some emerged from the darkness of a nearby store. Others deserted their spots in the adjacent line to swap pesos for dollars. Rather than taking places at the rear, the intruders inserted themselves ahead of me, in the middle of the line. Nobody complained.

Granma sold out when I was three places from the counter. The rest of the line melted away. Some of the people gravitated to the glass wall of the kiosk, where the vendors had posted the edition. The mob kept me four feet from the front page. That was close enough to make out the headline: FIDEL IS RECEIVED IN VIETNAM.

Vietnam? Vietnam wasn't part of the plan. Fly to China, stay eight days, come back to Havana. *That* was Castro's itinerary. What was he doing in Vietnam? More important, when would he be back? The Official Organ didn't say.

I sought another source. Camped in a back room of the Hotel Nacional was the staff of the film festival. With just a week to go before their party, they were sure to know whether the president planned to attend. I found the makeshift office occupied by a woman named Anita whose black hair curved a frame around the pronounced bones of her face. One of the festival's organizers, she was sure to know about the party.

"There's a party?" she said.

"That's what I'm asking you."

"Is there going to be a party at the Palace?" she asked a colleague.

The colleague shrugged.

"We don't know," said Anita.

I asked when they would know.

"Fidel is out of the country," said Anita.

"So?"

"If he doesn't return, there won't be a party."

"There's a party only if Fidel is there?"

"Yes."

"Will he be back?"

Anita shrugged. So did her colleague.

★

Waiting for Fidel's return, I met a woman named Laurie. She suggested that I accompany her to the foreign press center. The one-block walk gave her time to tell me that she was American, a filmmaker, and a regular at the film festival. Like Grandpa Munster, she had attended past parties. Like Grandpa, she had shaken the leader's hand. The president kissed her cheek. Laurie promised more details as she told me to wait in the basement of the press center, which doubled as an art gallery.

I needed fifteen minutes to ascertain that I had been ditched. During the interlude I met a Cuban whose manic hair and unkempt beard defied a face no older than mine. His immobile features and piercing green eyes gave him the focus of an assassin. Or an artist, which is what Eduardo was. The painter pointed to the wall, where an oversize canvas depicted fifty square feet of faces screaming in Munchian horror.

"Have you ever been on a camel?" he asked.

"A camel?"

The artist explained. Tugged by trucks built for pulling flat-beds, the trailers that transported Cuban commuters had two levels. The ends flanking sunken centers gave the buses a silhou-ette reminiscent of a two-humped camel. To understand the painting, he said, I had to ride one of the so-called camels.

"To understand Cuba you have to take a camel," added his wife.

"Camels" were hard to miss. True to Eduardo's rendition, the buses looked like nightmares on wheels. The carriages were packed, front to back, window to window, floor to ceiling. Movement looked improbable, breathing unlikely. Overcrowd-ing didn't stop the formation of lines longer than a city block on the sidewalks of Havana.

A shorter line formed at the door of the cafeteria, where the couple invited me to lunch. We claimed a place behind the last of twenty people. In Cuba, waiting was a given. Step two was to find out what we were waiting for. Eduardo began to quiz other would-be diners. What was for lunch? The folks at the back of the line didn't know. Near the front, a pair of women had heard a rumor: spaghetti.

"How's the spaghetti?" Eduardo asked a man leaving the cafeteria.

"Bad. Very bad."

"What else is there?"

"Nothing."

We left, I wondering how a restaurant could offer just one dish, Eduardo convinced that we needed a drink. The painter steered us into a featureless bar whose vacant counter and stools were visible from the sidewalk. The watering hole, like the cafeteria, had a one-item menu. It was rum or nothing. He ordered two glasses, each with three shots.

"*Se acabó,*" said one of two uniformed women slouching behind the bar.

Eduardo rose from his stool. I asked what was wrong.

"Sold out," said the painter.

It made no sense. I had already seen a bar with no glasses. Blackouts had forced me to grope my way home in the dark. But how could a bar — a bar selling only one item, rum — have depleted its stock by midday?

The news didn't affect my friends. The couple showed no hint of surprise. When I expressed regret about our failure to find either food or drink, Eduardo said, "This is Cuba." He approached a street vendor selling pizza and bought three. None had cheese. The patina of tomato paste failed to flavor the undercooked dough. Dessert, promised the artist, would be better.

"*¿El último?*" asked Eduardo when we reached the tail end of a line in a small park near his exhibition. A middle-age woman in a flowery blouse raised her hand, and the painter left his wife and me to hold our spot on the walkway into Havana's favorite ice cream parlor.

Coppelia was legendary for more than its flying saucer shape. Cubans had worshiped the quality of the ice cream since the place opened in 1966. They gushed about the variety of flavors. Was it twenty-four? Or forty? No two Cubans agreed. More uniform was the tone of dreamy reverence in which locals described the unimaginable array of exotic flavors. Coconut, banana, mango, guayaba . . . The list went on.

But Coppelia represented more than luscious ice cream. It was a magnet that attracted people from all corners of the capital. Teenage girls met there before the movies. The boys followed the girls. Once formed, couples kissed in the shade of tropical trees. Parents treated kiddies to triple scoops in a place that embodied the glory days of the Revolution.

"Sad" was how the painter's wife described Coppelia's present state. She called my attention to the structure's chipping paint and lifeless lights. The cheerful mural that once covered a long concrete wall had faded beyond recognition. Sadder still were the people standing in line. Ahead of us, thirty listless Cubans demonstrated every variation on the slump. The group's regular sighs were punctuated by dull moans — *"aye"* was a favorite — and tired exclamations, such as *"No es fácil."* It's not easy.

"This used to be a happy place," said the wife.

Looking to provide solace, I observed that the departure of the woman in front put us one spot closer to ice cream. Eduardo's wife shook her head. Cubans, she said, spent so much time in lines that society had developed rules. A person who had established a place in line was free to wander off. This allowed a Cuban to claim places in two or more lines or simply to ease the tedium of standing still. Nobody disputed the rights of a person who returned to an abandoned place.

An hour passed before an attendant herded us through the gate of a patio crowded with steel tables. There the waiting resumed. Who had time to spend the afternoon on an ice cream? Five schoolgirls in blouses and skirts surrounded one table. Another was occupied by a pair of mothers, who chatted while their children fidgeted. There were trios of women whose prim appearance suggested they had come from work. A handful of men, mostly alone, seated themselves in chairs left empty by the groups.

All eyes were on a cadre of stone-faced waitresses. One deposited four glasses of water and the same number of spoons on our table and left without a word. Her colleagues labored under the weight of tin trays carrying eight or ten plastic bowls, each heaped with three scoops of white ice cream. These were dropped, not placed, in front of customers.

"What flavor is this?" I asked after two spoonfuls.

"Vanilla," said Eduardo.

"Is there chocolate?"

"No."

"Is there any other flavor?"

"No."

Patience wasn't my forte. Twice a day I checked the pigeon-hole provided for each participant in the film festival. The box brimmed with invitations to screenings of obscure films. One filmmaker spotted my affiliation to British television and delivered a handwritten note asking to meet with me, the BBC producer. Missing was the invitation to the finale.

I suspected a plot. When not talking about herself or her documentary, Laurie told me about the previous year's finale. Everybody had been invited. Everybody, that is, except Americans. "Not so," said the festival's organizers when confronted with charges of discrimination. "The Americans' invitations just aren't ready." The invitations arrived at half past eight for a party that kicked off at seven o'clock.

I haunted the festival's office. The women in charge never failed to greet me with a smile. Nor did they tire of my increasingly shrill questions. Was the party on? Was I being excluded? Had others received invitations? Unable to answer, the pair downloaded other information. Did I know that Winston Churchill once stayed at the Hotel Nacional? Or that the American film star Matt Dillon was in town? How about Madonna? Had I heard the rumor that she was due to land in Havana? I hadn't. And she didn't.

Granma said that Cuba's commander-in-chief would spend four days in Vietnam. Finger-counting the days from his arrival in Hanoi, I reckoned he would leave on the Tuesday before the Friday-night party. Add a day for travel time. Another to compensate for my inability to understand the international dateline, and he would be back in plenty of time to host a party on Friday.

On Wednesday the tea leaves were rescrambled. FIDEL IN-TENDS TO DEVELOP RELATIONS WITH JAPAN, said the headline. The article elaborated: the leader was making a "transit" stop in Tokyo. Transit? I envisioned his pausing in the lounge of Narita Airport. The Japan stopover, I convinced myself, would only slightly delay Fidel's homeward progress.

There was no rationalizing the headline on Friday, the day I needed Fidel Castro to be in Havana primping for the party: FIDEL STOPS IN CANADA.

The president wasn't going to make it. The party was off. It didn't happen.

Disappointment was my first reaction. The weeks of waiting had taught me a lot about Cuba. Unlike the residents of other poor countries, Cubans looked healthy. Their intelligence was a tribute to free education. Underfed, they didn't seem to be starving. They *were* bored, but there were worse fates than tedium. Having decided that Cuba was a qualified success, I wanted to offer my compliments to the man in charge.

The news of Fidel's layover in Vancouver left me lifeless. Melancholy followed — the encounter with Cuba's leader wasn't meant to be. Then I spotted the Saturday edition of *Granma*. FIDEL RETURNS, said the headline. Below, a story recapped the statistics of the "historic trip." Fidel had covered 41,396 kilometers in the course of 18 days. Total time airborne: 48 hours and 58 minutes. The jet carrying the leader had touched down in Havana at 8:12 A.M.

On Friday.

9

FIDEL CASTRO SPENT most of his life making trouble. By the age of six he had stretched the patience of his Spanish father, who exiled the boy from the family's farm. Fidel landed in a boarding school in Santiago de Cuba, the biggest city in eastern

Cuba. There he cheated on math tests, beat up schoolmates, and punched a priest. Transferred to another school, he falsified report cards. During summer vacations he tried to coax his father's cane cutters to resist their boss.

Somehow he learned to read and write. The latter came in handy when, as a teenager, he wrote a letter to U.S. President Franklin Roosevelt: "I am a boy, but I think very much . . . if you like, give me a ten dollars bill green american in the letter, because I have not seen a ten dollars bill american and I would like to have one of them."

A Jesuit college in Havana brought Castro under control. At sixteen, he astounded classmates with displays of memory. Feats in basketball, baseball, and track won him the title of Cuba's top schoolboy athlete. Improved work habits made him one of his class's top ten students. The priests noted that the towering teen had the stuff of greatness.

Fidel found more time for trouble at the University of Havana. As a freshman studying law he joined the Anti-Imperialist League and the Committee for the Independence of Puerto Rico. He kicked off his second year with an antigovernment rant that became page one news. Fidel's extracurricular activities picked up in year three, when he trained for an invasion of the Dominican Republic. Back on campus, the big man's verbal attacks made the government cringe. The police tried to get physical with the critic, who packed a pistol. An ambush failed. Castro the troublemaker graduated in 1950.

Castro the lawyer favored hardship cases and political causes. The latter gave him more exposure. So did the bribery accusations he leveled against Cuba's president. Running for election to congress, he ended his campaign when the poll was canceled following a coup d'état in February 1952 by a former sergeant named Fulgencio Batista.

Castro saw red. At twenty-five, his goals were to oust Batista and revolutionize Cuba. He organized a band of like-minded patriots. One of the movement's members began to train the group to use guns. Meanwhile, Fidel crisscrossed the country to recruit and prepare other commandos. Short of guns, seeking a spark for nationwide revolt, he aimed to solve two problems with one attack.

The target was the Moncada barracks in Santiago de Cuba. On July 26, 1953, Fidel Castro and more than a hundred fighters assembled in a farmhouse outside the city and disguised themselves as soldiers. Their convoy included a Pontiac, a Buick, and a Chevy. Their weapons were a grab bag of shotguns and hunting rifles. Real soldiers shot back with better guns. Eight attackers died. Another sixty-one were hunted down, beaten bloody, and shot dead. The rest surrendered or were captured and tried. Bit players were sentenced to three years in prison. The ringleader, whom many Cubans considered a loudmouthed loser, got fifteen.

Nineteen months later, Batista released the prisoners. Castro went to Mexico to prepare another offensive. Scores of Cubans joined him. So did an Argentine doctor, Ernesto "Che" Guevara. About a year of training, planning, and fund-raising culminated when the heavily armed rebels set sail for eastern Cuba in a boat called *Granma,* whose previous owner, an American with fond memories of his grandmother, couldn't have imagined the later uses of his sentimentality.

Strong winds slowed the boat. A choppy sea sickened the passengers. The ship sprung a leak. An engine faltered. The yacht fell two days behind schedule. Food and water ran out. Worse, the rebels missed their rendezvous with supporters waiting on the shore to drive them to hideouts in the mountains. The navigator fell overboard but was saved. Nonetheless, the captain lost his bearings when *Granma* did reach Cuba's coast.

The journey ended at daybreak on December 2, 1956. At low tide, cruising near the shore, *Granma*'s hull stuck in the mud. Castro ordered his men to grab their gear and get in the water. "This wasn't a landing, it was a shipwreck," was how Che Guevara summed up the rebels' arrival near Las Coloradas, a village on the western edge of eastern Cuba.

★

"Fidel landed out there," said Francisco, raising an arm to indicate an area about a hundred yards from the concrete platform
beneath our feet.

I squinted at the aqua surface rippled by the faintest of
breezes. The calm made easy work for the shirtless men moving across our sightline. One took leisurely pulls on the oars of
a weathered rowboat. His mate reclined. Beyond the fishermen lay the Caribbean, more Caribbean, and a swollen sun
suspended thirty degrees above the horizon.

"And he went that way," said Francisco; his arm spun a semicircle from its first heading.

I tracked the gesture to the edge of a swamp. My eyes met
a wall of mangrove trees. Trunks no fatter than a fire hose
sprouted leaves the shape of paddles. Each shaft devolved into
an amalgam of crooked roots that disappeared into a tea-col-
ored murk. A mesh of vines connected the trees. Without a
boat, there would have been no way around the seamless tangle
before the construction of a manmade strip that penetrated
nature's mess.

The monument on the platform reminded me that others hadn't enjoyed the luxury of a walkway. Propagandists had
spray-painted WE WILL CONQUER on the stone marker. They
hadn't erased the scrawl of the amateur who had added, DOWN
WITH IMPERIALISM. A plaque embedded in the marker explained the significance of our position in Granma province.
It was here that Fidel Castro and eighty-one fellow rebels
launched their war against Batista.

The roots of my own journey to Las Coloradas were more
tangled. Frustration was part of the story. By skipping the film
festival, Fidel had drenched my dreams of a rendezvous. I spent
weeks devising other ways to meet, or at least see, El Máximo.
None panned out. Then the leader flew to Paris. I didn't expect
a speedy return.

There was little to keep me in Havana. I spent afternoons
visiting friends. A typical day included visits to Rodolfo, a mechanic, José, who worked in a café near Old Havana, and Os-
mani, an engineer who owned an art gallery. Sometimes I ate

dinner with Eduardo the painter. For rum, I could always count on Diego, the moviemaker. Like the Cubans, I spent a lot of time staring listlessly ahead. I waited for inspiration.

"Why don't you travel?" said the French journalist.

The suggestion made sense. Trying to meet Fidel had raised broader questions about Cuba. Was it a rich island fallen on hard times or a poor place returning to its natural state after the loss of its sugar daddy, the Soviet Union? Given their poverty, how did the locals keep smiling and dancing? Say Fidel died and recommended capitalism in his will. Would the country prosper? Maybe a road trip would provide fresh grist.

The east, said the Frenchman, was the Revolution's cradle. It was there that Castro concentrated his early efforts. Popular support grew. So did the size of his army. Only when the eastern foothold felt firm did the guerrillas begin to work their way west. Following his steps from Las Coloradas to Havana wouldn't get me an audience with the president. It might, however, amount to a meeting, albeit a metaphorical one.

Francisco glommed onto my plan the moment he overheard my sketch in the living room of Boris, his nephew. Wearing glasses and a baseball cap that covered a bald pate, the fifty-year-old exploded with enthusiasm. A road map of creases appeared on his burnished face. A thick black mustache couldn't disguise the yellow of his toothy smile. He immediately invited me to start the expedition with a visit to his family in Santiago de Cuba.

A week later, Francisco met me at the airport in his hometown and insisted on driving me to Las Coloradas. An engineer, he dismissed my concerns about his missing work. "It's more important for me to help you learn about Cuba," he said. Sensing my doubt, he added, "Don't worry, Cubans are always taking a vacation from work." Francisco spent the first eight hours of his vacation steering a Lada to the tip of Granma province.

"*Vamos?*" said Francisco, casting an eye on the setting sun.

"Let's go," I replied.

"Those poor guys," said Francisco as we reentered the swamp.

"Which poor guys?"

"The rebels. They didn't know where they were or how far they had to go. Their boat was ruined, so they couldn't go back. And they were in a swamp. The environment here is very . . ." He paused to find the right word. "Aggressive."

Francisco understated the case. Up close, the maze of mangroves was even more daunting. Sweeping away clouds of mosquitoes, I saw nothing but gnarled trees and twisted vines. The diabolic foliage hovered over shallow water and a gruesome bottom of mud. "Imagine," said Francisco at the end of our fifteen-minute stroll to shore.

The insurgents had taken longer to clear the swamp. Weighted down by supplies, Castro's men sunk to their waists in ooze. The water reached their chests. Extrication from one obstacle led to confrontation with the mesh of trees, roots, and vines. Leaves and branches ripped uniforms and slashed faces as the rebels stumbled through the swamp. Insects feasted on their flesh. Hours passed before the first of the filthy, bloody, exhausted army reached firm ground.

Francisco and I stopped at the shapeless building beside a deserted concrete plaza. He looked for a bathroom. I wandered toward a roof covering a boat. Only on spotting *Granma* painted on the ship did I recognize the replica. Less than fifty feet long, the wooden vessel couldn't accommodate a keg party. Anybody willing to load *Granma* with scores of invaders, plus their supplies, had to be gaga.

Three Cubans were standing near the stern. One held a brush, which he used to freshen *Granma*'s white coat. A coworker was minding a bucket of paint. Arms folded, the third man must have been in charge of quality. The human still-life brought to mind a Cuban friend's evaluation of labor relations on the island: "We pretend to work, and they pretend to pay us."

"Which way did the rebels go?" I asked.

The team took a break. The painter pointed across a narrow concrete road toward a line of low bushes and coconut trees. He said that the rebels had headed east, toward the Sierra Maestra. His mates noted that there were no roads linking their town to the mountains, not then, not now. They also told me where to find a man who had met the rebels when they left the swamp.

The man was out. Or so it seemed when we passed the black pig tied to the tree in front of the small concrete house. Francisco's repeated knocks on the weathered door brought no response. Nor did his shouts. Out back, we found only a barren yard populated by a half-dozen scrawny hens and a pair of piglets. Their squeals aroused a gray-haired woman wearing a long dress.

"Is this the home of Pablo Luis?" asked Francisco.

"PABLO," shouted the woman through the rear door before leading us back to the front.

The man holding the front door open with a callused palm looked well past his seventieth birthday. Lines crossed every inch of a face the color and texture of a baseball mitt. Scars and scabs marked other parts of his skin, which hung loosely from his bones. Whiskers reminded me of Bowery bums. So did his baggy shorts, a patchwork of blue cloth, black stitches, and brown soil. A soiled shirt retained only its top and bottom buttons. From his belt hung the trademark of the *guajiro,* a Cuban peasant, a scabbard carrying a two-foot machete.

"Come in. This is your house," he said in Spanish slurred almost beyond recognition. Asking neither our names nor our business, the old man gestured to two wooden chairs and seated himself in a third. He leaned forward to hear what we wanted.

While Francisco explained my interest in the *Granma* landing, I surveyed the home. The shelves carried no books. There were photographs of several children, three giant seashells, and a blowfish. A Soviet television resembled a safe. A chicken pecked for food in the cracks of the tile floor. A black-and-white shot of Pablo and Fidel Castro confirmed we had come to the right place.

"In 1956 I didn't know anything about communism," said Pablo. "I had heard of Fidel Castro. He was the young lawyer who went to jail after attacking Moncada. But that was all I knew." When I asked how he recognized Fidel, the chatty old man turned serious. "I wasn't the first one to see Fidel Castro. It was my neighbor, Angel Perez Rosabal."

"How did he recognize Fidel?"

"Fidel said 'Have no fear, I am Fidel Castro, and we came to liberate the Cuban people.'"

Pablo continued after reiterating that he was the second, not the first, local to sight the rebel leader. What he saw was a group of four or five men. The old man confirmed what I had read and Francisco had said: the guerrillas' uniforms were torn and dirty. Streaks of blood and scratches lined their arms and faces.

"I felt sorry for them," said Pablo, leaning down to scratch a piglet who had wandered indoors. "I asked if they wanted food but they said no. I asked if they wanted coffee. They said they had no time. They had to move on.

"Later I saw more men. One group was carrying a big machine gun and a lot of bullets. I offered to get them two trucks and to take them wherever they wanted to go. They said they couldn't accept because they didn't know me." Pablo paused, slipped his hand inside his shirt, and rubbed his ribs. "It's too bad they didn't know me. They would have had an easier time."

The leader stuck out from his group, said the old man. At thirty, he was older than most of the others. More striking was his size. "He was big, impressive," said Pablo, stretching his hand over his own head to demonstrate the height. The peasant remembered a handshake, followed by an embrace. "Fidel thanked me, even though I did very little."

"When they left, did you hope they would win?"

"Fidel hugged me. After that I was always on his side."

10

APPLIANCES DON'T BELONG in the Sierra Maestra. Impossibly steep, the mountains that form Cuba's southeast coast offer few flat surfaces on which to place, say, a big-screen TV. Rarer still are electrical outlets. Power lines stop short of peaks shrouded in clouds and blanketed by trees. So why, three, maybe four, thousand feet above sea level, was I looking at a squat American refrigerator?

The man who led me to Castro's wartime headquarters caught me staring at the antique icebox. Deviating from the monotone characteristic of Cubans mouthing the Party line, the guide said, "The refrigerator was for storing medicine, not food."

"They had electricity?"

"It uses gas."

But how had Castro lugged a fridge up here to Cuba's roof? Hadn't I had enough trouble just getting my body up to Co-mandancia de La Plata? My journey began in Bayamo, the capital of Granma province. At dawn Francisco and I were already in the bus terminal. The stationmaster, a pal of Francisco's, handed us a bottle of rum and two tickets to the foothills of the Sierra Maestra. Paying customers included a gang of unshaven farmers, a young couple carrying a chicken in a plastic bag, and a woman cradling a child. Given a seat by a drill sergeant, she, like the rest of the passengers, nodded off.

Kept awake by the rattling of a flimsy vehicle, I looked to the left of the rudimentary road. The rim of mountains behind the ridges looked too low to have hidden Castro's rebels. Even less suitable for a hideout was the area to the right. Cows grazed on browned grass. Weathered men wearing straw hats lounged in front of wooden houses with roofs of thatch or tin. Near one cluster of shacks a shirtless man raked the infield of a baseball diamond cut out of the rough plain.

Two breakdowns, twenty-five miles, and a hundred minutes later, the bus gasped to a halt in Bartolomé Maso. On my own, I would have gone no farther: the stationmaster said we had missed the only bus to Santo Domingo, a tiny town high in the Sierra Maestra. Francisco steamed ahead, breaking into a determined walk. A quarter mile later he flagged down a tractor. The ride lasted until an intersection a half mile away.

"We'll wait here," said Francisco.

"For what?"

"A truck."

Ten Cubans had the same idea. We gathered beneath the branches of the only tree in sight. During the next hour I was the only one to examine the six-foot sign bearing the profile of Castro. Dressed in fatigues and wearing a backpack, a rifle hanging from his shoulder, the commander-in-chief's message was TO ORDER. Nearby, smaller letters marked the spot where a rebel soldier had been shot in March 1958.

Other signs of the rebels appeared after a green truck stopped long enough for all twelve hitchhikers to clamber onto its rear tires, over sides higher than our heads, and into the cargo hold. We passed a billboard with wisdom from Fidel's brother, Raúl, the head of Cuba's military. A faded sign showed the names and faces of two guerrillas killed in July 1958. Farther uphill, a concrete monument remembered another fallen rebel.

"We're lucky," said Francisco, who spoke to the driver before boarding. "This truck is going to pick up coffee. It goes all the way to the top."

Lucky wasn't how I felt as rolling hills became severe inclines. Every time the driver shifted gears to cope with the ascent, the passengers jerked forward, then fell backward. Tight turns around rims carved into the mountainside sent us careening across the hold. A vehicle that rolled over the edge of the two-lane road would drop a hundred feet or more. My fear of falling multiplied when the other passengers began to gossip. The topic was the bus, which had tipped over the edge just a month before.

The ride got hairier after the other freeloaders jumped off at Santo Domingo. The inclines sharpened. The twists tightened. The truck belched exhaust and slowed to a crawl while negotiating the zigzag. The vehicle paused, then rolled a few feet downhill when the driver downshifted. Francisco shrugged off my plaintive glances.

The Cuban had spent the uphill adventure pointing out achievements of the Revolution. The phone cables, medical clinic, and reservoir we saw hadn't been in the Sierra Maestra before Castro came to the mountains. Jumping down from the cargo bin when we reached a flat patch called Alto del Naranjo, he announced triumphantly, "During the war it took three days to reach this point."

Arrow-shaped planks nailed to a post marked the crossroads. Pico Turquino, Cuba's highest peak, was a thirteen-kilometer walk. A community called La Platica was less than two. One arrow indicated that Santo Domingo lay five kilometers downhill. The fourth pointed into the forest: three kilometers to Comandancia de La Plata, Castro's headquarters during the war against Batista.

Francisco never stopped chattering. He talked about the trees that formed a tunnel around the path. One was a pine, another was unique to the Sierra Maestra. Coffee was the only tree I remembered. My mind was on my feet. Littered with round rocks that ignored the grip of hundred-dollar running shoes, the muddy trail demanded full attention.

The hike ended at a pen of chickens and pigs. Beside the yard stood a shack with a covered terrace overlooking a lush crease where two mountains met. Once the home of a peasant, it now belonged to the monitors of Fidel's former post. The man on duty served glasses of home-grown coffee. Then he pulled on his red and white cap and offered to show us the mothballed base. Francisco decided to rest.

I followed the guide higher into the hills. When mud oozed over the rim of my sneakers, he recommended boots. "Don't slip," he said on hearing the collision of my knee and the soggy earth. Two spills later the Cuban asked where I came from. My response elicited a comment: "Batista used American airplanes to look for the rebels. But the trees were too thick. That's why Fidel chose this place." Further harping about the genius of the Revolution and its father tired me more than the climb.

Post One was unremarkable. A simple cabin served as the way station for visitors to his headquarters. More striking was the Sierra Maestra. The rugged angles conveyed power. Blanketed in a patchwork of green, the peaks emanated a might that inspired rather than intimidated. To this was added a feeling of possibility. The slice of blue visible through a V-shaped gap was the Caribbean. Close enough to touch, the sea represented the tantalizing nearness of victory.

The guide led me to the rest of the camp. Sprawled across the side of the hill was the makeshift town where Castro spent most of the two-year fight. We visited a guest house for rebels from other camps as well as the cities. We walked by wooden shacks that had served as the kitchen, hospital, and storage house. The guide frowned while pointing at the grave of a dead comrade. He brightened when gesturing toward the top of the hill, where Che Guevara set up a radio transmitter. He beamed while showing me where Castro had signed Revolutionary Law 1, which granted tenants, renters, and squatters ownership of the land they worked.

The Cuban's voice fell to a hush when we reached the tour's highlight, Fidel Castro's house. Stilts kept the cramped cabin from sliding down the mountain. A ladder reached up to the entrance. Inside were a long table and benches for meetings and a smaller table that served as a desk. The guide showed me a wastebasket made of twigs. Behind a bookcase I found something almost as odd as the refrigerator: a double bed and mattress.

"The people brought the bed here so Fidel could be comfortable," said the guide. "For Cubans this place is the most famous, the most loved, of the war. It is where the first combatants of the Revolution . . ."

My thoughts drifted. The uphill journey had clarified the inaccessibility of Fidel's hideout. The canopy of foliage made it clear why the base was never spotted by Batista's aircraft. The high ground gave the rebels another advantage. Enemies struggling up the mountainside were easy to spot. Small forces could be ambushed, big ones sidestepped. A nest in the Sierra Maestra would give a king confidence.

Answers bred new questions. Batista's forces ambushed Castro's army three days after the landing. A few rebels were shot. Dozens were captured and killed or jailed. Some simply disappeared. Of the eighty-two men who landed, fewer than twenty made it to the Sierra Maestra. How did a handful of guerrillas defeat an entrenched dictatorship? Isolated in the mountains, how did they conquer the rest of Cuba?

The thought train stopped when I glanced at my watch. The truck driver had offered to carry us down the mountain. But he wouldn't wait. I cut short the gab — "the Sierra Maestra, and above all La Plata, was the place where Fidel and Che and the rebels" — and went to find Francisco.

Francisco and I sighed with relief at the end of the dirt road to La Platica, the village where the truck was to load its cargo. In the hold, we found the squat driver dozing on two sacks of coffee beans. Four other workers looked no more jazzed about loading coffee. Dressed in combinations of battered pants, soiled shirts, and decrepit shoes, the unshaven crew was taking a break from taking a break. Each chewed on his own four-foot stalk of sugarcane, whose tough skin had been shaved off with a machete.

I walked to the road's edge and looked at the village spread across the hillside below. Wooden shacks were scattered wherever a level patch had been found or built among the effusive foliage. The children playing in the narrow paths between the homes were the only signs of life. The only adult residents in sight were two men coaxing five mules to carry double loads of coffee up the road and the villager in charge of the produce.

The bean counter's arrival brought the truck's crew to life. The activity quickened as the sky turned an ominous shade of gray. Working in pairs, the men disappeared into the darkness of an unpainted shack. They emerged carrying sacks of coffee. These were swung onto the truck's tailgate, where the driver maneuvered them into stacks. Francisco helped.

I joined them. Paired with one of the Cubans, I began to shuttle into the warehouse. A pile of more than fifty sacks filled one side of the room. On the other side was a mountain of unbagged beans and a scale. The dirt on the bags turned muddy, meeting the sweat on my arms. After more than twenty trips in tandem, I tried lifting one of the bags on my own. My partner grabbed my arm.

"Don't do that," he said.

"It's not that heavy."

"We don't like to work too hard."

The bags of beans filled all but four feet of the cargo bay. Francisco and I climbed aboard when the engine rumbled to life. The workers piled into the cab. The clouds were opening. Drizzle turned to downpour as the truck began to crawl forward.

"The Sierra Maestra is a very rainy place," shouted Francisco.

I concentrated on hanging on as the Soviet truck bumped along the rocky road. Legs apart, knees bent, I grabbed the side with both hands. A yellow cord was all that separated me and a back flip off the vehicle's open tail. The rain slapped our faces. So did low-flying branches. The beating was a minor concern compared to the problems up front.

The road had become a river. The truck struggled over wet rocks. Small boulders pitched the rig on unnatural angles. Baths of mud caused the tires to slide sideways. No problem at sea level, the slippage was terrifying at altitudes. I looked over the side of the truck at wheels not two feet from the edge of a drop.

"Christopher, if the truck falls off the road, jump off," shouted Francisco.

I must have frowned.

"Don't worry, I've done it before."

I nodded.

"Christopher, do you want a drink?" he said, holding out his plastic flask of rum.

Keeping two hands on the truck was a higher priority.

I relaxed a bit when the wheels hit concrete at Alto del Naranjo. Traction improved thanks to corrugations in the pavement. Hair dripping, clothes soaked, I wouldn't unclench my teeth until we had cleared the corkscrew incline. Moving steadily downhill, the driver slowed on spotting an old man dragging a sack placed on a strip of bark.

We had seen the wizened man before. He had passed by during the workers' break. His blue work shirt and brown pants were in shreds. His toes showed through holes in his shoes. A head shorter than I, he was bent forward by the weight of a sack of oranges slung over one shoulder. He eased the load to the ground beside me, touched the machete hanging from his belt, and said, "It's not easy."

"The Struggle," I said.

"I'm sixty-six years old. I look sixty-seven, but I'm sixty-six."

"How long have you lived in the mountains?"

"Since 1950."

The old man had lived at ground zero during the birth of the Revolution. He must have seen the war, known the rebels. His memories might help me understand how a tiny band had taken over an entire country. Careful not to inquire too directly, I asked where he was during the fighting.

"On my farm."

I waited for more. The old man hoisted his sack and slung it over his shoulder. Turning to leave, he said, "The Struggle."

Leaving an hour later, the truck caught up to the old man. The driver stopped to offer a lift. The old man held out his hands so that Francisco and I could pull him onto the truck. After a long swig of Francisco's rum, he turned talkative. The subject was his farm. Pointing up the angled face of the hill to a flat patch high above our heads, he indicated the place where he grew yucca, beans, and rice. He also had a mule and some goats. What he didn't have was luck. The mule had shed its shoes and he couldn't afford a new set. Four of his goats had died the previous month.

"Rum?" said Francisco.

The old man tipped a swallow of rum into his mouth.

"Finish it. Finish it," Francisco insisted.

The last inch and a half of rum vanished. With it I saw the evaporation of my hopes of seeing the invaders through the eyes of an invadee. The old man would be too drunk to speak. Instead, the alcohol opened new doors.

"I knew the rebels. They were my neighbors, my friends."

"When did you see them?"

"They bought food from me. They paid for half."

"And the other half? Did they rob you?"

The old man pulled back, as if I had desecrated his daughter. He explained that the rebels didn't have much money. They were poor, like the people, and hungry, like the people. But they never, ever, stole from the people. Those were Fidel's orders.

Fidel had another standing order. His aim was to convert Cubans, one by one, to his cause. Robbed by a soldier, a peasant might become an enemy of the Revolution. Similar thinking bred the policy on prisoners of war. Executions of traitors and officers of the ruling regime were common. Not so with ordinary soldiers. When captured, Batista's soldiers were treated with kindness and, often, turned into rebels.

"So what about the other half?" I asked the old man. "Who paid for that?"

"I *gave* the food to Fidel."

FRANCISCO COMBED the remains of breakfast from his shaggy mustache and briefed me on life in his hometown, Santiago de Cuba. Blackouts, he said, were more frequent than in the capital. This mattered because the loss of power knocked out the city's hygiene system. Rather than make daily guesses about potability, the locals drank boiled water.

A different problem affected the bathroom of his home, whose innards were as Spartan as barracks. To save energy, the city pumped water through the system just twice a week. The residents stored water for the dry days. Topless oil drums held Francisco's reserve. Worried about my ability to cope with Cuban austerity, he showed me how to flush the toilet and bathe with a bucket of water.

Generosity overflowed. Francisco and his wife had vacated their bedroom for their guest. "It's your house," was their answer to my protests. When I woke up Francisco prepared a local specialty, a shake made from guayaba. His wife, Carla, a brown-eyed professor who dyed her hair auburn, cooked me enough eggs, toast, and coffee to feed a family of four. Then she spent more than an hour rehashing the history of the Revolution.

Instructive on the appeal of Castro to country folk and mountain men, the visit to Granma province hadn't explained how his movement had spread to cities such as Santiago de Cuba. Spotting my skepticism when she said, "It was the will of the people," Carla proposed a syllabus for learning about the Revolution. The historian listed the places where Castro stopped during his attempt to storm the Moncada barracks. Connecting those dots would teach me why the people embraced the rebel.

"Do you have a map?" I asked.

"Ask the people where to go," said Carla.

Strangers waved and shouted greetings as I walked down the street. A shoeless boy grabbed my hand and asked whether I liked coconuts. Hearing "yes," he clambered up one of the skinny trees beside his house and yanked down a football-size fruit. Two men interrupted surgery on a DeSoto to offer a tip to a visitor: "Santiago's sun is very strong. Walk in the shade."

The mechanics also steered me down a broad street lined with narrow, tin-roofed, wooden houses worthy of a frontier town. I passed a wall painted ¡CUBA SÍ. YANQUI NO! before reaching an intersection used mainly by scrawny horses pulling four-wheeled carts. The clicking of hooves was only occasionally drowned out by the rattle of trucks older than the Revolution. There were no cars on the road.

Roads built for horses, not horsepower, narrowed as the city center neared. Terra-cotta tiles baked on flat-faced houses years away from their last layer of paint. Residents along the slight but steady incline left open their elongated shutters and doors. Fresher than the residential street, the face of the downtown probably hadn't changed since the turn of the century.

A metal plaque on the side of one of the low buildings indicated that I was on course: "In this house was given protection to the men commanded by Fidel Castro Ruz during the glorious actions of 26 July 1953." Up a commercial street where shoppers ignored the empty shop windows, on the far side of a plaza bombarded by salsa coming from public loudspeakers, I found a similar plaque.

A blubbery man wearing a white shirt splattered with food stains confirmed that I had found the Rex Hotel, the place Castro slept before the attack on Moncada. Spread across the opening to a dark staircase, he wouldn't let me into the landmark, where I hoped to replicate the leader's last meal.

"Blackout," he said.

"Do I need lights to eat lunch?"

"The restaurant is only for Cubans."

The comment reminded me that the state divided Cuba into two worlds. Hard-pressed for cash, the government created a sphere where tourists could relax, enjoy the best of the island, and drop big bucks. Creating an ambiance conducive to spending meant keeping hotels free from hustlers. Cigar hawkers were no more welcome at the Nacional's bar than panhandlers at the Oak Room of the Plaza. Even though they benefited from the apartheid — tourist dollars financed social services — the Cubans grumbled. "Why are tourists treated better than I am in my own country?" was a common cry.

The desperation for dollars bred other policies. Cuban hotels offered no exchange facilities; many visitors never touched a peso. Keeping foreigners in the realm of hard currency meant keeping them out of peso places, where prices were low and subsidized by the state. When foreigners did enter Cuban restaurants, they were often charged a higher price, in dollars.

Blocked by the bouncer, I tried the truth. I said that I was an American with an interest in Fidel Castro. I was retracing the leader's footsteps. The path had brought me to the Rex, where I wanted to mimic the meal eaten by Castro and his cohorts before the attack: chicken and rice, salad, platanos, bread and butter, and mineral water or Hatuey beer.

"There's no chicken," he said.

"How about Hatuey?"

"There's none."

"What about salad? And platanos?"

"None."

Walking toward the stop for the bus to a town called Siboney, where Fidel's men assembled at a farmhouse before the attack, I stopped on a street dotted with vendors selling pots, earrings, and handmade shoes. A shirtless man sold me a roast pork sandwich. His friend, who had the day off from his job at an oil refinery, treated me to a bottle filled with powdered juice. A third man held open a shopping bag filled with palm-size bricks of ice cream.

Food was also the priority of the gray-haired mulatto standing beside me on the public bus to Siboney. The sturdy man's right hand held the handles of two buckets. His left hand gripped the feet of a live chicken resigned to its inverted position. A carpenter, the man was proud of his eye for poultry: the chicken in his hand had cost just forty pesos, less than two dollars. He thrust the animal toward me.

I took hold of the warm legs and pretended to judge the bird. Pleased when I agreed he had found a good one, the carpenter invited me to help him kill, clean, and eat the chicken. "I'm busy," I said. "And not hungry." Unruffled, he got off, but not before asking a round-faced girl in a school uniform to point out the farmhouse.

She forgot. A mile beyond it I disembarked across from a ramshackle home. The owner, whose shirt failed to cover his belly, introduced me to the pig at his feet. He led me to four more pigs in the pen behind the house. The jolly man offered lunch, an invitation that coincided with a display of the brown ooze he fed the animals. "This is your house," he shouted as I rode away in a horse-drawn cart whose driver had stopped to offer a lift.

I expected geniality to fizzle at the farmhouse. Painted white with red trim, the one-floor home would be manned by hacks spewing commie-speak. The sight of the red and black flag of Castro's movement affirmed my belief. The prim woman of forty at the head of the gravel walkway looked every bit the pedant.

Up close, however, she was like everybody else in Santiago de Cuba. My arrival didn't stop her from moving her feet in time to the salsa blasting from a radio next door. She beamed on learning that I was American and asked why I was alone. When I shrugged, the guide leaned forward, kissed my cheek, and said, "Now you aren't alone."

Nor was I alone during my return journey about an hour later. Joining a busload of passengers, I found myself pressed against a light brown man in a clean white shirt. He asked where I was from. I told him. He asked where I was going.

"Moncada," I said.

"The place Fidel went *loco.*"

"Crazy?"

"Fidel is a good man. But he was crazy the day he attacked Moncada."

The passenger ticked off a list of bad judgments and bad luck. The second biggest fort in Cuba, Moncada housed more than four hundred soldiers. They had machine guns. Fidel attacked with a hundred and twenty-three men armed with hunting rifles and pistols. Unfamiliar with the streets of Santiago de Cuba, two of the drivers in the caravan of cars lost their way. Another car got a flat tire. The Buick in which Fidel rode stalled outside Moncada's gates, where the group was surprised by a patrol.

The Cuban wasn't criticizing his president. My reading was that he viewed the incident as a blip in the career of an indisputable hero. Still, that sixty-one men had died during or after the attack was tragic. "Those poor guys," sighed the speaker. Nearby passengers nodded soberly, as if their own sons had died.

A sleepy man had replaced the armed sentries at the entrance to Moncada. No longer a barracks, the fifteen-acre sprawl had become the 26th of July School. Inside the perimeter of pastel yellow walls I found a coach with a clipboard putting thirty shoeless boys through soccer drills. At the far end of the former rifle range were dozens of boys standing in formation and pounding drums. A corps of girls kept time with their feet.

Two fleshy, middle-age women emerged from the ground floor of the former barracks, a long, two-story building pocked with replicas of the bullet holes left by the attack. The heavier of the pair asked what I was doing. "That's beautiful," was one woman's response to my story about following Fidel's footsteps. "Forget your plan. Come with us for ice cream," said the other woman. "We have passes. We won't have to wait."

The inside of the farmhouse and the fortress made as deep an impression as the locals who shepherded me from stop to stop.

At Siboney, black-and-white photographs made clear Batista's brutality. The poster-size pictures showed dead attackers, guns placed at their sides. Dark blotches spotting the backs of corpses turned facedown indicated that the men had been shot from behind. The bloodied faces of the men on their backs suggested beatings before execution. No further explanation was needed for the men whose shattered skulls lay in pools of blood.

Signs of the attackers' ineptitude magnified my view of the previous dictator's cruelty. One of the many glass cases containing the counterfeit uniforms used by Castro's men included footwear. One attacker had worn wing-tip shoes. Another wore black high-top sneakers with white laces. The guide showed me the bathroom where Fidel quarantined four university students who got cold feet.

At the museum inside the Moncada barracks I came across a group of thirty schoolchildren gathered around a pretty woman in a white blouse and red skirt. Cast in the roles of educator and inquisitor, the guide spoke briefly about the history of the rebellion in Cuba. Then she began firing questions.

"Who were the leaders of the 26th of July Movement?"

A forest of little hands shot up. The proud tyke selected to answer named Fidel and Raúl Castro and Abel Santamaría, whose eyes were gouged out with a bayonet before his summary execution.

"Against whom were they fighting?"

"Batista," barked the obedient child chosen to speak.

"Was this a fight to help the rich?"

"No!" cried a chorus of kiddies.

"Who did Fidel want to help?"

"The poor!"

The last stop on the tour prescribed by the historian showed the underside of Cuba's glitz during the Batista era. Across the street from Moncada was the former hospital where Castro, acting as his own attorney, defended himself and his attack on a regime he deemed illegitimate. The cramped nurses' lounge–turned–courtroom still contained a skeleton hanging in a glass case. A portrait of Florence Nightingale hung on the wall. Here, amid the clutter of chairs and desks, the leader delivered the two-hour speech that became the canon of the Revolution.

Exhibits in the hospital's other rooms depicted the plight of the average Cuban. One room showed the sorry state of education. Giant photographs showed public schools where frowning children sat at outdoor desks. Writ large was a quote from Castro: "It is inconceivable that 30% of our compatriots cannot sign their name, and 99% do not know the history of Cuba." A chart on the wall detailed an illiteracy rate of about one in four Cubans.

The display condemning health care was no less biting. A picture showed naked children with distended bellies. In another, a mother used a straw hat to fan a sleeping child. A third photo showed a woman crying over a dead baby. Advertisements for a funeral home were juxtaposed with ads for an air-conditioned kennel.

The museum fleshed out other points Castro made while arguing that a revolutionary government should replace Batista's rule. A country of 5.5 million had 600,000 unemployed. Another half-million peasants worked just four months each year. According to Fidel, the pension funds of 400,000 industrial workers had been stolen, while 100,000 small farmers worked land that wasn't theirs. Teachers and professors were badly paid. Graduates went from classroom to skid row.

Summing up his defense, Castro said, "Condemn me, it does not matter; history will absolve me."

★

A cabbie in Havana had provided my first glimpse of life before the Revolution. Like others in the capital, the middle-age driver did his share of griping about the shortages of food, fun, and everything else. But, he said, life was better than during *La Tirania*.

"The Tyranny?"

"The time of Batista."

The driver said that as a teenager he was afraid to leave his house after eight P.M. Criminals were one reason the streets weren't safe. The driver mimed a knife slicing his throat and a pistol put to his head. The police made little effort to stop crime. In fact, the cops were reason number two to stay home after dark.

"Before the Revolution, the police did whatever they wanted," said the driver. "They would stop people and take their money. If a person had no money, the police might beat him. They would walk into stores, grab cigars, and not pay. To be a policeman was to own a gold mine."

Another Habanero told me that the enforcers grew more lawless as the Revolution built steam. The police suspected young people of complicity with Castro, whose associates were fighting a clandestine war in the capital and other cities. Students were particularly vulnerable to random arrest. Many were jailed. Torture was common. The accounts of misery under Batista increased in Santiago de Cuba.

Take Francisco's mother. Walking to her home, Francisco and I turned right off a paved road and onto a street of packed dirt. The Cuban pointed to an empty lot where his father's store had stood before its wooden walls collapsed. He also showed me where the family built a sturdier shop and a house, which his mother had vacated to make room for her daughter and three grandchildren. Mrs. Matos's current place was around the corner.

The old woman welcomed me. Then she apologized: because the one-room house had no kitchen, she had no food to offer. Pulling at her long gray hair, the wrinkled woman asked me to excuse her lost beauty. Nor was there anything she could do about the lack of chairs. Seating me on the edge of the double bed that occupied a third of her home, Mrs. Matos opened an album filled with old photographs.

The snapshots painted a romantic picture of life before the Revolution. A younger, lovelier Mrs. Matos posed beside children and their frosted birthday cakes. The well-groomed boys wore shorts, the girls frilly blouses. As adults, they switched to white suits and satin dresses and posed beside multilayered wedding cakes. A picture of a small wooden building sparked a narration:

"This is our first store. We sold food, drinks, and other little things." Outside stood two men wearing broad-brimmed hats, shirts with neckties, and khaki pants tucked into boots. "Those are the police of the Tyranny. They used to come into the store and ask for ham sandwiches and beer. Sometimes they asked for cigarettes. But they never paid."

"Did you ask for money?"

"No, no, no," said the old woman. "They would have beaten me like they beat my friends. Or maybe they would shoot me. No, you never asked for money."

Mrs. Matos's story reminded me of a phrase I had read at the Siboney farmhouse written by José Martí: "Tyranny stirs the virtues that kill it." Another Cuban convinced me that the nineteenth-century nationalist had it right.

We met in Marte Plaza. The small park opposite the Rex Hotel was one of the places people gathered in the late afternoon. Trees kept the sun off those who weren't ready to go home. A group gathered around four men playing dominoes on a portable table. Others listened to a baseball game broadcast from the public loudspeakers or examined statistics and schedules posted on boards and dangled like Christmas ornaments from the branches of a tree.

Conversation was Santiago's main diversion. Pairs of women talked quietly. Men, who formed larger groups, tended to jump to their feet and flail their arms when making a point. Seated alone on the edge of an argument about Omar Linares, Cuba's biggest baseball star, I found myself drawn into orbit by a deeply tanned man whose head was covered by a short gray stubble.

My talk with Tato started on familiar ground. He asked about America and told me about relatives who lived in Miami. He asked my impressions of Santiago. Effusive about the locals' sociability, I wondered aloud how people dared to share their food. They appeared to have so little.

"We had less during the Tyranny," said Tato. "But more political problems."

"Political problems?"

"The police killed one of my brothers. After that we were scared to go outside. They made it impossible to live in Santiago de Cuba. To resist, we joined the 26th of July Movement. Later we went to the Sierra Maestra to help Fidel. Life was hard there in the mountains. Some days we marched from five o'clock in the morning until ten o'clock at night. Rain fell every day. At night it was cold. We didn't have much food. But that life was better than living in constant fear."

Tato noticed that his cronies had tuned in to his monologue. Evidently pleased to have an audience, he raised his voice and made a sweeping conclusion: "Batista was an asshole. Cuba is much better without Fulgencio Batista."

"Instead we got thirty-seven years of misery," chimed a man of thirty.

"Misery!" cried Tato, rising to his feet. "You're too young to know about misery. Misery is no education, no job. Misery, no food. Misery is when you can't walk on the streets because the police will kill you."

Tato hammered his fist on every beat of the key word, "misery." Having proved his point, he folded his arms and relished the silence of the listener he had dumbed. But he saved his best for last: "Fidel came here and saved us all."

12

"POLICE . . ."

"MONEY . . ."

"LET ME IN . . ."

"POLICE . . ."

The pounding of a fist on a wooden door accompanied the words invading my unconscious. The stew of sounds thickened when a dog started barking. Within seconds a canine chorus was in full throat. A guest soloist, a trotting horse, clip-clopped through the scene. The animal left. The howls continued.

I opened my eyes and tried to focus. Where was I? No answer presented itself. The dull light pulsing through the half-angled shutters made it difficult to judge the hour. Sleeping in my fifth bed since coming to Cuba, I found nothing familiar to help me place the room. A minute passed before I recalled that I was in Santiago de Cuba.

The stir in the street refreshed old worries. Diffused by the soupy air, the pounding sounded close, very close. The desperate voice lacked the precision I would expect of jackboots on a sweep for illegally housed foreigners. Slurred shouts might, however, belong to an informer. It wasn't impossible that the man was downstairs and demanding money from Francisco. If he didn't get it, he was going to the police.

The inference wasn't far wrong. I tiptoed to the window and peered into the night. I saw a silhouette across the street. Focusing, I made out the backside of a bulky man wearing a baggy white suit. He pressed one palm to the door of a narrow, two-story home. His other hand slammed the entrance.

"MY MONEY," he bellowed. "LET ME IN. I'LL CALL THE POLICE."

The creditor tripped his way back to the sidewalk. Dogs barked as he grumbled to himself. He grabbed the rough club, lumbered back to the door, and resumed pounding. Nobody answered. He stumbled to the adjacent house and beat the neighbor's door.

"THIRTY PESOS. THEY ROBBED ME OF THIRTY PESOS."

Twenty minutes later a white police car arrived. The appearance of two officers in light blue shirts and dark blue slacks brought people out of both homes. The attacker didn't see the folks he had been trying to rouse, for he was occupied with pleading his case — "THEY ROBBED ME OF THIRTY PESOS" — to the policemen, who listened long enough to see the trouble.

"He's drunk," said one of the neighbors.

"Like always," said another.

"I WANT MY THIRTY PESOS."

The police tried to calm him. Five minutes of patience produced no result. The man continued to shout about his money. He criticized the cops for not getting it. An officer placed his hands on the man's meaty shoulders. The drunk shook himself free. The cop braced for a tussle.

The tension lasted for the few seconds it took for a small man wearing shorts and a tank top to intervene. Claiming to be a friend of the drunk, he spoke softly to the policemen, who nodded. Then he slung the big man's arm over his own shoulder and led him away like a medic supporting an amputee. The drunk broke free and raised a fist.

"FEEE-DELLL," he screamed.

The friend pulled him back on course.

"FEEE-DELLL." The cry faded into the night. "Feee-delll."

"Fidel was up there."

Juan pointed north, toward the two-story structure across the street from the park where we sat. As long as the city block, the building's fresh white paint and smooth tiles stood out in Santiago's faded downtown. Through the ground floor's arched doorway were the offices of the Poder Popular, the People's Power. Attached to the face of the city hall's second floor were three wooden balconies, painted blue.

"He was on the balcony," said the aging Cuban, indicating the center of the building. "The people were all around here. Every-where."

The sweep of Juan's gesture covered the whole of Céspedes Park. Halfway up the hill separating Santiago de Cuba's horse-shoe-shaped harbor and the edge of the downtown district at Marte Plaza, the square had long been the home of the city's power brokers. The first was Diego Velázquez, the Spanish conquistador who established Santiago de Cuba, Havana, and five other settlements. Built in 1522, the stone house from which he ruled the island still occupied half of the park's west edge.

The Catholic Church set up shop on the south side of the square. On a base above street level, the cathedral had twin towers flanking a domed center. Its wooden doors looked too heavy to open. A different sort of clout resided a quarter turn counterclockwise. Converted to a cultural center, an elegant building had once been a club for merchants and landowners. Beside it stood a hotel.

The park's shaded benches began filling up late in the afternoon. Old men came to pass the time in groups of four or five. Women brought their children to play on the broad walkways. University students favored the edge nearest the cultural center. Guitarists, alone and in pairs, strummed too softly to disturb the calm, which made it hard to picture the contrasting scene described by Juan.

"It was madness. The park was full. Full! So many people I couldn't count them. And not just in the park. All the streets were full. And people were cheering. I was cheering too. The joy that I felt was the greatest of my life."

"Your whole life?"

"Greater than the day I married. Greater than the day my son was born."

The previous night, Batista decided that his 46,000-man army was no match for a few thousand bearded rebels and fled Havana with his wife, three children, and enough money to last a lifetime. Receiving the news at the sugar mill where he was spending New Year's Eve, Castro left to "liberate" Santiago de

Cuba. Other guerrillas streamed down from the mountains. The victors reached the city in the wee hours of January 2, 1959.

Santiago de Cuba was wide awake. Too excited to change out of pajamas and hairnets, residents lined the streets to cheer the arrival of the men who toppled the tyrant. Not everybody could fit into Céspedes Park. Those who managed to squeeze in saw Fidel Castro appear, like a messiah, on the balcony to deliver his first speech as the leader of Cuba.

"What did he say?"

"I don't remember. It was enough just to see him."

"But why?"

"I wasn't a *communista*," said Juan. "But I was a *Fidelista*."

How long did the spell last? Having seen bits of Juan's life in the days since our first meeting, I reckoned the sixty-year-old had scratched his name from the list of Fidel's fans. First, there was his job. A retired professor, Juan received a pitiful pension. To make ends meet, he went into business with his sister, who lived in the countryside. She brought fresh eggs to the city, where Juan sold them to friends and neighbors.

Split two ways, weekly profits of about a hundred and fifty pesos didn't buy luxury. Juan invited me to visit his home, five blocks from Céspedes Park. Five steps up from the sidewalk, the front door opened to a living room furnished with three lawn chairs, a record player, and a stack of vinyl disks. A velvet portrait of a ship passing through a canal covered most of one wall. Opposite was a poster of a woman in a swimsuit.

Crowding was a bigger problem than decor. Up a concrete staircase from the living room lived one son, his wife, and their four-year-old boy. Their bedroom provided the only access to a second bedroom, which housed another son, an engineer who worked in a hotel, plus his wife and infant. On the ground floor, a doorless room occupied by the daughter's family provided access to the bedroom of the master, who slept beside the kitchen. An ancient woman and the fifty-year-old daughter with whom she shared a double bed in the back brought the tally to thirteen.

"Can't your children get their own homes?" I asked.

"There's no money to build new homes," said Juan.

We left the claustrophobic quarters and walked a block to the bodega, where a crowd of twenty waited their turn to buy subsidized groceries. "¿El último?" asked Juan. A position established, the Cuban settled on the sidewalk opposite the rations store. The tedium of waiting was broken by a voluminous black woman who screamed "Fuck," "Asshole," "Whore," and curses I hadn't yet learned at the toothless biddy who disputed her place in the line.

Juan didn't gripe about the line. Nor did he complain about the quantity of food provided by the government, which failed to deliver two pounds of the previous month's sugar ration. I heard not one moan about the crowding in his home. Incredulous at his composure, I prodded Juan to comment on his life.

"I feel rich," he said. "The cost of living in Cuba is very low. I own my home. Even if I didn't, the rent to the government is very low. I need only twenty pesos per month to buy food with the ration book. With my supplementary income I can buy extra food at the market. I don't have much money. But in the Cuban system, one doesn't need much money. I have everything I need."

Cuba's system had other fans in Céspedes Park, where I spent a week of afternoons engaged in Santiago de Cuba's favorite pastimes, ducking the sun and shooting the breeze. Tentative at first, I discovered just how little it took to start a conversation. "Hot day" never failed. "The Struggle" earned bonus points. Saying nothing worked too: a lone foreigner was a magnet for a local with time to kill.

The attraction intensified the moment I revealed my roots. The retired men circled around to pose their backlog of queries about life in the United States. "Does everybody have a car?" was a common question. So were "Is it too dangerous to go out after dark?" and "Do you own a gun?" My failure to explain snow, a wonder Cubans had seen on television, didn't diminish my expert status.

I had a question of my own. I looked at a man old enough

for his first gray hairs but too young to spend the rest of his days in a shady park and said, "You aren't working?"

"I'm sick." He held up his left hand. The thumb and index finger were intact. The other three digits had been reduced to stumps. A carpenter, Luis said that seven months had passed since his buzzsaw snapped and mangled his hand. The pain, said the amputee, was the worst of his life. Or so he thought until the doctors reversed their prediction that the fingers could be reattached. He suffered throbbing depression until another solution surfaced.

"They are going to give me new fingers," said Luis.

The news surprised me. Expensive in the free world, prosthetic fingers seemed beyond the means of a poor country's medical system. But Cuba's cash-strapped doctors had a cheaper way to put the carpenter back to work. The following month, Luis was due for an operation that promised to replace the missing fingers with digits lopped off the hand of a dead man.

"And you don't have to pay?"

"In Cuba, hospitals are free."

An older man named Tomás was more explicit about his gratitude to the system built by Castro. Dressed in a plain white shirt and polyester slacks, the pudgy park dweller beckoned for me to join him on a bench. Was it true what they said? Was I really an American? Tomás spent a half-hour describing a poor boy's lifelong fascination with a land that seemed infinitely rich.

"Do you know anything about medicine?" he asked.

"Not much."

"I'm going to tell you something. In 1981 I had cancer." He pointed to the base of his neck. "I went to a good hospital, with good doctors. Cuban doctors. They operated. I had cobalt treatment. Thanks to the Revolution, I'm alive."

Tomás named another debt to his president. Nearly twenty when Castro stood on the balcony overlooking our spot in the park, he had never gone to high school. But schools built in the years that followed assured an education to all. Proud of his country as well as his offspring, Tomás told me that his children held university degrees. Two worked as veterinarians. The

other was a translator. But for the Revolution, all th
have been field or factory workers.

The retired laborer asked me to take a look at
around us. I saw boredom. Blank stares were the or
day for the people in Céspedes Park. Recreational
only occasionally broke the tedium under the trees. Tomás saw
something else. He pointed to a pair of policemen scolding a
teenager for resting his feet on a bench.

"Before the Revolution, that boy would have been afraid of
the police. They would arrest him, beat him. But not anymore."
Pleased with his first point, Tomás made a second one. "The
city used to be full of prostitutes. And gambling. Fidel cleaned
the city. He made Santiago de Cuba a beautiful place again."

I reminded Tomás about the dire present. What about the
shortages of power, water, and housing? What about food rations that left stomachs rumbling? Grown men begged for soap.
I told him about a long conversation with a furloughed laborer.
That talk ended with the news that it was his birthday. Opening
his identity card as proof, he asked for a present, my socks.

"My socks!" I said. "Can Fidel be doing a good job if a man
begs for my socks?"

"In thirty-seven years, a man will have good years and bad
years," said Tomás.

"Which is this?"

"Bad. But Fidel is a good man. He brought democracy to
Cuba."

"Democracy?"

"Fidel is for the people."

13

THE SHRIVELED WOMAN shuffling across Céspedes Park
stopped to consider an oddity. Draped in an unhemmed dress
held together by stitches and soil, she confirmed that there was
in fact a foreigner on the bench nearest the cathedral. She

shuffled my way. When the toes of her tattered sneakers touched the tips of my running shoes, she lifted a limp index finger to stress the simplicity of her request: "Give me one peso."

I looked into a face as dark and wrinkled as a raisin. No doubt about it, she needed the peso. And more. My hands tightened around the coins in my pockets. Frozen by indecision, I stared and hoped the beggar would go away. She held her ground.

"Just one peso, my love. Please."

Shifting my gaze past her left ear, I fixed my eyes on the balcony from which Castro had addressed Santiago de Cuba.

"The poor woman," said a voice to my left. "She has nothing."

I looked down the bench at the pudgy man with whom I had shared a laugh not ten minutes before. The tanned Cuban had been watching prepubescent girls trying and failing to interest their male classmates in salsa steps. When I grinned at one boy's refusal to gyrate in time to the music wafting over the park, a smile broadened beneath my neighbor's mustache. With a nod we agreed that the boys would learn. And the girls would wish they hadn't.

"How much are *you* giving her?" I asked.

He pulled a peso from the pocket of his cotton pants and placed the coin in the beggar's palm. I doubled his donation, and the old woman shuffled away without saying a word.

The man did speak: his name was Roberto. Thirty-five, he was an electrical engineer with three children and as many ex-wives, all of whom had remarried. Roberto regularly visited the kids in their new households. The support provided by the other fathers let the jolly divorcé help the poor.

"If I have one shirt, I won't give that away and leave myself naked," said Roberto. "But if I have two shirts, and I see somebody who needs one, I will give the other one away. If I don't, I feel bad."

Roberto also loathed the thought of a visitor underrating his hometown. He recommended a visit to El Morro, a seventeenth-century castle perched on the cliffs overlooking the mouth of Santiago de Cuba's bay. Another must was the birthplace of General Antonio Maceo, one of the martyrs of Cuba's wars against Spain. Nor should anybody miss the factory where the Bacardí family turned sugarcane into rum until the Revolution, when they moved to Puerto Rico.

I got another lesson in civic pride while hiking past the lifeless neon signs above a street of unlit shops. About half of the windows were empty. Stores that displayed clothing, toys, and plastic flowers had more sellers than buyers. The customers who did enter the caverns appeared more interested in conversation than commerce. Inside the Vietnam Bookstore, I found a copy of *Nothing Can Stop the March of History*, by Fidel Castro, *The Fertile Prison*, a book about Castro's years in jail, and a volume about the leader's memories of Ernest Hemingway, whom he met just once.

"Fidel is a great leader," said a man wearing a yellow guayaberra, the loose-fitting shirt favored by older Cubans. "But he is not the only great leader in Cuban history. Before Fidel there was Martí. Fidel himself said that Martí was the author of Moncada. Both men were fighting for the liberty and sovereignty of their own land. And before Martí there were others."

The angular black man needed no prodding to provide a roll call of national heroes. The summary ended with the conclusion that Cuba's was "a noble history" and a statement of the obvious: he was a retired professor of history. Math and science were important, he said. But now, more than ever, was the time for Cubans to study history. "Because so many things are changing in Cuba, it's vital for us to stay in touch with the essence of our society," said the professor, who limped out of the bookstore saying, "Wait here."

He returned with a worn paperback called *History Will Absolve Me*. The text of Castro's defense following the Moncada attack ran ninety-eight pages. Why had the stranger brought it for me? The inscription scrawled inside the cover provided no clue: "I dedicate this book to a friend and colleague, Christopher. You now have in your hands a valuable instrument for understanding the place where you find yourself."

The woman assigned to guide me around the museum

founded by the Barcardí family was less subtle about her love for the city. For half an hour, the slim mother of two answered my questions about exhibits that included conquistadors' helmets, machetes used by the Cubans who fought to expel the colonialists, and the oil portraits that remained when the Spaniards left the island. The guide then posed some questions of her own.

"Have you noticed that here the sun is different, more resplendent, than in other provinces?" she said.

"It is very hot."

"And have you noticed that the sea is richer, bluer, here?"

She was right. The sun *was* brighter, the sea *was* bluer, in Santiago de Cuba. Like the rest of life, the elements intensified when reflected off the locals. Theirs was a romantic vision of life. Yes, they were poor. Yes, their lot was unlikely to improve much. What distinguished so-called Santiagueros was their ability to love what little they did have.

The museum guide wasn't the only one eager to share with a foreigner. In the atrium of the cultural center a painter explained the religious images he had painted on rectangles of wood. Ripped from their homes in western Africa, the slaves brought to Cuba retained their beliefs — heresy to their Catholic owners. To worship without punishment, the slaves dressed their gods as Christian saints. The figures, said the painter, were the gods of the religion that came to be known as *santería*. His explanation of the web of legends linking the deities left me confused.

I looked away from the speaker. My eyes met the soft gaze of a young woman. She twirled one of the dozens of long, thin braids into which she had twisted her afro. Her skimpy blouse left exposed a tummy roll as dark as unsweetened chocolate. She didn't avert her eyes. I did.

My thoughts spun to the forecast of friends in Havana. No fewer than five men had told me that the girls in Santiago de Cuba were *caliente*. What sounded like "hot" really meant "horny." A friend in the capital put a gentler spin on the eastern city's reputation: "Love awaits you in Santiago." Was this love at first sight?

"Do you want to buy this?" said the woman, who approached as I drifted away from the painter. Spread across her palm was a leather band decorated with bite-size seashells, the symbol of one of the *santería* gods. She promised that the bracelet brought good luck.

"I'm not a believer," I said.

She stared.

"We don't have *santería* where I come from."

The woman, Ana, asked me to walk with her. Talking as we wandered uphill, she told me that she played the congas in an all-girl group that played folkloric music. Her proof was the leathery palm she rubbed across my cheek. She laughed when I asked about her pay, which was about six dollars a month. She pointed to her feet and said that these were her only shoes. To keep them pretty and herself presentable, she cleaned them every night. I involuntarily connected her words to the propaganda painted on a building: "Poverty passes. What doesn't pass is dishonor."

The drummer talked about asking her boss for new clothes for performances. Certain he would say no, she had a backup plan. She was going to make an offering to her saint. Ana fell to her knees to show me how she would pray. When she rose, I wondered whether there wasn't a third scheme.

"I'm a contortionist," she said as we settled on a bench in Marte Plaza. "Do you know what that is?"

I did.

"Would you like to see?"

I wasn't sure.

Ana scanned the vicinity. Twenty yards away, five men were absorbed in their own chatter and the salsa buzzing from the radio of a sleek Chevrolet. The distance and the twilight kept the group from noticing a pretty woman lifting her left leg and placing it behind her head. Ana duplicated the feat with her right leg, framing her torso with fishnet stockings.

"Do you like this?" she asked, pressing her chest forward.

What did a man say to a woman with her ankles behind her ears? Did he confess that images of twisted sex were racing through his brain? Did he admit to fearing a tryst with a contortionist? I held my breath until Ana lowered and crossed her legs in a more conventional pose.

"I can also split my legs like this," she said, using two forefingers to demonstrate a hundred-and-eighty-degree angle. "To see that, you have to come to my house."

Hospitality knew no limits in Santiago de Cuba.

It was hard to reconcile Santiago's self-love with the critical glare that Habaneros cast over their city and the rest of the island. The capital was a beautiful place; it was a shame I hadn't seen it "before." Coppelia served excellent ice cream; too bad there weren't as many flavors as "before." Sentences that began "Cuba has all the ingredients of paradise" ended with "but Fidel doesn't know how to cook."

So which way was it? Should I subscribe to the dark view of the Habaneros or the brighter picture presented in Santiago? Was Cuba on track or off? Perplexed, I needed more information.

I had a plan. Fidel Castro left Santiago de Cuba the day after his late-night speech in Céspedes Park. But he didn't rush. His cohorts controlled Havana. So he moved to consolidate his power by building popular support. Like a slugger in his home run trot, Fidel shared the victory by driving cross-country at the head of a train of jeeps and trucks. He entered Havana riding on a tank.

The "Liberty Caravan" came to my attention on New Year's Day. Printed beneath a headline — WE TRIUMPHED BECAUSE WE BELIEVED IN THE PEOPLE — was a description of the crowds that lined the route. The story also noted where Castro stopped to speak and included a map of the rebels' victory tour.

Say I followed the route. I would see what Fidel saw, stop where he stopped. Doing so was no guarantee of learning how, or whether, the Revolution had succeeded. Hoofing across

Cuba might not even help me decide where on the spectrum of grays to place Fidel. But it might.

Transportation posed the biggest obstacle to duplicating the leader's journey. Heading east, I had hoped to see the country through the window of a train. Or a bus. Two days before my departure for Santiago de Cuba, I walked to the government travel agency nearest my apartment. There I found a line of twenty-five listless Cubans ignoring both the scalding sun and the strains of "Material Girl," a Madonna tune, wafting from a window across the street.

"Where are you going?" asked a stubbled man.

"Santiago de Cuba."

"When?"

"Sunday."

The man, Oscar, shook his head. Frowns crossed the faces of the two men with whom he was waiting. A middle-age woman wearing thick glasses sucked in a quick breath of air. The quartet spent the next ten minutes agreeing that the odds of getting a bus ticket on two days' notice ranged from slim to none. Energy not spent trashing my plans went into offering advice.

"Never take the train," said Oscar. "The trains never leave on time. Sometimes they are two days late. Trains make many stops. And they are slow. Buses are faster."

An hour later our group was herded into the office. Beneath a Cuban flag rested a bust of José Martí. On the chipping wall hung three pictures of Fidel, a portrait of Che Guevara, and a black-and-white photograph of Fidel and Che together. ALL OF OUR ACTION IS A CRY OF WAR AGAINST IMPERIALISM read the faded words on one wall. On another wall SOCIALISM OR DEATH was painted near a steel box marked COMPLAINTS AND SUGGESTIONS.

My complaint was that there wasn't an empty bus seat for eight days. Trains were booked solid for more than two weeks. The woman behind the counter suggested that I fly to Santiago de Cuba. "It only costs ninety," she said. Dollars? Pesos. But only Cubans could claim the subsidized air fare. Foreigners paid more, and in dollars. There were no good alternatives.

My spin through Granma province deepened my under-standing of Cuba's transport woes. I traveled the first leg in style: Francisco's son skipped two days of work to drive us from Santiago de Cuba to Las Coloradas. When the lanky engineer left us to negotiate the Sierra Maestra on our own, Francisco's gift for hitching rides got us to the peak. But the descent was more troublesome. The coffee truck dumped us at Bartolomé Maso too late to catch the bus to Bayamo. We joined five other stragglers and squeezed into a Ford bound for Yara, a nearby town with bus and train service. The tickets were sold out. The sun set.

Cuban truckers didn't work nights. The vehicles remaining on the road stopped picking up passengers after dark. After three hours of standing on the roadside, thumbs extended, we went to meet the nine o'clock train to Bayamo. At ten-thirty the conductor confirmed what the stationmaster had said: "Full." He rejected bribes for standing room. Sometime after midnight I nodded off under a tree beside Yara's main street.

Transport wasn't my only concern as I tried to get out of Santiago de Cuba. Habaneros had told me that eastern Cuba was a violent place; a series of gestures always accompanied the warnings. Wrapping two fists around an invisible machete, speakers took two or three savage swipes at the air.

"The east isn't just dangerous," said Diego, the moviemaker, "it's deadly."

The point was quickly proved. Seated in his home at Las Coloradas, Pablo skipped from the day he met Fidel Castro to the recent day when tragedy struck his family. His son had survived Angola, where thousands of Cuban soldiers died repel-ling South African attacks. He made it through the leanest years of the economic collapse. What did him in was a fishing trip with a friend. Alone in a boat, the pair began to argue. Words became blows. The fight ended when the friend grabbed his machete and chopped off the hand of Pedro's son.

Fernando nodded at the familiar ring of the story. He said

that such fights were common in the countryside. Why? Women were gravitating to Cuba's cities. When men got together, they argued over the females who remained. Add a few bottles of rum and the fact that peasants felt naked without their machetes, and you had a recipe for trouble.

Diego and others feared that I would be even more vulnerable than the locals. The moviemaker reiterated that these were Cuba's dark days. Already poorer than the capital, the provinces were devastated by the "special period." Cubans knew that visitors carried cash. How would a hungry cane cutter treat a lone foreigner? Like a camel treats an oasis.

But say highwaymen didn't rob me blind. Spoiled by my own apartment as well as the run of Fernando's home in Santiago de Cuba, I wondered where I would sleep. And what about food? Then there was loneliness. Hitchhiking across Patagonia, I went hours without seeing a soul. In Vietnam the problem was quality, not quantity. Weeks passed between coherent conversations. Would Cuba's hinterlands be any better?

"The people will help you," was Francisco's answer to every worry.

The middle-age engineer fingered his thick mustache and asked me to think back to our trip to the Sierra Maestra. Had I forgotten how we reached the peak? In Cuba, said Francisco, shortages were nothing new. True, the problems had been severe in recent years. But a history of poverty had taught Cubans how to survive. Locals knew how to make do with what they had. They also understood that helping one another was important to their own long-term survival.

"This is *sociolismo*," said the amateur orator.

"You mean socialism?"

"No. *Sociolismo*."

Francisco elaborated. The pun began with the word *socio*. Spanish for "partner," it was a common greeting among Cubans. *Socialisma*, with an *a*, was the system by which the state provided for the people. *Sociolismo*, with an *o*, was how locals referred to the way things really got done in Cuba, by one *socio* helping another.

Francisco was the Nobel Laureate of *sociolismo*. A buddy in Bayamo slipped him a bottle of rum from the bar of the bus terminal. Another pal loaned us a classified map of the mountains. Former colleagues working in Granma province arranged for us to spend the night near Las Coloradas.

I pointed out my own lack of *socios*. Francisco said that I had missed the point.

"The people will help you," he said.

"Do you think I can hitchhike all the way to Havana?"

"Of course."

"Where will I sleep?"

"The people will help you."

"What will I eat?"

"The people will help you."

One final question. What about safety? When I asked whether he thought it dangerous for a blue-eyed foreigner to hitchhike across Cuba, Francisco lowered his chin and pursed his lips. He stroked his mustache. Then he spoke.

"You can take my machete."

14

EVERY TOWN in Cuba had a bust of José Martí. So did schools and factories. The patriot's name was on Havana's airport. His face was on the one-peso note. His sayings, Cuba's "Confucius says," were painted everywhere. Martí was God. His word was gospel.

The pervasive image was of a frail man with a mass of dark hair swept back from a bulbous forehead. Heavy eyebrows, a tiny goatee, and a mustache that covered his upper lip created an air of intensity. His clothing was no more playful. Martí dressed like an undertaker: heavy black suit, high-collared white shirt, ribbon-thin, black bow tie.

José Martí was an oddball in Cuba's pantheon. He was an

egghead, not a general. He spent most of his life writing about Cuban independence and rallying others to the cause. He dreamed of an island ruled by social justice, a Cuba undivided by gender, race, or wealth, and forecast that American imperialism might one day replace Spanish colonialism. But theories weren't enough.

Martí organized an armed rebellion and, in 1895, left his exile in New York City. Like Castro, he returned to Cuba in a boat barely fit to complete the journey. Like Castro, he landed on the east end of the island with the intent of joining rebels already on the ground. Physically fit and mythically lucky, Fidel survived brutal marches, napalm attacks, and the ambush that decimated his band of rebels. Martí, the prototype of the ninety-eight-pound-weakling, struggled under the weight of a pack. Moments into his first battle, he was shot dead.

The martyr took on an additional role the day I left Santiago de Cuba: he was obstructing traffic.

The morning began with Francisco cooking me a massive breakfast — "To strengthen you," he said. He poured me two shots of rum. "To stimulate you." Then my mentor offered one last tip. He told me how to get to Bayamo, the first stop of the Liberty Caravan.

"Go to the bus station."

"There are no tickets."

"For the public bus, no. Take the private bus."

The "private" buses idled outside a narrow room jammed with battered baggage and comatose Cubans. They were trucks built by DeSoto and Wyllis, companies that went bust before I could drive. The dinosaurs that preyed on stranded travelers weren't pretty. Or comfortable. Passengers were loaded like cattle onto flatbeds rimmed by sides as high as my chest. Availability was their sole virtue.

"Where are you going?" demanded a grizzled man outside the terminal.

"Bayamo."

"Get up," he said, pointing to the ladder welded to the side of one of the jalopies.

I joined roughly thirty westbound Cubans. Beside me stood a mulatto carrying a piglet in a shopping bag. The creature was ignored by everybody except myself and a soiled girl. The conductor herded more people aboard. The passengers grumbled about the crowding and the delay. Ten minutes passed before the truck began to roll.

Drums drowned out the rumbling of the engine. Looking toward the military beat, I saw a horde of teenagers marching our way. A banner identified them as students. Behind them walked a pack of girls dressed in white and tapping a dance in time to the drums. Behind them was a group of boys in white shirts and red kerchiefs, a bunch wearing the straw hats favored by field laborers, and a unit in fatigues and berets. Up the street stretched an endless line of children and banners.

"Today is the birthday of our national hero," said the mulatto as the truck jerked to a halt. "All schoolchildren go to the cemetery. Workers too."

Going nowhere, I thought about my own visit to the place where José Martí was buried. The walk along Santiago de Cuba's waterfront boulevard had taken me past colonial customhouses. On the left stood another relic of the old days, a low-slung train station. Farther along was the factory where Bacardí rum was fermented until the Revolution. A mile later I came to Santa Ifigenia Cemetery.

A voluptuous woman freshened her lipstick before showing me Martí's tomb. En route, the stylish guide showed me the monoliths along the marble walkway, twenty-eight plaques, one for each of the camps where Martí stayed between his return to Cuba and his death at a place called Dos Ríos. Each stone bore one of the man's sayings. "Triumph is for those who sacrifice," said one. Another, "When a people divides it kills itself."

The guide became quiet when we reached an octagonal tower built over a sunken atrium. We looked down at a statue of Martí, seated and meditative, and a bronze urn covered by a crisp Cuban flag. I ended the silence with a question about one of the heirs to Martí's freedom fight.

"Where are they going to bury Fidel Castro when he dies?"

"We don't think about such disagreeable things."

"You don't?"

"Cubans don't like to imagine life without Fidel."

Cuba's so-called Central Road probably hadn't changed much since the day Castro rolled out of Santiago de Cuba. True, there were no cheering crowds on the road winding along the rim of hills on the edge of town. There was, however, a rear view of a natural bowl filled with colonial buildings overlooking a harbor. The city disappeared and the scenery turned to rolling hills whose spindly palms and green scrub baked under the relentless sun.

The truck chugged like a locomotive on the flat stretches. The roar multiplied whenever it hit an incline. Hills taxed the engine, which groaned during gear shifts. The vehicle slowed. The noise resumed when the gears gripped and tossed the payload of passengers.

I clung to the side rail. The man with the piglet steadied himself by grabbing my shoulders. His wife dislodged her sunglasses as she tumbled into two sturdy women who had braced for the shift. A preteen girl grabbed the strap of my duffel bag. Riders not struggling to keep their balance whooped like kids on a roller coaster.

The DeSoto became a mobile carnival. The passengers chattered quietly until the truck's collision with a bump in the road lifted the group off the floor of the cargo bay. Nobody fell. I was holding the rail. The mulatto's hands were on my shoulders. He, in turn, was in the grasp of his wife, who was linked to the rest of the web of mutual support. Everybody whooped.

The merriment multiplied my own joy. Having seen nothing but hurdles when it came to transportation, I was thrilled to be on the road. I felt my face begin to glow from the sun. Cuba, and life, looked good from the top of a DeSoto crawling along the Central Road.

The fun lasted for half an hour. Then the truck turned left onto a narrow road and into the plaza of a tiny town. The driver eased out of the cab. The other passengers also disembarked. I wasn't in Bayamo. But I wasn't going any farther. Not on that truck.

"Where are we?" I asked a youth in jeans and a flowery shirt. "El Cobre."

El Cobre was Cuba's holiest place, its Mecca. People saved money for years to make cross-island pilgrimages to the town twenty kilometers outside Santiago de Cuba. The goal of the pilgrims, such as my fellow passengers, was the local church. There lived the patron saint of Cuba.

The Virgin of Charity was the center of the legend, which I learned from Luis, the painter at Santiago de Cuba's cultural center. He said that the story began in 1606 when three men found a wooden statue floating in a bay on the island's north shore. About a foot long, the statue was of the Virgin cradling Christ with her left arm and holding a gold cross in her right hand. I AM THE VIRGIN OF CHARITY was inscribed, in Spanish, at her feet. A procession took the statue to El Cobre, where its powers had been revered for centuries.

Cubans spoke with reverence of the basilica built to house the Virgin. El Cobre was *the* place to ask for protection. Cubans also came to give thanks. Others asked for miracles. Take Ana. When the conga player wanted something, she prayed. When she *really* wanted something, she took an offering to El Cobre. "You can ask for anything," she said.

"Is this your first visit to El Cobre?" asked a man in jeans, a student named Aristide.

"Yes," I said. "You're a believer?"

"No. I'm not religious. But I feel good here."

Aristide led me up the inclined street to the basilica, a gracious, cream-colored edifice whose three domed towers shone like beacons against the chaos of green covering the mountain behind. He stopped to buy a bunch of flowers wrapped in pages of *Granma* and suggested I do the same. The student explained the need to leave a bouquet as an offering to the Virgin.

"I'm not religious," he repeated. "But this is part of Cuban culture."

Recessed from three arched entrances, the heavy wooden

doors were shut firmly when we reached the top of the drive. Aristide led me to the rear, where a parking lot overlooked the town and the brown gash that copper mining had left on the land. A gang of peddlers sprinted toward a foreigner who might need candles, crosses, or shiny stones. Evasive actions took us out of the heat and into the cool of a hall in the back of the basilica. To the right, a marble staircase led to a chapel.

At the top of the stairs a middle-age woman wearing a wooden cross around her neck held out her hands. She accepted my flowers and added them to the dozens of bouquets left by other worshipers. A sweep of her hand invited me to join the ten Cubans already in the chapel. I watched the pilgrims cross themselves and kiss their fingers before kneeling to pray. Then the men and women looked up, their faces open with the wonder of children listening to Grandpa's stories.

The becalmed gazes were directed toward the glass case holding the Virgin, who could be rotated to face the congregation in the cavernous chamber behind the chapel. Propped on a silver bowl on a marble stand, the statue looked like a doll, a doll dressed in a pyramid of a gold robe decorated with the national crest of Cuba. The Virgin also wore a crown, as did the baby in her arms. No amount of finery, however, could make me understand the evident devotion inspired by the wooden statue.

Back downstairs, I understood better. Cubans came to El Cobre bearing objects symbolic of their unfulfilled prayers. Cripples asked for mobility by leaving tiny legs cut from a sheet of metal. Amputees prayed by leaving symbols of arms and hands. Thousands of other dainty cutouts of cars, houses, and anything else a Cuban might want dangled from hooks on the wall above a silver altar. Some pilgrims left clearer signs at the Shrine of Miracles. High on the wall, crutches hung beside a set of leg braces.

But El Cobre wasn't just about requests. Another display showed offerings left by grateful Cubans. Several women gave thanks by leaving braided ponytails. Beside the hair lay a license plate and a guitar. A nurse left her diploma. A doctor left his stethoscope. Computer disks, salsa cassettes, and compact discs proved that modern life hadn't doused faith in the Virgin. Athletes left their medals. So did soldiers.

I paused over a letter attached to a photograph of a raft made by lashing planks to inner tubes:

> *This photo was taken on the coast of Florida (U.S.). It refers particularly to a boat (one of many) that arrived on the coast, logically, with nobody on board. Brothers, I, Victor Hugo Tomayo, advise you who have this mindless idea, not to do it, for life is worth much more than the dangerous trances that come to us at times. And remember always that where there is life there is also hope for a better future.*

I doubted that the heartfelt letter was real. Where better for the Party to discourage Cubans from fleeing the country than at Cuba's most sacred shrine? The author, in all likelihood, worked for the propaganda department. If not, he had been put up to writing the letter. Or so I thought until I noticed that El Cobre's keepers gave equal time to other views.

A typed letter from a woman thanked the Virgin for helping her survive years in the prison to which she was sent for her "political ideas" and asked that she help her outspoken husband and son, who were still in jail. Beside a picture of two young men in white T-shirts was a note thanking the Virgin for protecting them en route to the American naval base at Guantánamo Bay, a favorite spot for Cubans seeking to flee the island. A postcard dated July 1995 read:

> *To the Virgin of Charity.*
>
> *Thank you for having carried my husband as far as the Naval Base, Guantanamo, and keeping him safe and sound. I wish with all my heart that we can be together soon.*
>
> *I feel tears of devotion as I struggle to survive.*

I turned to a poster that listed the highlights of the basilica's history. Here, in 1801, slaves working in the mines were declared free. In 1868, Carlos Manuel de Céspedes spoke at El Cobre. Thirty years later a general came to celebrate a mass after the ouster of Spanish troops from Cuba. One name, however, was conspicuously missing from the hall of fame.

"Does Fidel come here?" I asked the chubby watchman seated near the poster.

"During the war he was nearby. But he never came inside."

"Doesn't he believe in the Virgin?"

The watchman's exaggerated shrug said it all. Like me, he didn't understand how the leader could have overlooked this facet of mainstream Cuba. Fortunately for Fidel, his mother was a believer. Asking the Virgin of Charity to protect her son from Batista's soldiers, she left a small gold guerrilla fighter.

15

THE SITUATION looked hopeless from my seat beside the Central Road. Minutes passed between cars and trucks. When vehicles did appear, they turned left, to El Cobre, instead of continuing straight, toward Bayamo. The bus stop's roof shielded me from the midday sun, but the sides turned the shelter into a kiln. Sensible people were safely indoors. The exception, a skinny man wearing running shorts and a pink baseball cap, had dressed for the heat.

"What are you doing?" he asked.

"Waiting for the bus."

"It won't stop here."

I pointed to the post beside the shelter. A sign showed the profile of a bus. A flip of the man's hand said, Oh, that old thing. Pointing west, he explained that the stop was down the road. He handed me a plastic bag containing several pounds of rice and a television picture tube and told me to wait for him to fetch his bicycle. Two minutes later he returned.

"Come to my house. Drink coconut juice. Then go to the terminal."

Pedro's home was a featureless block just a few yards from the road. Inside, I exchanged nods with his sister, an aunt, and an uncle. Three children hid themselves. When my host disappeared, I looked at the bare living room's only decoration, a shelf with eight empty bottles of local beer flanking a green Heineken bottle. When Pedro reappeared, he was carrying a machete.

"Let's go," he said.

Pedro grabbed two coconuts from a pile of ten by the door. He said they were fresh and proved it by pointing to similar fruit on the thirty-foot tree in the front yard, which is where he left me with the machete and the pair of yellow-skinned bowling balls. I sensed he expected me to have the drinks ready for his return. I suspected I might lose a finger if I tried.

He came back, frowned, and opened a hole in one of the coconuts with three swift hacks. I drank through a thin pink straw. When the juice ran out, Pedro split the coconut and handed me a spoon for scooping out the white pulp. He repeated the process for the second fruit without taking a sip or a bite of his own. Was I supposed to pay for the snack?

"No money," said Pedro. "One peso is nothing. One friendship is everything."

The friendship took me back inside. There, a tour of his life began with two black-and-white televisions, both out of order. "Soviet shit," said Pedro. More reliable was the Japanese boombox a relative had brought from Miami. Flipping on the radio, Pedro asked if I liked rock music. Billy Joel? John Lennon? Then he asked a trickier question.

"Are you a communist?"

"Not yet."

"Do you know . . . ?" Pedro stroked a long, imaginary beard.

"Not yet."

"We're lucky to have him," said Pedro, rewinding a cassette. "Cuba has no money, no economy. Still, he gets us things. Schools. Hospitals. He's very intelligent."

The man had a point. Fidel Castro took over a country whose cash cows were tourism, agriculture, and mining. Tourism fizzled when the leader banned gambling, prostitution, and Americans. That left the natural resources, which generally don't make countries rich. Turning the island into a Caribbean Hong Kong wasn't an option for a populist who despised free markets. A better, and perhaps the only, alternative to a man forced into a corner by Washington was to milk the Soviet Union for billions of dollars that the island could never have generated on its own.

Pedro demonstrated another point. Having located the song he wanted me to hear, he pressed Play. "Stairway to Heaven" crackled out of the cassette player. He leaned back, closed his eyes, and rocked himself. I thought about how right Francisco had been to dismiss my concern about loneliness.

When I couldn't drink more coconut juice or stand more Led Zeppelin, Pedro put me on the back of his bicycle and pedaled me to a cluster of dusty buildings opposite a hospital. Spotting a familiar face in the shade, the Cuban told me to wait while he talked to a man with a gray beard and greased-back hair to match.

"This is my uncle, Luis," said Pedro, returning with the old man in tow. "He's going to Palma Soriano. He will help you."

I checked the map. Palma Soriano was just halfway to my destination. On the other hand, I appreciated that rides might be rare. Francisco had flagged down three vehicles to get us into the Sierra Maestra. Because puddle-jumping seemed the way to travel in Cuba, I would be grateful for any westward movement.

Luis skimmed the highlights of his life while we waited for a truck. The government had sent him to do construction work in Libya, one of the outlaw countries Castro supported. Luis boasted that he had once spent five hours in Madrid's airport. Now a postman, he made extra money by growing flowers to sell to pilgrims to El Cobre. A discussion of the profits was interrupted by the appearance of a truck whose passengers were packed tight as bowling pins.

"Too crowded," said Luis.

Switching subjects, he warned me to beware of Cubans. There were lots of "bad ones." Thieves were everywhere. Rubbing his fingers together, the old man said that Cubans were especially keen to rob foreigners. He recommended that I keep an eye on my bag, which he grabbed on spotting a small truck with a blue hood.

Luis couldn't do enough for me. He handed my bag to the passengers already on the Soviet truck. He pushed my fanny as I clambered over the tailgate. Following me to the front of the narrow cargo hold, he shouted, "Watch your bag. Watch your bag." He placed my hands on the rail behind the cab when the truck jerked into action.

A squat tank mothballed beside the road was the only sign that Castro's caravan had passed this way. The rest of the view was all rolling hills and peaceful valleys. Trees were sparse and the grass was dry, a condition overlooked by the grazing cows. The engine rumbled on the inclines and went quiet when the driver coasted down hills. The teenage busboy clanked the rail with a wrench when passengers wanted to get off. The truck slowed, three young men jumped down, and the conductor shouted, "Hit it!" before asking newcomers for their fare. I paid three pesos.

A young woman looking to do likewise rifled the contents of her plastic shopping bag. Flustered, she spilled a brush, brassiere, and other items into her lap. More fumbling failed to produce three pesos. Or any other money. Her wallet was gone.

"How much did you lose?" asked the conductor, who waived the fare.

"Fifty pesos."

Twenty Cubans moaned. After the chorus of sympathy, four groups formed to analyze the disaster. Others grilled the woman, who recalled seeing the wallet just before boarding, when she handed her bag to young men on the truck. The coincidence of their exit and the disappearance of the wallet led the makeshift jury to convict the trio in absentia. I told you so, said the look Luis shot my way.

IN EVERY HAND A TOOL AND A GUN, said the billboard on the edge of Palma Soriano, which we reached after about a half-hour. Pointing to a set of Stalinesque buildings on the edge of town, Luis indicated his apartment. But he stayed aboard. Having promised to look after me, he would accompany me to the bus station, a place he considered a cesspool of crime. He promised to wait with me until another ride appeared.

The shepherding never stopped. Luis introduced me to the stationmaster. The squat, middle-age Cuban said that the four o'clock to Bayamo, due in two hours, was full. He pointed to sixty Cubans waiting in the stark, steamy terminal. His pessimism cooled, however, when Luis told him that I came from New York. He had a brother in New York! He owned a restaurant in the Bronx! Grabbing my forearm, the boss pledged to get me on the bus.

Luis killed time by taking me to visit his mother-in-law. He led me to the mouth of a narrow alley. The path of dirt ran between a row of rotten shacks. Several twists into the impoverished maze, the postman stopped in front of a crooked door, which swung ajar when he knocked.

"It's your home," he said.

A small girl wearing shorts but no shirt came to the door of "my home." Others stirred. A pig and a goat emerged from beneath one of three beds, the only furniture on a floor of packed dirt. A pretty twenty-year-old in a thin nightgown sat up and rubbed her brown eyes. I did the same. Had the Revolution missed this spot?

The answer hadn't come by the time a tiny old woman shuffled through a door in the back. The mother-in-law pulled her long gray hair into a tight bun. Her top teeth were gone. Those remaining in her lower jaw had rotted brown, something I learned when she beamed during Luis's rendition of my story. When he finished, she scurried out the back and returned with three oranges.

"Take these for your trip," she said.

I couldn't take food from the poor.

"You will be in a truck," said the wizened woman. "The fumes will make you sick. You may want to vomit. The oranges will calm your stomach."

"I don't have a knife."

ʼnkled hands grabbed back and peeled one of the

ɔ daughter, the sleepy twenty-year-old, returned. Out of
ʌ nightgown and into black heels, blue jeans, and a white
blouse tied to expose her navel, she joined her father's tour of
the town. Walking up the empty main street, she said she was
a dancer in a local cabaret. Her dream was to dance in Havana.
But her love for her family kept her close to a home she considered dull. "There's not much here," she said.

Dad disagreed. Two blocks from the main road Luis stopped
at a street corner. He pointed to a sturdy building whose doors
were shut. This, he said, was an important stop on Castro's road
trip. It was here that the leader delivered his first radio address
as Cuba's new leader. Sweeping his arm across the dusty, empty
intersection, the postman boasted that the streets had been
packed the day Fidel came to town. He moved to a plaque on
the wall and, following the words with his finger, read aloud the
tribute to his hometown's place in history.

Luis had learned to read after the Revolution, when Fidel had
battled illiteracy by arming thousands of young patriots with
primers and sending them into the country. Before then he had
had no opportunity to learn. He went to work at eleven. Regularly beaten by Batista's police, he joined Castro's underground
movement. Later he joined the rebels in the Sierra Maestra,
which he continued to guard for five years after the victory.

"Palma Soriano is more beautiful than before," said the old
man. "We have two hospitals. And schools. Now Cubans learn
to read when they are still children."

Luis saddened as we neared the bus station, where he
planned to leave me in the care of his friend. Times were changing, for the worse. In his day young people fought for a better
Cuba. Today's youth seemed bent on destroying the society he
had fought to build. "We were honest," Luis said. "Now the
young are thieves."

The bus boss renewed his promise. When the bus to Bayamo
left town, I would be in a seat. What he couldn't say was when

the bus would arrive. Or whether it would come at all. Dead engines and gas shortages caused cancellations, which weren't always relayed down the road.

I crossed the vacant street and approached a cluster of food stands. Two pesos bought me a drink of sugar, fruit, and ice mixed in an electric blender. Another road-food staple, pork sandwiches, cost five pesos. Extricating chunks of fat and skin from the meat between my bread, I heard a man shout, "Contramaestre. Ten pesos. Contramaestre."

Contramaestre wasn't my destination. It was, however, thirty-three kilometers closer to Bayamo. Doubtful that a bus would arrive, I spoke to the driver, a man wearing aviator sunglasses, who loaded me into his clunky station wagon. The forty-year-old Ford already had seven passengers who, like me, had turned to the private sector. Two women and two men piled out of the back seat so that I could climb all the way back, where I squeezed between a pair of men, one thick and one thin. The front seat belonged to a girl in a yellow blouse until a man wearing a straw cowboy hat stumbled up and asked the fare to Contramaestre.

"*¡Shit!*" he screamed when told that a ride cost ten pesos. The vulgarity drew stares from a thirty-yard radius. Clearly drunk, the man apologized to the ladies and collapsed in the front seat. He paid up and dozed off as the Ford began to bounce west along an uneven road that wound gently between fields of sugarcane.

Exhaust began leaking into the cabin. I looked at my neighbors. The muscular man to my right was asleep. The slim youth to my left nodded when I held my nose. But he said nothing. Nor did he gripe about the music, crackly salsa blasting from an exposed speaker beside his left ear. The twenty-year-old did smirk when the drunk's hat blew off his head and out the window. We also shared a swig of the rum bottle passed around by the coarse cowboy. By the time we reached Contramaestre, Rafael was trying to pay my fare.

"Where are you going?" he asked.

"Bayamo."

"Do you have family there?"

My answer puzzled him. Rafael had visited Santiago de Cuba. Havana seemed impossibly far. New York might as well be Mars. When I said that Americans traveled for its own sake, the young Cuban laughed. "How weird."

Rafael wanted the weirdo to meet his wife and mother, who lived on a farm outside Contramaestre. He begged me to stay the night. Or a few days. Would I like that? Incalculably generous, the offer frightened a city kid. Before I could contrive an excuse, the young farmer was leading me to the bicycle on which he planned to pedal me home. Twenty minutes later, the day's fourth ride veered off the main road onto a bumpy dirt path that twisted through a series of gentle hills.

The sight of Rafael's home bred second thoughts. Sitting on a patch of bare land beside a pond, the farmhouse was a squat rectangle made half of brick and half of wood. A lattice of poles supported a roof composed of metal sheets. Inside, a plastic table, four chairs, a crib, and a manual sewing machine crowded the living room. Curtains separated the space from the three rooms with double beds. Out back, a covered area with an open grill served as the kitchen.

Rafael's mother was stirring the contents of a pot propped above burning wood. A small woman with short, dark hair, she smiled shyly and wiped her hands on her soiled dress. Rafael's stepfather wasn't much more talkative. A gaunt man who wore thick glasses, he identified himself as a retired bureaucrat and returned to listening to a boxing match on the radio. When the farmer's very young — eighteen years — and very pregnant — eight months — wife proved just as reticent, I wondered how we would pass the time.

The farmer grabbed a bucket and asked me to follow him down a path that led past a pigpen, through a cloud of chickens, and across the path of a turkey. We trudged through a field of dirt awaiting rain, which would let the family plant corn. He stopped at a forest of tall, thin stalks. Pulled from the ground by three mighty yanks, the plant was a yucca, whose roots Rafael hacked off with his machete.

We filled the bucket and walked to a grove of coffee trees, where Rafael pulled off a red bean for me to taste. The sweetness didn't resemble coffee. He explained that the beans needed to be dried, toasted, and ground. There was, he said, no substitute for fresh coffee: "If you don't grow your own, you never get a good cup."

Other fruits rated less deference. Rafael climbed a nearby tree and dropped down six fat oranges, which he sliced open with his machete. He repeated the steps at a coconut tree: climb, drop, hack, eat. Stuffed, I asked whether the produce belonged to them or the state.

Both, was the answer. The family, which owned its land thanks to Castro's agrarian reforms, was allowed to sell about half of the food it grew at market prices. The rest had to be sold to the government at a fixed, low price. Not that Rafael thought this unfair. He said that the state helped farmers like him with advice, fertilizer, and credit. Also, low prices were a tradeoff for free schools and hospitals. Didn't Americans understand socialism?

I understood that Rafael was an endangered species. Not only was he well fed. Not only was he content with his lot in life. The farmer was one of a dying breed of Cubans willing to live in the Sierra Maestra and its foothills.

It was Francisco's wife who first told me about the exodus from the mountains. The problem, said Carla, stemmed from Cuba's successes. Bumpkins finished high school and went to urban universities. Few graduates wished to return to homes without electricity, plumbing, and gas. The outflow worried a government that considered coffee, a mountain product, an important export.

The state sent researchers to study the mountaineers. What would it take to keep them in place? What would make them happy? "Batteries for my radio" was a typical request. Food was also a big motivator. Thus the government devised the Plan Turquino. Named for Cuba's highest peak, the scheme of increased rations and regular meat aimed to stem the departures and stimulate a return to the Sierra Maestra. Winding up the road to the rebels' command post, I had seen a billboard saying:

THE REPOPULATION OF THE SIERRA MAESTRA IS THE WORK
OF EVERYBODY.

Almost nobody was moving back. Built to entice lowlanders,
new apartments in the Sierra Maestra sat empty. People in Havana said they preferred idleness and hustling to hard but honest work in the mountains. Elsewhere, laborers were given the
choice of working part-time in the mountains or losing their
job. When the carrots and sticks failed, the state sent soldiers to
pick coffee.

Rafael's stepfather offered his opinion after a dinner of rice,
beans, yucca, and two kinds of meat, chicken and pork. The
angular man's bare torso glowed beneath a kerosene lamp as he
sat outside the house and talked about country pleasures. With
the exception of three years in Havana, a place he dismissed as
inhospitable, he had lived his whole life in and around Contramaestre. He liked the tranquillity. He liked that one could
walk without fear at night.

The old man paused to tune his Soviet radio. He skipped past
an interview with a bureaucrat discussing the sugar harvest. A
station playing salsa didn't last much longer. The surfing
stopped when he found a station playing Benny Moré, a velvet-
voiced singer from the 1950s. The stepfather leaned his stool
against the house and continued.

"Cuba is changing, getting worse. Young people get so much
for nothing. There are jobs, but they don't want them. Instead,
they steal. They can steal more in one day than they can earn
in a week." After stopping to swill his own rhetoric, the gaunt
man added, "Cuba is becoming a country of crooks."

16

MORE THAN AGRICULTURE guided Party policies in the Sierra
Maestra. Coffee mattered. But the government would sooner
kick the habit than give an inch on an obsession as old as the
Revolution: security.

The surveillance system was alive and well when I landed in Cuba. The men who detained me at the airport checked my name against a list of known enemies. Every block still had a Committee for the Defense of the Revolution. Towns had officers from the outfit dedicated to seeking and destroying enemies, the Ministry of the Interior.

I visited the watchdogs' hall of fame during my time in the capital. The faded mansion housing the museum was stuffed with counterintelligence memorabilia. Gear used by the bad guys filled the glass cases. One contained machine guns and pistols as well as a bomb detonator in a box lined with the Stars and Stripes. A chess set had some connection to sending codes. Both a briefcase and a box of Hershey's cocoa had false bottoms for hiding radios. A phony rock transmitted signals.

The exhibits showed that Cubans couldn't be fooled. Photographs showed an American in sunglasses hiding a package in the bushes. Other pictures showed large caches of captured weapons. One counterespionage operation netted an airplane. "The enemy began to use new methods, but none worked," said a label.

The curators dedicated a separate room to the CIA's attempts to kill Castro. During Kennedy's presidency, the agency once hired the Mafia to bump off the leader. An exhibit described the discovery of a plot in which thirty men would ambush Castro's car. In each of the three years that followed the ministry claimed to have foiled schemes to lob grenades at the leader when he attended baseball games. My favorite was the plot to slip him a cigar laced with toxins.

The shenanigans were old enough to be funny. The Cold War was over. The CIA had given up on killing Castro. Laws banned privately funded attacks by Cubans living in Florida. A picture of Howard Hunt underlined that the chapter was closed. A key player in the war against Castro, the agent had moved on to incarnations as Watergate burglar, prison inmate, and junk novelist. But did the Cubans know that the fight was over?

The first indication that Americans remained suspect came

from Alberto, a muscular mechanic in his early twenties. Breakdowns of my Chinese bicycle made me a regular at his workshop in Havana. Our conversations were predictable. He asked whether a mechanic might find work in America. I asked how to meet Castro. When he mentioned that his grandfather had fought in the Sierra Maestra, I asked whether we might meet. Neither of us could imagine an old man unwilling to tell his war stories. Both of us were wrong.

"I have to tell you something, just between us," said the mechanic a few days after my first inquiry. "My grandfather is *very* revolutionary."

"That's why I want to meet him."

"You don't understand. When I told him that I had an American friend he became angry. He said that the Americans will never be friends of Cuba, that they only want to come here to get information."

The suggestion struck me dumb.

"My grandfather says you are a counterrevolutionary."

Did Alberto agree? And what about the old man? Would he report his suspicions? The weight of the accusation kept us quiet.

"Can I tell you something in confidence?" said the mechanic, turning his back to the sidewalk. "I don't get involved in politics. I only want to make money and fix up my home. But I don't want you to get hurt. So I have to tell you that you are going to have trouble in the east."

"What kind of trouble?"

"Havana is a big city, with lots of foreigners. The east is different. The towns are smaller. You will be more noticeable. People will wonder what you are doing."

"I won't be doing anything."

"Cubans won't believe you, especially if you are in the Sierra Maestra. They will follow you, investigate you. People will think you are an infiltrator."

Five letters told me that Alberto might be right. Painted big and bold, the white letters on the billboard beside the bus stop in Granma province said SUERC. Smaller yellow letters spelled out the words behind the acronym, which, when translated, stood for REPUBLIC OF CUBA'S UNIFIED SCOUTING SYSTEM. Finer print described the organization's mission: "It consists of reporting all that you hear or see that could be an enemy activity, a catastrophe or natural disaster, fire, floods or earthquakes." Beneath the explanation an outline of Cuba was surrounded by three icons: a warship, an airplane, and a tank.

Back in Santiago de Cuba I saw more SUERC signs. One showed a pair of eyes spotting painted icons of five signs of fishy activity: spy planes, enemy propaganda, warehouse fires, dead animals, strange objects. Why hadn't I seen such signs in Havana?

"The Sierra Maestra is a strategic zone," said Carla, Francisco's wife.

She said that the Sierra Maestra had twice been the center for guerrillas. First came Castro. Later, Cubans backed by the CIA copied his playbook and used the peaks as a base for contesting the communists. Both sides understood that the mountains were the only place to hide in a small, heavily policed country. Bent on prolonging their reign, Cuba's rulers stepped up their patrols and banned photography in the sensitive area.

But the government wanted more eyes looking out for enemies. Thus the concern about the depopulation of the Sierra Maestra. The emptier the region, the greater the opportunity for insurgents. The state was desperate to keep the mountain people in place and to lure others to join them. Extra food and clothing, and a bit of meat, was a small price to pay an occupying force.

Rafael's family spent the evening hours chatting and greeting neighbors, who roamed a countryside illuminated by a brilliant moon. At nine o'clock Rafael showed me to the bed vacated by his older brother. The family of five shouted down my protests that I was equally able to sleep on the mattress in the living room.

The sound of morning chores awakened me before dawn. I heard Rafael spreading feed for the chickens. He led the family's five cows to a pasture near the house. The farmer's mother started a fire. The smell of homegrown coffee had me out of bed before six A.M.

"Did you sleep well?" asked the mother, smiling with her eyes.

"Of course."

"Good. Stay another night."

Rafael upped the offer as he stood among the pecking chickens and ducks. Wearing tattered shorts and rubber boots, he invited me to stay for a few days. We could talk, he said, adding that I needed to learn more about farming, to see "the real Cuba."

In the real Cuba, a trip to the bodega followed the chores. Located beside the Central Road, the supply store was a room with eaves that covered a broad porch. None of the twenty men, women, and children gathered inside and out looked hurried. Armed with empty Baggies, the deeply tanned peasants spoke softly about rain, sports, and other neighbors. A half-hour passed before Rafael presented his ration book and paid for sugar and soap.

Other neighbors shouted greetings as he pedaled up the road through the fields. He stopped and gabbed. I shielded my eyes from the sun and looked around at stalks of yucca, clusters of coconut trees, and furrows of parched earth awaiting seeds of corn. Rafael's wasn't a romantic world. At twenty, he could count on nothing but forty-plus years of the same routine. Novel to me, the farm life had me leaning toward another day in rural Cuba.

A motorcycle parked in a patch of naked dirt in front of the farmer's home clouded the likelihood of an extension. The bulky bike had a sidecar. Its green paint was weathered and chipped. In a region where locals traveled by bicycles and horses, I couldn't imagine that a farmer could afford a vehicle.

"The police," mumbled Rafael.

Curious, he ambled toward the front door. Getting there meant pushing his way through a crowd of eight neighbors attracted by a commotion inside the house. Rafael's mother appeared just before her son reached the rear entrance. The smile was gone from her eyes.

"Rafael, the police want to talk to you," she said.

The farmer looked puzzled, but I knew why the police had come. They had come to find an American.

How had they found me? Who had snitched? None of the half-dozen neighbors who had seen me the previous night had a telephone. I doubted that Rafael's brother, a bureaucrat in Contramaestre, had reported me. Equally trustworthy was the stepfather, who left early to visit a sick friend. There was no way to know.

I did know that I wouldn't be the only *Yanqui* nabbed in recent times. Before leaving New York I spoke to an American named Adam. A filmmaker, Adam had gone to Cuba with a videocamera and a plan to interview dissidents. Days after touching down he heard a knock on the door of his hotel room. In the hallway stood a squad of policemen, who took him to their headquarters. An interrogation ended with charges of counterrevolutionary activities. Adam was put on a plane, minus his camera and film.

A Cuban told me about another American who came to Havana to dig up dirt. The locals who arranged for interviews with dissidents gave him an address for a late-night rendezvous. A crew of clean-cut thugs trounced him as he stepped out of a taxi into the unlit street. Beaten bloody, the American didn't doubt that he had been set up.

I worried more for Rafael than myself. Deportation was my worst-case scenario. He, on the other hand, had to live in Cuba. The police were sure to frown on the farmer's encounter with an American. He might also be jailed. Even if he did no time, his record would be marked black. And it would be my fault.

Rafael didn't look worried. Watching from the kitchen, I saw him settle into a lawn chair and answer the questions of the strangers in his sitting room. There were three of them, all men in their forties with deep tans and Stalinesque mustaches. None of them wore a uniform. Nobody was smiling. Not even my normally cheerful host, who rose and walked to the kitchen.

"They want to talk to you," he said.

If guilt wasn't written on my face, my awkward shuffle was sure to damn me. Stopping in front of the three-man panel, I felt like a man facing a firing squad.

"Shake their hands," whispered Rafael.

The policemen were less interested than I in pleasantries. Seated in the lawn chair farthest to my left, a man in a plaid shirt asked for my passport, which he handed to the chunky officer to his left. My eyes flicked right, to the stony face of a skinny man in a light blue guayaberra. His hard stare sent my gaze back to the man in plaid.

"You're an American?" he asked.

"Yes."

"Where is your group?"

My group? The question sounded serious. Translation: Where were the other intruders? What about our equipment?

"Are you traveling with a group? A tour?"

What followed was a moment that I thought happened only in Hollywood. The prisoner spills his guts. My confession began with the journey from Santiago de Cuba to Palma Soriano. I described my doubts that there would be a bus to Bayamo and my decision to take the gypsy cab to Contramaestre. I recounted meeting Rafael and his family. They were good people, I said. And I hoped that they weren't in trouble for showing kindness to a stranger.

The man in plaid nodded and smiled. I had won him over. His partners didn't look convinced. The chunky man leafed through my passport another time. The man in the guayaberra simply stared at me.

"Did I do something wrong?" I asked.

"We're the police," said the chunky man. "We have to know who is in our country and what they are doing here."

"Of course. That's the duty of the police in any country. You have to guarantee the security of the people. If a Cuban came to my country, our police would do the same."

A knowing nod indicated another conversion. Two down,

one to go. Could I crack the third nut, the officer with the petrified face? He looked deeply skeptical. His fingers knit in a tight pyramid, the man had yet to react to anything I said.

"Do they know you are here in Cuba?" he asked.

"They?"

"Your government."

"My government doesn't permit us to come to Cuba."

"So why did you come to Cuba?"

The wrong answer — to high-five Fidel — was on the tip of my tongue, which I held. Instead, I prattled on about how Cuba and America were neighbors, and everybody ought to know their neighbors. Right? I had been to Canada and Mexico, but not Cuba. Strange not to know people who lived just ninety miles away. Right?

Nods from my two converts confirmed that I was on a roll. They looked toward the holdout, who appeared unsure of my innocence of whatever charge they had in mind. Having taken my visa from his partner, the tough officer pointed to a discrepancy. My travel permit listed my occupation as investor. Rafael's family, however, said that I claimed to be a writer. Was I writing things about Cuba?

"One day I'll be old," I said, searching for words likely to appeal to Cuban machismo. "I'll want to remember what I saw in Cuba."

"Exactly," said the officer in plaid.

Something in my comments had touched the patriotism of the man in the guayaberra, who began to talk about Cuban history. Like a lecturer at reeducation camp, the wiry man stressed the importance of studying and understanding his homeland's past. He spun a story about the bravery of the Mambises, the slaves-turned-rebels who had only machetes to attack the Spanish soldiers. He traced the path of José Martí, then drew comparisons between the intellectual and Fidel Castro.

The silence of the other two suggested that the holdout was their superior. I wasn't going to interrupt the man who controlled my fate. Moreover, the top cop wouldn't jail me as long as he was talking. After twenty minutes, the monologue ended with a test.

"What sort of propaganda did you hear about Cuba?"

All Americans, I said, knew about Cuba's president. I also knew that they were a poor country of people who, like myself, loved baseball. When it came to music and dancing, Cubans were second to none. Right?

"And the blockade? What do you think about the blockade?"

A deep breath preceded what sounded like a test of my political colors. I started slowly. The blockade was an old law, I said. And the American people realized that it was an old law, a leftover from the past. We wanted to lift the blockade. We were just waiting for the right moment. That moment, I said, would be soon. Very soon.

"Are you a friend of Cuba?" asked the senior officer.

I knew the wrong answer. But this was no time to point out the hunger of people living on reduced rations, to complain about a country with no visible means of transport, to ask why a state needed a security apparatus able to ferret out a foreigner staying miles from the outskirts of civilization. But I lacked the energy to give the right answer. An hour into the grilling, I was out of bull. Or was I?

"You have so much in Cuba," I said. "Music: you have salsa. Rum: you have Havana Club. But look at this family. They are poor but they took me in their home. The people, that's what I love most about Cuba."

I thought I had him. No easterner could resist a compliment about hospitality. I sensed a softening in the man's rigid mien. I went for the knockout.

"And Cuban women," I said, "are very hot."

"Hotter than the Cuban sun," smiled the man in the guayaberra.

17

ANOTHER FARMER PASSED Rafael's house shortly after the departure of the security officers. He halted the horse-drawn cart he drove between his fields, which were up the road, and his home, on the opposite side of Contramaestre. Would I like to visit? Perhaps stay a few days with his family?

I looked at Rafael. He downplayed the run-in with the police. "They were just worried for you," he said. "They wanted to know whether you were eating well." Still, the lawmen had instructed my friend to escort me to the bus station and to notify them when the American was out of town.

Not that I wanted to linger. The hour-long interrogation had scared me. I worried that the cops would reconsider my spiel and conclude that I was, in fact, a counterrevolutionary. Rafael agreed that a quick exit was a smart move. We sat among the sacks of yucca in the bed of the cart and headed to town with the farmer.

The horse pulling the buggy performed a transport miracle. Its feat wasn't lugging us six kilometers in under an hour. And there was something more extraordinary than its instant responses to the driver's words. Plodding steadily down Contramaestre's sleepy central street, the horse reached the bus stop just two minutes before the departure of a vehicle marked TRAIN-BUS, a truck cab attached to a long carriage with plastic seats.

The swift connection left little time for good-byes. I wanted to wait on the sidewalk. Rafael insisted that I board the Cuban way: space, so rarely available, had to be grabbed fast. He shoved me aboard and paid my two-peso fare to Bayamo. As the bus pulled away, he waved weakly. Looking out at the sea of sugarcane along the Central Road, I immediately missed him.

My funk was brief, thanks to the girl standing beside me on the sluggish bus. No older than eighteen, no higher than my chin, she wore baggy shorts and a flannel shirt that dropped off a shelf of heavy breasts. She tied back a bush of black hair from a pale face dabbled with freckles. Seeing me yawn, she looked up and said, "Hunger or sleep?"

The icebreaker led to chit-chat. Bayamo was just a stop for Rosa. From there she had to find a way to get to Holguín, where she was studying to be a hairdresser. Not one to let logistics stand in the way of a good time, she was returning from a mountain town's annual four-day drinking and dancing binge. Ninety-six sleepless hours later, she was keen to get home.

Rosa pulled her identity card from a cloth bag. Tucked into the plastic folder was a photograph of a little girl wearing a white diaper and a toothless smile. She admired the photo from all angles before handing it to me and saying triumphantly, "My daughter."

"And your husband?"

"I don't have one." She added, "Cubans do a lot of things without thinking."

Rosa did have a boyfriend. Or so I deduced when she whispered in the ear of the young man seated in front of us.

"What was that about?" I asked.

"The Struggle."

Rosa had bought twenty-four pounds of roasted coffee during her stay in the mountains. Cheap at the source, the beans would sell fast on the black market in Holguín. The teenager reckoned she would net ten pesos per pound if she weren't caught; raw coffee was contraband in the hands of Cuban lowlanders.

I thought back to the grizzled man who had flagged down the truck carrying Francisco, me, and more than a ton of coffee down the hill from Castro's wartime headquarters. Standing behind a chain stretched across the narrow road, he had no obvious authority to stop traffic. He wore no uniform. He was, however, holding a rifle.

A second highwayman jumped into the truck's cargo hold. One by one, he opened the bags belonging to the folks sprawled on top of the coffee sacks. When I hesitated to expose my belongings, Francisco explained that the men were inspectors who ensured that only the state carried coffee out of the mountains. The checkpoints were new, said one of the other hitchhikers when the truck was stopped by another pair of armed men. As recently as two years ago, smuggling wasn't a problem.

"Your bag wasn't checked when you left the mountains?" I asked Rosa.

"They don't check your body."

The teenager rubbed her stomach before sliding her hands around her waist. She then took hold of my hands and placed them under her baggy shirt. Expecting flesh, I felt burlap. Moving my palms slowly around her torso, Rosa gave me a tour of the coffee strapped to her body. But she skipped one stop.

"I also have coffee inside me," she whispered. "For stimulation."

A forgotten worry resurfaced when Rosa and I parted company in Bayamo. Pedro had shown me to the pickup point near El Cobre. His uncle steered me through the next town. Rafael fed and housed me. Rosa carried me the final yards to Bayamo. More than a day late reaching the place where Fidel Castro spent his first night on the road, I was on my own. Would the people help me?

Standing behind the terminal, I watched a bony horse clip-clop down an otherwise deserted four-lane boulevard. The animal pulled a wooden wagon guided by a driver with a whip. His cargo was three passengers seated on parallel benches. I looked at another horse-drawn taxi, which displayed a list of destinations, such as Ice Cream Factory, Children's Hospital, and Cemetery, as well as the fare to each stop.

Two turns took me into a web of narrow streets down which the locals ambled without worrying about cars. Faded plaster was losing the struggle to cling to the brick underpinnings of one-story houses. As elsewhere, shutters and doors were swung open and converted to storefronts. What distinguished the market here was *guarapo*. Produced by cranking stalks of sugarcane through a steel wringer, the juice was served in lidless beer cans.

Streets bore the names of local heroes. One was Perucho Figueredo, the composer of Cuba's national anthem. Another was Francisco Vicente Aguilera, a leader of the 1868 uprising, which became the First War of Independence. A bronze plaque set in a cracked wall called attention to the home of a martyr of Castro's movement. "History," mumbled the cigar-chomping man who saw me reading a plaque marking the spot where a member of the underground was shot in 1957.

I passed three boys playing baseball on a stoop. Two wore weathered mitts. The third held a bat fashioned from scrap wood. Calling for a chance to throw a pitch, I was tossed the chunk of rubber posing as a ball. Farther along the tranquil street a boy and a girl were batting balloons the size of grapefruits. Learning to make do at an early age, they had inflated reservoir-tipped condoms.

Nearby, a freelance barber trimmed the dark locks of a teenager in his sidewalk salon. A woman had set up a table where she painted fingernails. Beside her a shirtless codger earned pennies by filling cigarette lighters. Hard work for tiny returns didn't keep the self-employed from keeping up a steady if quiet banter.

Yelps around the corner broke the calm. A wave of shouts moved toward us. A black youth whizzed past on a bicycle. Seconds later, a pack of men followed. Their cries alerted bystanders down the street. Men lunged for the rider, whose increasing speed kept him ahead of the alert. Nearly a hundred people were in the street by the time the bike disappeared from view. One of them was a red-faced man whose short legs and massive tummy kept him from snagging the teen who snatched his bicycle.

"I nearly got him," said one pedestrian.

"My hand touched his shoulder."

"My God!"

People loitered in the street after the excitement died down. Strangers formed clusters to discuss what they had seen. Ten minutes later the groups were reaching similar conclusions.

"The crime in this town."

"Cuba is lost."

"The Struggle."

The uproar in the street contrasted with the quiet of the central square. Leafy trees and marble benches ringed the rectangular plaza, whose centerpiece was a bronze statue of the hometown hero, Carlos Manuel de Céspedes. Colonial buildings surrounded the oasis. The tenant mix reminded me of Santiago de Cuba. The town hall, on the rectangle's long side, faced the cultural center. A department store and a café occupied another side. Opposite were the province's museum and the house where de Céspedes was born. In the center, a goat led by a white-haired man pulled tiny tots in a cart. Three more kids, none older than twelve, joined me on the bench.

"Where are you staying?" asked the cutest, boldest boy.

He led me a few blocks from the square to a small wooden door that opened into an unlit living room kept cool by fifteen-foot ceilings. A chandelier hung over furniture carved from dark wood. Two televisions were the only signs of the twentieth century. Tall doors opened into a dining room, which looked onto an internal yard bordered on the left by a long patio. Beneath the eaves of the internal walkway I found the home's owner.

Pushing seventy, Mrs. Tamayo was a fleshy woman who wore a housecoat and thick glasses. Her main activities were rocking in a chair, listening to the radio, and griping about her health. The old lady received a constant flow of friends and cousins. Had I known up front about the traffic, I might have sought other lodgings. Ignorant, I snapped up the offer of a bed for five dollars a night.

My room was behind one of the three doors along the covered corridor. There I found three single beds as well as the entrance to the only bathroom in the house. Sinking into a midafternoon nap, I was awakened by a young woman who barged in, excused herself, and scurried toward the toilet. Back against the pillow, my head lifted to follow the chirping sound of eight downy chicklets wandering into the room. Mrs. Tamayo cut short my third attempt to snooze. She wanted to talk.

She boasted that her house was in a historic district. Keen to beautify the area, the state had patched and painted the outside. Inside, beneath the floor, they found bones and bottles that archaeologists later determined had belonged to the Mambises who fought in the First War of Independence. Those same Mambises, said the old lady, first sang Cuba's national anthem directly outside her door. Ignoring my pleas of fatigue, the sturdy woman muscled me out the door.

It was four o'clock when I resettled on the bench in Céspedes Park. The preteens I had met earlier took up spots on opposite sides. One of the boys was glum: his coach had canceled baseball practice. Another was dreading going home to find there was nothing to eat. Alexis, the cute kid who took me to the house, carried a school text.

The book's introduction promised to increase students' knowledge of their continent and others. It aimed to expand their horizons and introduce unknown places. Every chapter would be a "voyage" to a distant land. A country-by-country analysis followed a section on the mountains, minerals, and rivers of the Americas. First up was the United States.

The section started with innocuous facts. The U.S. has fifty states. The capital is Washington, D.C. Also presented as fact was that the U.S. "dominates places such as Puerto Rico and the Virgin Islands." Reading on, Cuban school kids learned that *Yanquis* had turned the Panama Canal into a military base and, against the will of the Cuban people, occupied a corner of their turf, the naval base near Guantánamo.

American domestic policy fared no better. Topic by topic, the text trashed my country. The economy was characterized by militarization and the development of arms. Regarding population, the book said the U.S. lured professors and scientists without considering the consequences of "the robbery of brains" on underdeveloped countries. It called New York a city of great social differences, where workers and others in the majority were exploited by multimillionaires. Racism was rampant, illiteracy high.

"Do you have a car?" asked Alexis.

"No."

The boy turned glum, as if I had said that I was no Wizard and there was no Oz. Lifting his head, he asked tentatively, "But you have flown on an airplane?" My response brought a smile back to his face. News that I owned a motorcycle lifted him to a high that swept him off to study his text.

Uncle Sam was in vogue. Walking down a commercial street where Cuba's capitalists were hawking chopped pork sandwiches, corn fritters, and cotton candy, I saw a pair of Cubans wearing baseball caps with white lettering. I knew that USAF stood for United States Air Force. Did the local police? Less subtle was the T-shirt worn by a middle-age man running a food stand. I'M PROUD TO BE AN AMERICAN said the English text printed above the bald eagle on his torso.

My landlady was pro-America too. Seated with two friends when I returned to her house, Mrs. Tamayo told me about her trip to New Jersey in 1990. The old lady's eyes widened as she described the wealth accumulated in the ten years since the friend who sponsored the visit had left Cuba. Her friend owned a car. He also owned a gas station with a small supermarket on the side. "Imagine!" The old lady lost her breath recounting the moment when her friend confided that he was worth four million dollars. "Four million dollars!" The friend's fortunes triggered despondency about her own city.

"Bayamo used to be tranquil. I felt safe," she said "Now there's so much crime . . . I don't recognize the place."

One of the old lady's friends provided an example of Bayamo's crime wave. Her home had been burglarized the previous week. While she and her husband slept, thieves stole a bicycle and her children's clothing. The other visitor topped the story with one of her own. Her neighbor was a doctor. One evening, while he and his wife were out, thieves loaded their refrigerator, television, and stereo onto a truck. The couple returned to find their home empty. The victims couldn't even keep out other intruders: the thieves had stolen the front door. Mrs. Tamayo and her friends shook their heads.

Bayamo wasn't the only place where crime shocked Cubans.

na, Boris told me a "shocking" story: walking through ʳana, he saw a youth snatch a foreigner's bag. Santia- varned that I might be jumped were I to walk in a neighborhood called Martí. Crime had even come to Contra-maestre, where rustlers had made off with one of Rafael's pigs.

To me, rising crime was a good news, bad news story. The bad news was that Cubans were desperate. Left poorer and hungrier by the withdrawal of Soviet aid, they were resorting to stealing to support themselves and their families. The good news was that there was more to steal. Now able to own dollars, more Cubans received money from relatives in the U.S. Economic reforms let Cubans start tiny businesses. Crime, in other words, was a sign of prosperity.

Cubans failed to see the silver lining. For more than thirty years they had lived in a virtually crime-free society. Soviet-subsidized socialism reduced their need by providing food, clothes, and housing. Suffocating security made it hard for those hoping to cover up a theft. Fed but watched, Cubans felt free to leave their doors unlocked. So crime's comeback meant more than the loss of a bicycle. Crime symbolized the disintegration of a way of life.

"At least we don't live in Santiago de Cuba," said Mrs. Tamayo. "That place has the Mafia."

"The Mafia?" I asked.

"Blacks. Those people don't want to work, so they steal. They will leave you naked in the street."

The racist remark represented another wave of "crime." Castro had outlawed discrimination when he grabbed hold of Cuba's reins. But reducing prejudice proved trickier than, say, nationalizing foreigners' property. Like other white people in the New World, Cubans with Spanish blood had been passing pigment-based judgments since the day slaves began arriving from Africa. As elsewhere, bias didn't die with the abolition of slavery.

The wife of a friend in Havana provided the first sign that racism lived on in Cuba. "Take care of yourself around black girls," she said, making a slashing motion against my pockets.

Other Habaneros moaned that the influx of black easterners was spoiling life in the mostly white capital. People too prudent or shy to say *"negro,"* or black, indicated their distaste for darker comrades by rubbing a finger on the skin of the opposite forearm.

Fair-skinned Cubans weren't the only ones given to stereotyping. A mulatto, Boris showed neither shame nor irony when saying that he never had, and never would, sleep with a black girl. In Santiago de Cuba, a dark brown laborer advised me to avoid local street parties: "Where there are music, rum, and blacks, there will be fights." The coffee-colored taxi driver who drove me home one midnight made an assumption of his own. "See that," he said. "Two blacks on bicycles at this hour. They are thieves."

The driver offered another insight. Much as he loved his leader, he couldn't overlook the gap between Castro's practice and preaching. The man who ordered the end of racism counted no blacks among his wartime commanders. Nearly forty years later, the Party's heavies were still as white as the Ku Klux Klan.

I put question marks beside crime and racism on my list of issues addressed and, allegedly, tackled by the Revolution. Lying down for the nap that had eluded me earlier, I wondered whether other totems would tumble as I traced the trail of the Liberty Caravan. The Revolution looked good when I left Santiago de Cuba. Would that feeling survive the trip to Havana?

A chubby woman wrapped in a brown towel interrupted my thinking. She rattled open the towering door to the bedroom beside mine and disappeared into the bathroom, whose thin walls failed to hide the sound of a shower. Peeking through the door she had left ajar, I saw the naked torso of a lean man who, like the woman, looked to be in his twenties.

About an hour later another young couple stumbled into my room and began to kiss. Seeing me, they ducked into the adjacent bedroom. The next morning I counted four sets of sheets hanging on the clotheslines stretched across the courtyard. It was then that I saw Mrs. Tamayo's game. The old lady was renting her spare bedroom by the hour to locals who, because they lived in crowded houses, had no place to share their affections. I had checked into a love hotel.

18

"I REMEMBER THE DAY he came here. The people were so happy." Mrs. Tamayo rocked her chair and resumed her tale. "Everybody went to the park to see Fidel. I went there too. He was only one block from my house."

"Did he give a speech?" I asked.

The old lady felt certain that Fidel had spoken in Bayamo. She just couldn't remember what he said. Hoping for more information, I walked to Céspedes Park and into the narrow colonial edifice that housed the province's history museum.

The woman assigned to steer me through the exhibit was quick to note that Bayamo was founded in 1514, before Havana. Sugarcane, and slaves to cut it, arrived ten years later. "A city of patriots" was the catchphrase she dropped before naming several homegrown heroes. The guide was prouder still of an odd bit of history. Rather than risk losing Bayamo to Spanish troops, the Mambises torched their hometown in 1869. A photograph of Castro chatting with local men during his stop in 1959 provided a transition to my question.

"Where did Fidel spend the night?"

"Fidel didn't stay in Bayamo."

"He didn't? Are you sure?"

The guide decided that she wasn't sure whether Fidel had stayed or even spoken in Bayamo. She called over a colleague, Aldo, who had undertaken personal "investigations" of the history of the Revolution. Dressed in light slacks and a clean white shirt, the history whiz immediately reversed his colleague. Fidel, he said, had spent the night in town. I wasn't sure whom to believe.

I did believe Aldo's story about an obstacle that stalled the

Liberty Caravan outside Bayamo. A group of Batista's officers drove east to meet the Havana-bound rebels. Aldo reckoned that at that time the army brass commanded five thousand troops armed with bazookas and Sherman tanks. The officers demanded a deal.

"Fidel Castro said, 'No, I will only accept unconditional surrender,'" said Aldo. Childlike, he added, "Do you know what he did next?"

Legend had it that a few hours after reaching the impasse, the rebel leader swaggered into Bayamo alone, armed only with the pistol on his hip. Making a beeline to the army's quarters, Fidel explained the Revolution's roots and goals. Then, one by one, Batista's soldiers stood up and turned in their weapons. That night, January 2, Fidel spoke from a balcony overlooking Céspedes Park.

"Fidel slept in Bayamo," said Aldo. "Then he went to Holguín."

I didn't expect much from Holguín, a city seventy kilometers north and slightly east of Bayamo. Tips from two young men I met in Céspedes Park failed to pique my interest.

"Holguín is known as a city of parks," said a pimply carpenter.

"Holguín is famous for blondes," said his pal.

Getting worked up about Holguín was only half as hard as getting a ride there. I knew better than to waste time at Bayamo's bus terminal. Seats would be sold out. And if they weren't, the odds were even that the bus would break. Trucks had proven more regular and reliable. But where could I find one?

"Go to the Amarillo," said the carpenter.

"The Yellow Man?"

"Just tell a taxi. They know where to take you."

"Taxis" gathered outside the city's train station. Formed in front of a row of homes whose owners had converted their yards into shops that served travelers, the line of horse-drawn carriages stretched more than twenty long when I arrived early the next morning. Its ribs protruding, the beige horse at the front of the rank showed no interest in work. The teenager lounging on the attached buggy was equally apathetic when I asked him to take me to the Yellow Man.

"Holguín exit," he shouted. "Holguín."

No takers. The teenager offered a tip. Horse-taxis traveled only when full. The alternative was a bicycle-taxi. He pointed to the sidewalk, where our conversation had attracted the attention of a slight man whose bicycle had a padded rack in the rear. For three pesos, the cabbie agreed to pedal me to the place that trucks stopped for westbound passengers.

More than thirty Cubans gathered at the pickup point on the outskirts of Bayamo, sitting on three rows of benches behind a chest-high fence of steel. A concrete roof shielded them from a white-hot sun. The haze over the flat expanse behind the shelter made ghostlike silhouettes out of the mountains south of the city. Judging by their stares, my fellow travelers looked a breath away from becoming ghosts.

My eyes landed on a man standing beside a sentry stand twenty yards up the road. With a clipboard in his hand, he had the deep tan of somebody who worked in the sun. His cap had mesh sides. His sunglasses had mirror lenses. Most important, his dusty pants matched his loose, short-sleeve shirt with epaulets. Both were yellow.

The carpenter had explained the Yellow Man's job. When the loss of subsidized Soviet fuel paralyzed Cuban transport, the government began posting people at the exits of all the cities and many towns. The goal was to maximize the use of those vehicles that continued to operate. The Yellow Men had the authority to stop any vehicle with one of the blue license plates used by the state's cars and trucks, and they loaded travelers into the empty spaces. It was hitchhiking for socialists: Karl Marx meets Jack Kerouac.

I felt funny about approaching the Yellow Man. Cubans earned very little money. The flipside of low pay was low prices as well as plenty of free services. No contributor to Cuban socialism, I had no right to claim any benefits. But would the Yellow Man treat me like a Cuban?

"Is this where I get a truck to Holguín?" I asked.

"Wait under the roof," he said. "The sun is very hot today."

The Yellow Man moved into the shade of the concrete sentry post, where he joined a colleague dressed like him. I shuffled back to the shelter and asked who was last in line. None of the zombies flinched. When I asked again — "¿*El último?*" — a solid man with two stripes on the sleeves of his faded fatigues raised his hand. I sat down beside the corporal on the back bench of the shelter.

Slight stirrings and deep sighs were the only sounds. Some travelers watched the air before their eyes. Others looked at the Yellow Man, as though watching him would speed the appearance of a ride. The Yellow Man stared down the vacant lanes. Every face bore the uniquely Cuban look of resignation to an indefinite wait.

The Cubans lifted their heads to watch the approach of an empty flatbed. A few shifted in their seats. When the truck rumbled through the checkpoint a man shouted, like a fan berating an umpire: "*AMARILLO,* what about that one?"

"How are we getting out of here?" grumbled a heavy woman.

"*Aye Cuba,*" moaned another traveler.

When more trucks passed I asked why, in thirty minutes, the Yellow Man hadn't stopped a single vehicle. "He knows those drivers," said the corporal. "They work nearby." He rose to his feet and marched over to lean on the steel fence.

I walked over to a youth selling bottles of powdered juice. When I needed another break from the sweltering tedium, I visited a squat concrete structure marked Bathroom. The stench of fermenting urine didn't surprise me. Nor did the floor-level commode. Squatting, I looked ahead and found, in red letters, ¡VIVA FIDEL!

I emerged to find the Yellow Man flagging down a dump truck. He strolled around to the driver's side, engaged in a brief chat, and announced the vehicle's destination, Cauto Cristo, a town less than halfway to Holguín. The words enlivened the Cubans, who arranged themselves in the order of arrival. The soldier, who I knew was headed to Holguín, didn't budge. So I stayed put.

The Yellow Man placed a set of four steps beside the truck. The passengers mounted the metal staircase and climbed over the side after dropping twenty centavos through the slot of a rusty, sealed box in the cab of the vehicle. When twenty of the shelter's citizens had climbed aboard, the truck rumbled away. The cruise director marked his clipboard, returned to the shade, and opened a copy of *Granma*.

A tank-shaped Ford shook to a stop in front of the shelter. The driver jumped out and shouted, "Holguín. Fifteen pesos. Holguín."

"Where is a man like me going to get fifteen pesos?" shouted a man older than seventy. "You rich people have money, a car. Look at the poor. We have nothing."

The driver put his Ford back in gear. The old man sat down. I tried to disappear lest the critic scold me for having too much money. Or for being too stupid to spare myself further waiting and sweating.

It *was* silly. Sixty U.S. cents was nothing for a seventy-kilometer ride. But I couldn't let the Cubans see me spending big. The two-hour wait had bonded me to the other travelers. True, nobody had hugged me. On the other hand, nobody had suggested I didn't belong. To leave would be to betray my gratitude for being treated like another traveler whose luck had run out.

That thought bubble was pierced by the woman sitting to my left. About thirty years old, she had dozed off and leaned lightly against my side. Still sleeping, she emitted a sharp yelp. Her torso straightened as I turned toward the sound. Her hand leapt to the top of her red blouse as she gave out a longer cry. She slumped across my leg and slipped past my knee. Her skull thudded on the shelter's floor.

Three Cubans rushed toward her, and a pair of men lifted her back onto the bench. A middle-age mother abandoned her child and shook her chin. When the young woman's eyes didn't open, the mother cradled her head and spoke softly into her ear. But to no effect.

"Water," shouted the mother.

I handed over my plastic bottle. Put to the victim's lips, the water dribbled down her chin. Another woman wafted a perfume under her nose, but she didn't respond to the makeshift smelling salts. None of the ten people surrounding the lifeless body knew what to do next.

The Yellow Man did. "Hospital," was his only word as he lifted the woman and carried her across the road. A jeep appeared within two minutes. Small black letters on its yellow license plate said *"particular,"* private. The hero stood in front of the moving vehicle, whose driver agreed to take the woman to a hospital. The men loaded her into the passenger seat. She hadn't revived by the time the jeep drove away and the Yellow Man returned to the shade.

"Hunger," said one speculator.

"An attack," said another.

"She's too young."

"The Struggle."

A long silence followed five minutes of head-shaking about the fate of the young woman in the red blouse. The quiet broke when a horse-drawn taxi dropped a woman and two children in front of the concrete shelter.

"*¿El último?*" asked the mother of two.

I hesitated to follow the corporal onto the Chevy truck that the Yellow Man flagged down three hours after my arrival at his station. The owner asked five pesos for passage to Holguín. The price didn't put me off. The vehicle's condition did. Faded red paint covered the truck's hood as well as the lattice of bars covering the cargo bay. A cow would have balked before entering this cage on wheels. A person had no choice but to pay the privateer and squeeze into the herd of more than fifty desperate travelers.

Pressed against the grill on the truck's right side, I looked at the billboard outside a lumberyard: MEN ARE PROVED BY DIFFICULT TIMES. The rest of the countryside was unfettered. The plain grew nothing but dry grass. Past a giant gear beside concrete letters that spelled Holguín, the name of the province as well as the city, an expanse of cane filled my field of vision. Miles passed before the tin roof and smokestacks of a sugar refinery broke the seamless sea of brown and green stalks.

More remarkable was the composure of the passengers. The woman to my right seemed not to notice my armpit in her face. I said nothing about the chest pressed to my back. If the other passengers' calves were burning like mine, they didn't say. Crammed like cordwood, the Cubans stood quietly as the truck rolled along the Central Road.

The stoic spell ended when a Yellow Man stopped the Chevrolet. Standing beside his own brood of travelers, the man looked for space in the cargo cage. The eyeballing sparked an outcry — "There's no room." "We're already suffocating." "No more" — which convinced the inspector not to add passengers. "Never again" was the unkeepable promise I made once off the Black Hole on wheels and on the firm ground called Holguín.

A bicycle with a homemade sidecar carried me to the center of the city, a park named for General Calixto García, a nineteenth-century hero. I sat on one of the park's dozens of shaded benches. I reckoned it was only a matter of time before somebody offered to help a foreigner. Indeed, the time was a quarter-hour. The somebody was a dark brown woman who flopped down beside me and said, "I've been cleaning floors all day."

She was no older than thirty. Her clothing was simple — a red T-shirt and knee-length skirt — but clean. But what Anna lacked in style she made up for in friendliness — broad smiles looked at home on her face — and flattery. "I sat next to you because you are handsome," she said. I ignored the red flag and let the woman lure me into her life. A devout Catholic, she described her training as a metalworker and a quality controller. All for naught. She cleaned floors for a living.

"Where are you staying?" asked Anna.

"I don't know."

"I can help you."

We walked out of the square, just as I had done with the boys in Bayamo. Two blocks away we came to the entrance of a private home, just as in Bayamo. This, Anna explained, was the home of a friend. For five dollars I could have my own room. I could bring in all the girls I wanted. No problem. I smiled both at Anna's assumption and at the ease of finding lodgings.

I stopped smiling after a longer look at the house. The front door was at the foot of a narrow alley I wouldn't enter after dark. Outside sat three men tough enough to unnerve me in broad daylight. They shifted their chairs to let us pass. I felt like I was entering a den of thieves.

"I don't like this place," I said.

"No problem," she said. "Meet my friend."

The friend was out. We did find a young man with a thin black mustache. Tinkering with a cassette player in a living room whose only furnishings were a small sofa and a velvet wall hanging, he said he was the owner's son. Anna took the youth by the arm and led him out of earshot. Unable to hear a word of a conference that lasted five minutes, I considered bolting. Then the Cubans returned.

"Do you want a beer?" asked the son.

"No thanks."

"Cuban rum?"

Anna led me out the back door, through a courtyard surrounded by neighboring houses, and into a brick building attached to her friend's home. An afternoon power failure left the room dark, but there was enough light to see that the walls were bare and the only furniture was a double bed covered with a white sheet.

"You can stay here," said Anna, resuming her cheerful demeanor. "It's very private. You can bring girls."

"Why do you think I want to bring girls here?"

Anna sat on the edge of the bed and said, "I'm menstruating. Do you know what that is?" Concerned about the limits of my Spanish, she pulled my hand to her crotch.

I had no response.

"It's no problem. It means we don't have to use a condom. That way it will be better for you."

I couldn't move.

"Unless you want to use a condom. For hygiene."

I finally reacted when she pulled me onto the bed and pulled off her shirt. After a frightened glance at two brown breasts, I managed to say "But we just met."

"No problem," said Anna.

But there was a problem. A big one. It shouldn't have mattered that Anna was no great beauty. But it did; I was in no way attracted to her. Then there was the room, which felt more like a jail cell than a love nest. Above all, the alley, the toughs, and the whispered conference left me nervous. No, scared.

"Don't worry. You can pay my friend five dollars. Then you can help me."

The penny dropped. "Help," I had learned, meant "shower with money." Like Mrs. Tamayo, Anna's friend rented rooms to young lovers. Like hustlers in Havana, Anna had spotted a sucker. The plain mulatta wasted little time in luring an American to a place where she could multiply her monthly salary in less than an hour. How would she react to the news that I wasn't keen on paying her or her friend? Anna began to sob.

"I'm sorry. I've never done this before," she cried. "I'm very religious. Catholic."

I made no move to console the topless woman.

"I live in an apartment with my mother and two sisters. In one month I earn only one hundred pesos. That's . . ."

"Four dollars."

"Four dollars a month. We can't survive on that. Today I don't have one peso. If I go to the market I can't buy anything. Here is the only food I will eat today."

Anna showed me a wad of mashed yucca. She opened and overturned her dusty change purse. She had one more thing. Pulling her ration book from her pocket, she showed me a picture of the Virgin Mary.

"Please pardon me," she pleaded. "I'm not a bad person. I didn't realize that you didn't understand why we were coming here. I only brought you here out of necessity. Please pardon me."

I said nothing.

"Please pardon me."

Only the hardest heart could have withheld what Anna now needed more than money: forgiveness. After we parted, I remembered something I had heard on Mrs. Tamayo's terrace. Referring to her thieving compatriots, the old woman had said, "Cubans are good people. But we're in a very bad state. The Struggle is turning good people into bad."

19

HOLGUÍN'S MAIN PLAZA differed little from the centers of other eastern cities. At the heart of the square stood a statue of a hero, in this case Calixto García. Late in the afternoon the park filled with Cubans who had finished school or work. Gray-haired men and bleached blondes passed the bench where I settled after leaving Anna.

The environs were also standard issue. The colonial buildings surrounding the park housed a cultural center, a history museum, and a shop where visitors could pay dollars for postcards and knickknacks. Pedestrians examined the posters in front of the Video Room, a cinema that showed bootlegged videotapes on a television set. Locals pondered paying two pesos for "A double explosion of martial arts!"; on tap were *Time of the Intruders* and *Bad Blood*. As elsewhere, the hub was a place where Cubans welcomed foreigners.

"Do you need help?" asked a college-age man.

I was no longer sure about the help offered by strangers. I sidestepped the question by asking about his footwear, a pair of sandals held together by nylon straps. Styled in California, they looked expensive.

"In Cuba there is a choice," explained the youth, Wilfredo. "You can eat or you can buy clothes. I didn't eat for many weeks so I could buy these shoes."

Wilfredo sat down and skipped to another topic, his hometown. Established in 1523, Holguín was laid out in a grid whose precision was best appreciated from the hill at the north end of town. The highlights were parks and a brewery. Holguín also had a beer-drinking burro. Nonetheless, the man was keen to leave.

Medicine was Wilfredo's ticket out of Holguín. Now in his fifth and final year of medical school, he owed the state two years of social service. Graduates typically went to rural clinics before returning to learn a specialty. Looking ahead, he hoped to specialize in pediatrics in Havana, not Holguín. "It's the place all Cubans want to live," he said.

I trusted Cubans who acknowledged discontent. So when Wilfredo suggested I stay with his friend — a man whose honesty would be immediately recognizable — I agreed. Besides, darkness was falling and I needed a bed. There was little choice but to follow the affable student to a narrow house several blocks from the center.

A flabby woman wearing a sundress and plastic sandals beamed as she opened the door. She led us through a living room dotted with family photographs into a kitchen. There, at a formica table beneath naked fluorescent bulbs, sat a shirtless man whose helmet of black hair didn't budge as he pumped my hand with the joy of a paroled prisoner. Ernesto wasted no time telling me about his passions, English and music.

He was also determined to convince me of his virtue. The little Cuban called himself a devout Catholic who prayed several times a day. He didn't smoke or drink rum or coffee. Nor did he give in to another temptation, stealing from the state. Cubans survived by filching cheese, candy, or whatever else their factory produced and reselling the haul on the black market. Ernesto thumped his chest — literally thumped his chest — and boasted that he never, never stole. He made ends meet by giving music lessons.

The sermonizing was quick to grate. When, in the days that followed, I felt my patience fraying, I reminded myself of Ernesto's dilemma. Too poor to afford three daily meals, the trumpeter was going against the flow of Cuban society. He was

a good man struggling to stay decent. And I thought
daughter. At twelve, the tall girl already had her mother
brown hair and her father's inability to smile. She also
unstudied charm.

"What are your favorite things?" she asked. Uncritical of a
grownup's inability to find an answer, she said, "I like the beach.
And I like the sea. I like picking up the little shells. And I like
music. When I'm playing the piano I'm happy."

Innocence was unknown in other parts of Holguín. Or so I
deduced when I returned to the center of town the next morning.

A crowd had gathered on a narrow street linking the main
plaza to a smaller square called Flores Park. Closed to cars, the
strip was chaotic. Street vendors sold ice-chilled drinks, cotton
candy, ice cream bars. Clusters of Cubans gathered around the
stands to buy or to watch others buy. Dozens more loitered
without apparent purpose.

Not everybody was idling. Faced off in two rows in the center of the street, women presented goods for inspection by the
pedestrians who ran their gauntlet. A middle-age woman held
out a pair of new shoes. Beside her a teenager had a pair of
neatly folded jeans whose tags hadn't been removed. Down the
line I saw shirts for men, dresses for ladies, and sneakers for
children. Expressionless and quiet, the people were human
mannequins. But what were they doing?

I also failed to grasp the meaning of the mob near the end of
the block. But for the presence of six policemen, I would have
suspected that the five-layer semicircle of people on the sidewalk were watching a beating. The group's calm and the string
of people stretching around the corner suggested that there was
something else afoot. The mystery ended when I saw a sign that
said, in Spanish, Panamerican Stores.

Stores that accepted only dollars were nothing new in Cuba.
Yes, Castro had banned private shops and western goods after
taking power. Ration books provided clothes and shoes. Televisions, radios, and other frills were dispensed as prizes for hard

work. But people who didn't work for the state had another option. The government maintained special stores for foreigners as well as Party bigwigs.

Dollar stores also attracted ordinary Cubans, who would risk arrest to procure, say, a toaster. The brazen entered the forbidden premises and hoped to duck security. More cautious and better-connected Cubans asked diplomats and visitors to accompany them inside. The safest approach was described by Dan, a Canadian I had met in Havana:

"Things were different when I came here in 1993. I was stopped by a woman, attractive, who asked me to help her buy some things. She gave me forty dollars and a list of what she wanted from the diplostore. Her stuff only cost thirty-eight. She was so grateful that she took me home and fed me a small meal. Then she led me to the bedroom and fucked me. Can you believe it? And she let me keep the two dollars' change!"

Cubans no longer needed foreign fronts. Now allowed to hold dollars, they were also granted the right to spend them. Some stores sold everything from clothing to hardware to beer. Others specialized in jewelry, appliances, or shoes. To meet the demands of the people and to take in more money, the government was opening dozens of dollar stores. The cities had several. They also cropped up in small towns, such as Contramaestre. Wherever they sprouted, the outlets attracted long lines. But mobs?

"There's a sale today," said a man standing apart from the two hundred people seeking access to the store.

"How did they know?"

"People know things. They hear a rumor and wake up early, before the store opens. Some sleep here. Some pay other people to stand in line for them. We have little money, so it's important to get a good price."

"And if what they want is sold out?"

"They buy something else." He pointed to the gauntlet of women. "They bought things they don't want because the prices were reduced. Maybe ten shirts. Now they're waiting for someone to buy them for more than they paid, but less than the normal price."

The tactic made sense to me. Buy low, sell high, was the strategy behind fortunes all over the world. But in Cuba? Impressed that the people were spotting and seizing an opportunity, I was surprised that the state was doing nothing to stop the resurgent middlemen.

"What did you buy?" I asked.

"I have another business."

The Cuban, Jorge, was surfing the demand for dollars. A money changer, he spent his time trying to buy dollars cheaply. He charged twenty-five pesos for a buck he had bought for twenty-two. Sales meant a bonanza for the money changer. Desperate for dollars, people would pay twenty-seven pesos or more to get their hands on greenbacks.

"But it's illegal, right?" I asked.

Jorge said that the penalties for changing money were prison or a fifteen-hundred-peso fine. He was not worried about the police. Ditto the dozen or so other money men working the shopping street. In New York, the clean-cut hustlers would have been bankers braying for bonuses. In Holguín, the financiers were more subtle. Clustered at the ends of the strip, the young men whispered the argot for hard currency: "¿Divisa?"

The police's blind eye was logical. The state set up the first exchange kiosks in the capital, but plans to extend the experiment to the east were still on the drawing board. Until more booths were built, Jorge and his colleagues were the only game in town. That left the cops and their bosses with an uncomfortable choice. One was to watch money changers flaunt the law. The other was to arrest the arbitrageurs, a move that, by making dollars less available, would stem the tide of cash into state coffers.

I followed an eastbound street from Calixto García Park through a corridor of airy homes onto Calixto García Boulevard. I stopped when I spotted more than a dozen food stalls set up in the parking lot outside Calixto García Stadium. The vendor who sold me a chopped pork sandwich had a question for an American. According to *Granma*, the U.S. had blocked the export of computers for Cuba's health system. Why, he demanded, would the *Yanquis* stop a humanitarian shipment?

Nearby, I came across another reminder of the diplomatic antipathy between Cuba and the United States. Abandoned among the car park's trees was a trailer used in the army's shooting drills. On the side a propagandist had painted a tanned soldier standing over a pale man seated beside a helmet that said USA. "The truth is that Cubans are ready," said the words beside the cartoon. The trailer's other side carried a tip for trainees: "The Marines wear bulletproof vests, so practice shooting at the face."

The unsettling message kept me from noticing the approach of an old man wearing a straw hat. His appearance startled me. A white beard covered half of his puckered face. Large patches of his bent body were visible through tears in his filthy clothes. Focused on the callused toes protruding from his shoes, I heard his meek voice: "Young man, I'm dying of hunger. Some money." I dropped a handful of coins into his palm and watched his painfully slow exit.

Back in the lot beside the stadium I inquired about another local spectacle. Was it true that Holguín had a burro who drank beer?

"Mayabe," said a skinny man in a tank top.

Mayabe was the local beer. The man, Juanito, said that Mayabe was also the name of the burro who drank bottles of the brew. Quartered in a hotel, the animal was a big draw. People came from far and wide to buy a beer and watch Mayabe chug. He noted that the original Mayabe had died, perhaps of liver failure, a fate to which the current Mayabe appeared doomed.

"You need a car to get there," he said. "It will cost you fifty, maybe sixty, pesos."

Eighty, or maybe one hundred, pesos was the estimate provided by Juanito's buddy Rubén. The slimmest of three men leaning against a green Lada at the north end of the lot, the

man of thirty had the sculpted face of a fashi
He stroked his mustache and aimed his piercing eyes
nearby grove of trees before elaborating on the price o
to Mayabe.

"I would never take you in my car," said Rubén.

"Not even for a hundred pesos?"

"Not even for two hundred. Here, foreigners aren't allowed
to ride in private cars. The government wants you to ride in
their taxis. If the police see me, they will fine me. And they will
take away my car."

Rubén's friends nodded.

"See this beer," he said, holding up a brown bottle with no
label. "I'm not supposed to have this. Because I'm Cuban I'm
not supposed to have good beer. If the police catch me, they
will fine me."

Not willing to drive me, Rubén appeared unconcerned about
an arrest for drinking. He lifted the bottle to his lips and tipped
the contents down his throat. His friends made no effort to hide
their bottles. I was the only one checking the area for policemen. I saw two, about fifty yards away, engrossed by their pork
sandwiches.

"You don't have to worry about them. You're a tourist. If the
police come here, they will probably buy you a beer. In Cuba,
tourists can do whatever they want. Last year my friend's cousin
came from Miami. He bought three whole pigs and had a big
party. If I did that the police would put me in jail."

"For buying pigs?"

"For *peligrosidad*."

"Dangerousness." The word turned Orwellian when used by
the state's security. Cuba was meant to be a country of equals.
Centrally planned salaries let field laborers live nearly as well as
the country's heart surgeons. For decades, all work outside the
state sector was illegal. That had changed. What hadn't changed
was the assumption that excess wealth was a sign of crime. A
conviction for "dangerousness" could rest entirely on the evidence of high living. The prosecution didn't need to prove the
deed.

Mrs. Tamayo was the first Cuban to tell me about this crime. She introduced me to her neighbor, a balding man who had spent his life making furniture. The carpenter nodded as Mrs. Tamayo described the years of work that allowed him to save enough to buy a refrigerator, two air conditioners, and a pickup truck. These were all carted away by the police, who said that Cubans weren't supposed to be that rich.

"If Cubans don't have enough money, they have a problem," said Rubén. "If they have too much money, they also have a problem."

"So you're fucked."

Rubén's eyes widened at the sound of my snap analysis. He reached into a straw bag beneath the Lada and pulled out a beer. The handsome man handed me the bottle after popping the top with his teeth. "We're fucked," he said, clinking his bottle against mine. He waved a brick of notes in mock defiance of the police. I asked where he got the money.

"Beer," he said.

The Cuban was part of a syndicate of bootleggers. The kingpin was a friend working in the Mayabe brewery. Every day he pilfered a few beers, which he sold for five pesos. Rubén's crew stored and chilled the brew for resale at eight pesos. A three-peso profit? Not quite. The bootleggers had expenses. None lived close to the stadium, which was known as the place to buy beer. Nor did any of them want to warehouse stolen goods. They solved both problems by paying a local who was willing to risk storing contraband in his refrigerator.

"Three more," said Rubén to a teenager on a bicycle. "Cold ones."

Minutes later the teen returned carrying beers in a basket. I reached for my wallet. Rubén also reached for my wallet. The black marketeer stuffed the money back into my pocket and pronounced: "When I have *wanikiki* I spend it on my friends."

A pattern repeated itself over the next two hours. Rubén, Juanito, or one of the half-dozen others who had gathered around the Lada sent the teenager for beer. I tried to buy a round. The group shouted down my offer. They also spotted my attempt to stem their generosity by drinking slower. Whenever a fresh beer arrived, Rubén snatched away my current bottle, tipped out the warm contents, and forced a cold one into my palm.

He did make one demand: "Give me a number."

"Thirty-three."

He jogged over to a vintage Chevrolet near the stadium. He exchanged a few words with the man seated on a stool beside the car. When he jogged back, he thanked me.

"For what?"

"Most people use the same number every day. I like to change numbers. So I put three hundred pesos on thirty-three."

"My number is twenty-five," said Juanito.

"Seventeen," said another beer buddy.

The other Cubans all identified their lucky numbers in Holguín's favorite game of chance. Banned by Castro, gambling was alive and kicking in the shadow of Calixto García Stadium. The Chevy was a mobile casino. Bets were placed with the "bank," a man who noted, mentally, numbers ranging from zero to ninety-nine. Paid off at sixty to one, winners were determined by taking the last two digits of the winning number in Venezuela's lottery, whose result could be picked up by radio in Cuba.

"If I win I get eighteen thousand pesos," said Rubén. "We'll have a big party."

The car park was a free-for-all. The only thing that didn't fly was stinginess. Slurring his increasingly abusive words, Rubén shouted at a rival beer baron, a mulatto carrying a plastic bucket filled with bottles on ice: "Why don't you ever treat me to a beer, faggot?"

"Faggot?" cried the mulatto, dropping the bucket and clenching his fists.

"All you think about is money. What about friendship?"

"You're not my friend. My friends don't call me faggot. Faggot is what you say to sugarcane! But what do you know. In this country the blacks are only good for cutting cane. Right? Only white people are allowed to make money. Right?"

The mulatto moved toward Rubén. Rubén turned his bottle upside down and gripped its neck. I stepped sideways. Better men, Juanito and the rest of the syndicate, jumped between the would-be brawlers. The shouting and finger-pointing lasted five more minutes, after which the mulatto marched away grumbling.

"I'm good with the good, and bad with the bad," said Rubén.

I said I had to go.

"Where are you going?" he slurred.

"Home."

"Let's go get some girls. I know two good ones."

"What if the police see me in your car?"

"Fuck the police."

20

"CHRISTOPHER, is Harlem the poorest neighborhood in the United States?"

Talks with Cubans often focused on their questions about the U.S. Though they sounded simple, they revealed the bias of both the source and *Granma* as well as their doubts about information in the Official Organ.

"Christopher, are dollars the only money in America?"

I lavished extra patience on Ernesto, who was determined to take advantage of the time I spent in his home. Keen to ask me about English grammar and pronunciation as well as life in America, he picked my brain at least once an hour.

"Christopher, in New York how much does a trumpet cost?"

Six A.M. on a Sunday morning was where I had to draw the line. That was the time Ernesto chose to switch on the radio in the kitchen, a room separated from mine by a sheet draped across the doorway. I heard Ernesto mumbling English phrases while feeding the ducks he raised behind the house. Stuck on a word, he wandered into my nook and asked me to pronounce "carburetor."

"Ernesto, can we talk a little later?"

There were other reasons that Ernesto's house felt odd. One was the constant presence of his parents, a gray-haired woman bent like a question mark and a squat old man who Ernesto said was almost blind and mostly deaf. Also, the trumpeter's humorless determination to work hard and live clean made me nervous. What if the puritan learned about my drinking and gambling buddies?

Ignorant of my extracurricular activities, Ernesto didn't want me to leave. Not that his heartfelt appreciation of my help with his English was enough to keep me in town. Nor was I swayed by his offer of trumpet lessons, free. The clincher was the warning that travel was tough on Sundays. Buses were packed. Most truckers had the day off. The Yellow Men knocked off at noon.

Not everybody rested on Sundays. Walking toward a church in the town's center, I noticed residents dressing their windows with price lists for the snacks they sold. On the way back from the morning service, I stopped to watch a chain of four men, two women, and a child pass buckets of gravel from a pile on the sidewalk to a pile on the roof, where two more men were laying bricks on a one-story home. Down the street a shirtless man tinkered under the hood of a car with a rumble seat.

Ernesto's home was also abuzz. Returning after lunch, I found a crowd around the kitchen table. Four neighbors had joined the house's five residents. All nine Cubans wriggled in anticipation of two o'clock. At that time, every Sunday, Ernesto's brother telephoned from Miami.

"Answer! Answer!" squealed the neighbors as Ernesto's wife reached for the ringing telephone. The trumpeter fumbled with gadgets near the handset. A small speaker would amplify the sound of Miami. A tape deck would record the conversation.

The old man got first crack. The phone pressed to an ear that allegedly couldn't hear, he smiled and nodded while his son prattled on about the house he was buying for $100,000, a figure that elicited gasps from the audience. Next came Ernesto's wife, who reported on the father's health. The serious little girl told her uncle about their American visitor. Like children waiting their turn with a kaleidoscope, the neighbors itched in anticipation of their turn to talk to Miami.

Cubans had a history of moving to Miami. Expelled from Cuba in the late 1800s, José Martí took refuge in a community of expatriates in New York City. Desi Arnaz, the costar of *I Love Lucy,* was the son of a former mayor of Santiago de Cuba who landed in Florida before World War II. Decades later, Castro honeymooned in Miami as well as New York.

The new regime drove thousands more to Florida and other parts of the U.S. Army officers and government officials who ducked the firing squads were among the first to leave. Rich Cubans fled as the government seized their property or banned their business. They were followed by thousands of professionals who didn't care for Castro or his polices. By the time the president stopped the exodus, a quarter-million Cubans had left.

Rare was the day I failed to meet a Cuban with relatives "up north." A middle-age cabbie in Havana told me how an aunt in New York had treated his mother to a visit to the Statue of Liberty. A doctor told me that her father owned a travel agency in Miami. Later waves of refugees — 120,000 Cubans left in 1980, another 35,000 in 1994 — meant that Cubans were quick to befriend a man who came from the country filled with their brothers, sisters, and cousins.

At Ernesto's, the excitement outlasted the thirty-minute call. His wife and neighbors rehashed every detail of the conversation. The trumpeter rewound the recording of the call. Hearing themselves and Miami for a second time, the group laughed at the sound of my reluctance to get on the line with a man I had never met. ("He lives in a country full of people like me," I said.) It wasn't until the end of the tape that I heard what was missing — Ernesto's voice.

"I don't talk to my brother," the trumpeter told me later. "He doesn't help me. He knows that I need to buy food for my family, but he still doesn't send money."

A Cuban exile could commit no greater sin. Enthusiastic though they were about the success of relatives in America, Cubans went stone silent at the mention of a person who ignored the folks back home. Have your fun in Florida, went Cuba's unwritten family law. Just don't forget the family. Emigrants who didn't look back were said to have drunk "the Coca-Cola of Forgetfulness."★

"This is soap. We use it to wash."

I lifted my eyes toward a man whose voice I was hearing for the first time. Seated across the kitchen table was Ernesto's father, Angel, who was stroking back the final strands of his thinning white hair. His uniform was a pair of plastic sandals, a white undershirt hanging over the beltline of baggy pants, and glasses so thick they obscured his eyes.

"You can go to the bodega to look for soap," said Angel, "but you won't find it. Not in Cuba."

Ernesto had said that his father was out of touch with reality. Because the old man never spoke, I accepted the analysis at face value. Now I wondered whether the blind-and-deaf story was spun to prevent my talking to him. Indeed, the trumpeter cringed as his father began to speak. And the longer he spoke, the more I suspected that his son had something to hide.

"Here there's nothing. No food to eat. No buttons for a shirt."

A Cuban carping about rations was nothing new. Not so the words that followed.

"Yesterday I went to the bodega. They only gave me two pounds of rice. There's nothing there. Nothing that a man wants to eat. I went to the black market and bought a small piece of beef."

Ernesto placed his forefinger on his lips.

A market in Havana is where I first heard about the dangers of beef. Stationed beside a pile of pig parts, a cheerful butcher went quiet when I asked for steak. He alternately clasped each wrist with the opposite hand and said that selling beef would

---

★The large number of people who depend on cash from relatives bred the joke that Cubans live by *fe*. Literally "faith," the word is an acronym for *familia exterior*, family abroad.

earn him five years in prison. "Seven years," interrupted his helper, who also mimed manacles. The men couldn't agree on the penalty. They did agree that selling beef had been a serious crime ever since the loss of Soviet feed halved the size of Cuba's herd. Still, steaks and burgers could be had, for a price.

Ernesto's father said that the police monitored farmers with cows, and people who "lost" animals often landed in jail. Harder to punish were peasants whose animals were injured. Hungry farmers developed a knack for smashing the front leg of a cow and calling the cops. Once an inspector determined that the animal couldn't be saved, the owners were free to kill and eat the beast. As with other farm products, some meat found its way to the black market.

A taste for beef wasn't all that distinguished the old man from other Cubans. He told me how he had worked for one of the American corporations that, together, controlled more than half of Cuba's land and industry before the Revolution. He was overjoyed by the fall of Batista and looked forward to living in a Cuba run by Cubans. For years after the Revolution he joined the cheering and dancing masses on holidays such as July 26, the anniversary of the attack on Moncada.

"People used to put out flags on the twenty-sixth," said Angel. "Now there are no flags. The people have lost their enthusiasm for the Revolution. They have lost their enthusiasm for life."

The loss of animus explained the old man's candor. The eighty-year-old had given up caring. That's why he had rejected his son's offer to bring him to Miami. "What's the point," he said. "I'm on the road to heaven." Apathy bred bravery: "This communism is worthless."

I had heard a similar damnation from Mrs. Tamayo. She, like Ernesto's father, was old enough to remember life before the Revolution. She had also been part of Cuba's middle class, a group that though not rich, was educated enough to earn a good living. The old man had been a translator. Mrs. Tamayo's husband had owned a store in Bayamo. Both had a habit of referring to *antes*, before.

The old lady dwelled on her health. Seated in her rocking

chair, she lifted her housecoat to show me a thigh th
shape of a fire hydrant. Pointing to the Ace bandage w
around her knee, she said that the pain kept her from w
and asked me to help. When I returned to the U.S., could I
back a balm that would ease her trauma?

"There's nothing here in Cuba. No medicine, no food, nothing." Mrs. Tamayo folded her arms across her chest and nodded
knowingly. She rocked her chair and added, "So now you know.
There's no milk, no underwear, nothing," she said before repeating her mannerisms. "So now you know. There's no gaso-
line, no electricity, Cuba has nothing." Fold. Nod. Rock. "So
now you know."

The old lady talked about the days before the Revolution.
People were happy, she said, because they could have their own
business. Bayamo had "stores and stores and stores." The
shelves were stocked with clothing, perfume, and food. Families
could find and afford the goods they needed. She rocked some
more before comparing the glorious past to the miserable present: "Now there is nothing. People here are starving. There are
people who go days without cooking."

"But you said you were cheering when Fidel came to Bayamo."

"We didn't know," she said.

"Know what?"

"That they were communists."

The clearest example of the disillusion of older, richer, and
whiter Cubans came near the end of my trip. In Havana I met
a professorial man whose pale face made him look more European than Cuban. French would have been my guess in light of
his preference for wearing a black beret.

"It's all a lie," he shouted as his son and I watched the education minister speaking on the television news.

The son tried to hush his father. I braced for a wave of storm
troopers.

"I can say what I want. I can say it in the street, on the corner,
anyplace I like. I have the right because I have my medals in my
room."

His father, my friend explained, had been a hard-core revolutionary. He served in the army after Castro came to power. He was on the beach during the battle at the Bay of Pigs. Terrified by the blizzard of bullets and the roar of bombers, the soldier fought until a bomb exploded near him. The wounded hero then came home and headed his local militia. For thirty years he worshiped Fidel and cursed Americans.

Then came "the special period." Cubans began to go hungry. Without foreign aid, Cuba could barely feed itself. Communism's strongest supporters saw that the system didn't work. The good times had been a Soviet-sponsored illusion. The realization left men and women who had spent their life believing Castro inconsolably bitter.

"It's a lie," repeated my friend's father. "And they are all liars."

No less bitter about the effects of communism on his country, the old man in Holguín relished speaking his mind. Knocking the system brought a grin to Angel's face. Candor was an elixir that improved his hearing and returned his eyesight. He prolonged his pleasure by softly singing a song: *"Viva Cuba. Viva Fidel. Y ellos que lucharon, juntos con él."* After one repetition I translated the ditty: "Long live Cuba. Long live Fidel. And all those who fought, together with him."

"That's a song the communists used to sing," said the old man, smirking. "You don't hear it anymore."

21

AN OLD MAN PEDALED me to Holguín's Yellow Man. I felt sheepish. But the sixtyish driver showed no sign of resenting either his load or the fact that he fed his family by operating a bicycle-taxi. His complaint was the weather. A chilly drizzle had forced him to wear a wool overcoat.

"This cold front comes from the U.S.," he said.

The cyclist wasn't the only one pointing a finger at my country. Past a road sign that said SOCIALISM OR DEATH, beyond a low building whose face bore the message TO DIE FOR THE HOMELAND IS TO LIVE, we came to a memorial for six medical students who died fighting for freedom. Painted on a wall nearby was CUBA WILL NEVER BE ADDED OR SOLD TO THE UNITED STATES.

I paid closer attention to the sign hanging over the road. White letters on the blue background said "Havana 774 [kilometers]." The capital seemed impossibly far away in light of what I had learned about Cuban transport. My destination that day, Camagüey, was nearer. Ernesto, my host, had treated the journey like a polar expedition. He told me to rest up and carry provisions. My driver thought I could complete the two-hundred-kilometer stretch in a day. But it would take a lot of luck.

Luck looked elusive when I approached the swarthy man wearing a faded yellow jacket. Consumed with filling the hold of the truck he had just stopped, the Yellow Man ignored my inquiry about where to wait for transport to Camagüey and motioned to a crowd on the opposite side of the Central Road. As Cubans began streaming toward the vehicle, he pushed me aside and, like a teacher scolding a pupil, told me to wait there.

I followed Adonis, a sturdy youth who shepherded his mother and grandmother toward a crowd of forty huddled beneath a concrete roof. He called out for el último to Camagüey. I claimed the place behind his threesome. Together, we watched the Yellow Man load passengers onto two trucks bound for a city called Las Tunas. I raised an eyebrow. Adonis shook his head. His only worry was how the rain would affect his granny.

"This damn cold front came down from the United States." He changed the subject. "Where are you from?"

"The United States."

"Don't worry. The front will pass soon."

The wait also passed quickly. Thirty minutes after our arrival, a Soviet truck eased to a halt in front of the shelter. Furniture filled the front third of a cargo bay rimmed by waist-high sides. After a brief chat with the driver, the Yellow Man rolled a ladder to the side of the vehicle and shouted, "Camagüey." A scramble ensued. People who hadn't claimed a place in the long-haul line raced for the ladder. So did those seeking a short hop. The travelers who had made the right choice called for order.

"The line," shouted Adonis. "The line."

"Don't kill yourselves," called the Yellow Man.

The last four places on the truck went to Adonis, his family, and me. But the blessing was mixed. The truck's wet bed was full by the time I climbed over the side. The first aboard had claimed seats along the rim. Their baggage, and more passengers, filled the center. My only choice was to place my feet in the gaps between the bodies and the bags, and find a way to steady myself.

Adonis had two hands on the side of the truck. I rested one hand on his shoulder. A pair of rough hands gripped my shoulders from behind. That stranger's waist was held by Adonis's mother and grandmother, who were stranded in the dead center of the hold. We all wobbled when the truck jerked into motion, but the human chain didn't break.

Fraternity bloomed as the truck steamed west along the Central Road. Bumps lifted the thirty-plus passengers into the air. Hard landings were followed by a round of moans and exclamations. As my calves began to cramp, a middle-age man offered me a seat on his bag. I continued to stand and loaned my windbreaker to Adonis's mother. Suffering from the chilly drizzle, the Cubans warmed themselves by huddling together.

The country was no beauty. Flat but rugged terrain flanked the straight and narrow strip of asphalt. Adonis pointed out the different types of fruit trees: stocky trunks that grew green platanos, spindly stalks rising to yellow coconuts. He also filled me in on the fauna. The animals grazing on the browning grass were cows. The beasts idling amid the shrubs on a hill were horses. Out of information after noting the virtual absence of traffic on the road, Adonis embraced the silence that enveloped the other travelers, many of whom had fallen asleep.

The group came to life in Buenaventura, where a Yellow Man stopped the truck. Using the rear tire as a step, the designated hitchhiker peered into the cargo bay. Met by a blast of protest — "We're already in here like chickens." "Are you blind?" "No more!" — he descended almost immediately. Did the expert testimony affect his judgment? Moments later a bag fell into the hold. Sets of fingers appeared on the gunwales. Like buccaneers, more travelers joined a hostile crew.

The frowns died when the Yellow Man and another bystander hoisted a septuagenarian up to the cargo bay. Wearing a straw cowboy hat and brown sunglasses, he was pulled into the hold by Adonis and another passenger. The others called out "Welcome, old man" and "Look at him. Old but still strong." Once among the group, the old man and the rest of the newcomers were inducted without further hazing.

We stopped again on the far side of Las Tunas, where my map said that Castro "greeted the people" during his cross-country drive. Few of the hitchhikers missed the chance to stretch when the driver paused. Some headed for a row of food stalls beside the eastbound lane. I followed but decided to pass on food that looked bad and smelled worse.

The Cubans didn't share my feeling. The man who held my shoulders, a tractor driver who worked south of Camagüey, emerged carrying a roll filled with pork paste. He spotted me, tore his sandwich in two and held out half. My insistence that I wasn't hungry was neither believed nor accepted. He pressed the food into my palm.

A man who earned six bucks a month was treating me? It should have been the other way around. Adonis doubled my shame when he brought me a sandwich of my own. I was speechless when a thin twenty-year-old handed me a cardboard box containing rice, boiled platanos, and two pork ribs. We hadn't exchanged a word or even a glance before he bought me lunch.

Named Raúl, the thin man was a soccer coach. Back on the truck, we counted down the final kilometers to Camagüey, shivering as a stiff wind exacerbated the effects of the damp air.

Four hours after leaving Holguín, the truck paused at a fork in the road. Raúl told me to jump down. He paid my ten-centavo fare when we boarded a local bus for the city center. He pointed out the baseball stadium and indicated a monument to two local heroes whose feat was to pilot a plane to Camagüey, in central Cuba, from Seville, Spain. Late for work, Raúl showed me one last point of interest, a winding street where dollars were traded.

A disheveled man blocked my path down the narrow street. He handed me a slip of paper on which precisely written words said, "I lost my ID card. I have no social services. I need 40 centavos." A pair of young women watched me give him two pesos. They continued to stare after he crept away. When I walked, they followed. When I walked faster, one, a teenager with a hairy mole, caught up.

"We know each other from Havana."

"I don't think so."

"I'm José's cousin. We went to a cabaret together."

My friend's cousin couldn't do enough for me. She introduced the woman with her, an aunt. She offered to carry my bag. And she took me by the arm and led me to the home of a friend with a spare room.

"Listen to him," shrieked Pepé, who agreed to put me up. "He's Cubanized."

My diction caused the outburst. Cubans weren't used to foreigners who said *wanikiki*, not *dinero*, when they meant money. Pepé, his wife, and the women who took me to the house decided that a command of Cuban slang wasn't the only sign that I had adapted to life on the island. They howled at an American who traveled courtesy of the Yellow Man. The judges agreed that, thanks to tanning under the eastern sun, I even looked vaguely Cuban.

They were right; I did feel at ease in Cuba. My comfort in a country that initially unnerved me became clear as I walked down Camagüey's main drag, República, a narrow strip where I traced the faint smell of sewage to the trickle beside the sidewalk. Looking up, I saw a rigid row of two-story buildings. The image of a European sailor beside a wooden ship identified the Columbus Hotel. Other signs advertised a baby supplies store called the Age of Gold, a hairdresser called Venus Institute of Beauty, and a bookstore called Vietnam. Locals walked by windows with dusty displays. The shops were empty but for employees and friends who stopped to chat.

The action was in the street. An old man seated on the curb offered passersby double-edged razor blades and individual cigarettes. Beside him another pensioner was selling boxes of matches. A younger man hawked homemade brooms and mops. The cart caught the eye of a group of women spooning ice cream into paper cups.

A smoke-spewing tractor chugged to a stop in front of a cavernous cafeteria filled with empty chairs. The driver dismounted and strolled back to the vat on his trailer. He attached a thick hose, and water gushed from the vat to a metal canister. No longer shy about approaching Cubans, I asked about the load. Did the special delivery mean that the city's tap water was undrinkable?

"It's not water," said the driver. "It's rum. The strongest rum in Cuba."

He dipped into the canister. "For a friend," he said, handing me a jar containing two inches of the colorless liquid. I tipped the rum between my lips but tasted nothing. Then my mouth began to tingle. Then my throat burned. "The strongest in Cuba," repeated the driver before knocking back the remainder of a drink I couldn't finish.

I had more luck with a free-lance vendor near the north end of República. The wiry man shrugged when I noted the shortage of tomato and the utter lack of cheese on what he called pizza. He came to life when, after I bought the baked dough, I said, "The Struggle." Confirming that he had indeed met a foreigner who saw his situation, the vendor told me a story:

"A few days ago I was sitting in my home, which is opposite the art museum. There was no gas. I had no coal to make a fire. And I had very little food left for the month. A bald tourist looked in and saw me. He lifted his fist and cried, 'Cuba, resist!' 'Resist!' I screamed. 'You in your fucking tour bus can resist. I have no food, no gas, no coal . . .' You should have seen how fast that guy ran away."

The south end of República took me back into Camagüey. A cluster of dollar stores attracted customers. Like decorative lions, money changers flanked the doors. The police patrolling the street paid no attention to the young men riffling fat wads of bank notes. Nor did the cops break up another obstruction, the gauntlet of men and women holding up the brand-new shoes, shirts, and sweaters they had bought at recent sales.

Life was quieter a few blocks away, in Workers' Square. The Bank of Cuba occupied two of the buildings that defined a triangular space around a car park and a tree. A cultural center filled a third, stylish building. Another was the birthplace of Ignacio Agramonte, a nineteenth-century hero and Camagüey's favorite martyr. I sat on a bench in front of an eighteenth-century church and watched twenty Cubans waiting for ice cream.

The price explained the line. Having stopped his cart in the car park, the state's ice cream man was charging about a penny a scoop. Two scoops were the minimum anybody bought. The driver of a bicycle-taxi bought a six-scoop pyramid, which dribbled a white rivulet down his arm. A woman carrying a bowl asked for twenty scoops. So did a housewife, who loaded her ice cream in a plastic sack to take advantage of opportunities to hoard.

"Don't you like ice cream?" asked a leggy woman whose miniskirt didn't pretend to cover the tops of her dark brown thighs.

"I don't like waiting."

"Me neither. Can I sit with you?" When I consented, she sat down and said, "Friendship is very important. Right?"

"Right."

"Do you want my address?"

Sitting with a stranger wasn't unusual in Cuba. Striking up a conversation was a survival tactic in a place where waiting and idleness were a way of life. But a half-dressed woman giving her address to a man with whom she had shared no more than a few sentences? It reminded me of the floor cleaner in Holguín.

The woman, Laura, ran another play from Anna's book. A cabaret dancer, she used a sad story to kindle my sympathy. One night, after a show, she had been hit by a car that veered onto the sidewalk. The driver fled, leaving her with injuries that kept her hospitalized for more than a month. Physical therapy rebuilt her damaged knee but couldn't erase the eight-inch scar.

"Do you like my legs?" asked Laura, standing to improve my view.

"They're good legs," I understated.

"The manager of my nightclub doesn't think so. He says clients don't want to see a scar. He wouldn't give me my old job." After a brief frown she turned hopeful. "I'm going to look for a job at another club. Do you think I will succeed?"

"Sure."

"Would you like to see me dance?"

"When?" I asked.

"Now."

"Here?"

Laura pointed toward the cultural center, opposite the church. She knew the staff. They would let her use a room to show me her dancing. Another setup? I hoped not. Laura's smile was genuine. Her brown eyes sparkled. Inside the body of a runway model was the charm of a schoolgirl. I fought off a cynical sense that a scam was in store as we walked through an airy atrium and up a broad staircase. Two flights up we came to a long, empty ballroom, where the story took an unexpected twist.

Laura began to dance. The coltish woman didn't need music to put on a show worthy of a Las Vegas revue. Her arms spread like a swan's wings, she took several measured steps toward me. She swiveled, rocked her hips, and kicked a foot above her head before dancing in the other direction. Flowing arm movements accompanied increasingly intricate steps and twists. She closed her eyes as if listening to an internal orchestra. Sexy? Yes. But suggestive? No.

"Did you like my dancing?" she asked at the end of her five-minute routine.

"I love your dancing."

Laura beamed as if I had repaired her broken dream.

22

PEPÉ APOLOGIZED for the lack of water in his home. Sporadic when functional, Camagüey's water system was down for the day. The dry faucets reminded my host of the well in his backyard. The well, in turn, reminded him of the pain of pulling up buckets of water. He resolved to renew his earlier search for a turbine to pump the water. Would I join him? I balked.

Pepé worried me. He was a fat man in an underfed country. His curly white locks were at odds with the smooth pink face of a thirty-year-old man. He was friendly bordering on intrusive. "Do you need help finding a girl?" he asked as I unpacked my bag. His pants were imports. Beer bottles filled his refrigerator. Such signs of prosperity didn't jibe with a man who never worked.

"Come," he said, pointing to bicycles by the door. "I'll show you everything."

A series of turns on broad dirt streets took us to a concrete house. The home of a friend? Pepé had never met the owner. He got the address via the grapevine, which said that the owner had a turbine which, though needed, was less important than money to feed his family. A shirtless old man told us to return later to speak to his son.

A few blocks away a housewife told Pepé that she had a turbine but, because it was broken, he would need to find spare parts. At stop number three, nobody answered repeated knocks on an open wood door. I frowned at the results of our half-hour quest. Pepé took a different view. Where I saw three strikes he saw two maybes and one inconclusive. Even if these tips didn't pan out, those people would spread the word. "If you search, it will appear," he said.

The chunky Cuban led me back to Camagüey's center, a web of winding streets designed in the sixteenth century to disorient invaders. We stopped at a plaza where freshly painted homes lined one side of a cobbled space as big as a football field. A cluster of neighbors watched policemen leading a teenager whose hands were cuffed behind his back. When the minidrama ended, the locals resumed staring at a long structure with a central tower. We walked the bicycles to the side of the building, where Pepé pointed to a plaque. This, said the marker, was the spot where Castro delivered a tribute to Ignacio Agramonte in 1986.

Pepé took me to the south side of the thin river that ran through the city. A few blocks from the main street, he found the plaza where Castro spoke in January 1959. The backdrop was a church whose high facade bore an image of the Virgin Mary. She overlooked the raised yard that served as the podium where the victorious rebel told the people: "Everybody here is going to learn how to handle a gun."

Between stops Pepé shouted and waved to friends. He devoted more time to women he didn't know. Slowing the bicycle and veering toward the sidewalk, he might say, "Look how beautiful she is" or "That is a body." Other compliments targeted specific parts — "What strong legs" — or thoughts, such as the suggestion that a schoolgirl wait four years and marry him. The girl didn't blush. I did.

Pepé's manners improved when a slight woman opened a narrow door on a street near his home. She led us into a one-room house jammed with artwork. Four paintings hung on one wall. Three canvases occupied most of another wall. Poised pensively between two sculptures and a table littered with brushes, paint, and unfinished canvases was the creator of the art and the mess, Pepé's cousin Roberto. A slim man with dark hair and fine features, the artist skipped the greetings.

Roberto had a problem: paint. He lifted one of the dozens of half-squeezed tubes, shook his head, and said in soft, steady tones, "This one is no good." He praised a tube of paint made in Britain. A tube from France also rated well. No, he said, the problem wasn't the paint itself. The trick was simply finding enough paint, in enough colors, to do his work. Canvases were even harder to come by, particularly outside Havana.

The most drastic shortage, however, was in the materials for sculpture. Marble and other stones were all but extinct during "the special period." He pointed to a slab of stone lying flat among several chisels and electric drills on his worktable. A miracle had brought that marble to him. A family had commissioned him to design a headstone for a child who died at thirteen.

"If you look, it appears," he said.

Roberto held out similar hope for the resolution of another problem, his lack of work space. The state might give him another house, which would become his studio. "They owe me," said Roberto. "I did a job for them a few years ago."

Planning a monument at Revolution Square, the city had commissioned Roberto to represent the history of Camagüey in seventy meters of bas-relief sculpture. The artist showed me how the work was divided into a series of stone plates about three feet high. He also told me that Party officials had dictated the images they wished presented. His job was to execute the official version of history.

That was in early 1989. Communism had already collapsed in East Germany. The Soviet Union was wobbling. Unconcerned, the officials invited Castro to inaugurate the incomplete monument. The president promised that problems in the Eastern bloc wouldn't affect Cuba, and, seated among Party officials and other dignitaries, Roberto had no reason to doubt him.

Years later, the job finished, the sculptor hadn't been paid for work that a government specialist had valued at eighty thousand pesos. The state had a rule against paying artists in cash, giving them goods instead. But the death of Soviet communism killed the supply of new televisions and Ladas. The city, which acknowledged its debt, was leaning toward compensating Roberto with a house.

"Can I see the sculpture?"

"It's in Revolution Square," he said. "Go there and you will learn about Cuba."

Roberto lied. No, he misled me. Or it's possible that he led me exactly where he wanted.

Revolution Square wasn't what I expected, a sculpted tribute to Camagüey's glory. The spot where Castro had brushed off the collapse of the Soviet Union looked like a construction site. Weeds grew between the concrete tiles of the open space. Workers had abandoned piles of dirt and stone. Rainwater filled the bin of a rusty wheelbarrow. Goat droppings were the only sign of recent activity.

The animals had moved onto the monument, an amphitheater of steps and plateaus, with a bronze statue as the main feature. I guessed that the subject was Camagüey's designated hero, Ignacio Agramonte. What I couldn't guess was the function of the metal lattice that formed a rusty tiara around the back of the monument. A dust-covered man trailed by a dog ambled by and answered my question.

The frame, he said, was built to hold the sculpted plates that told the story of Camagüey. Local lore had it that part of the lattice collapsed. The planners considered repairing it, but then decided it would be easier to shorten history by twenty meters. All work had stopped when funds ran out during "the special period." "If they don't hurry and finish the monument, they will need more plates for the new history," joked the man.

Workers had propped Roberto's bas-relief against a wall. Unfamiliar with local history, I couldn't identify the carvings of stern-faced men from the colonial era. Nor did I know the significance of a scene of men riding horses beside a river. Another plate bore the familiar faces of men with only loose links to Camagüey. One was Che Guevara, an Argentine. Another was Camilo Cienfuegos, another rebel leader. A factory clearly represented post-Revolution prosperity.

The plates were stacked four deep. Nothing protected the face of one from the back of another. Pieces were chipped from

Camagüey's history. One hero had lost his nose. Looking at the weeds surrounding the display of negligence, I couldn't help but feel sorry for Roberto. I wondered whether a house was fair compensation for an artist who knew his work had been turned into a junk heap.

Pepé, a self-proclaimed ballbuster, was harder to pity. He turned me into a prop in his games, telling a neighbor that I was a cousin who, having moved to America at an early age, had returned to sharpen his Spanish. When the neighbor pointed out that Cuban men like black girls, my host said, "Not me. They're thieves. Their skin is rough. And they smell bad."

Nonetheless, I enjoyed the company of the white-haired bigot. Pepé was the most candid person I had met in Cuba. In a country where the walls had microphones as well as ears, he was a daredevil when it came to speaking his mind, and his insouciance provided thrills as well as facts. But why wasn't he scared, like other Cubans?

I learned the answer in the cramped library opposite my bedroom. I wandered into the nook and thumbed through the rows of dusty paperbacks. Turning to leave, I saw two photographs flanking the doorless exit. One was a black-and-white blowup of a young Fidel Castro, his sidelong glance betraying worry. The other showed a man with his hands firmly on the wheel of a tractor. A massive beard defied the evident youth of his face and smile.

"That's my father," said Pepé, who didn't scold me for snooping. "I'm going to teach you something."

He pulled a stack of photographs from the bottom drawer. One showed his father standing among armed men whose ragged clothes and sun hats made them look more like hillbillies than soldiers. Other shots displayed stone-faced men posing with pistols and rifles. The rebels, it seemed, spent more time in photo shoots than in shooting.

Pepé added commentary when he came to another picture of his father, a gun in his right hand. The glass in the left hand of the grinning rebel was touching a glass in the hand of a glum gent whose spotless uniform identified him as an officer of Batista's army. "They are toasting the end of the war," said Pepé.

The next photograph showed a line of farm trucks stopped in a dusty town where a sign advertised General Electric appliances. People packed the back of the vehicle. A handmade banner, reading WORKERS, decorated the front. The next shot showed bearded men posing with locals. More pictures showed an endless line of trucks and jeeps stopped in towns along the Central Road. Picture after picture of vehicles and streets packed with Cubans told me that there had been nothing phony about the enthusiasm for Castro and his Liberty Caravan.

Another handful of snapshots indicated what happened after the Caravan reached Havana and the euphoria died. Pepé showed me a picture of his father as an older, barrel-chested man whose short hair was standard military issue. He never left the army. Personal loyalty to Castro and a lifelong belief in the Revolution earned him the post of the boss of Camagüey. We looked at a picture of his father, in an olive-green uniform, waving to a crowd from the back seat of a car.

The revelation about his father's clout helped me connect the dots. Pepé's loud mouth was unusual. So were brown eyes forever dancing in search of trouble. A bulbous stomach proved his skill at finding fun. Normal for a frat boy, the trappings of the high life and a "what, me worry?" attitude made sense once I realized that my host belonged to Cuba's elite. Pepé was a Communist Party animal.

The oversize brat confirmed my assumptions. Born in October 1959, ten months after the postwar celebration, Pepé was raised in one of his family's three houses. Dad liked laughter and rum. So did his mom. Whether in Camagüey, at the beach, or in Havana, their home was party central. The arrival of an out-of-towner was reason enough for Dad to order his team of flunkies to roast a pig. Pepé was living large at a time that most of Cuba was sharing the wealth.

But privilege had its limits. Daddy's influence couldn't save Pepé from a stint in Angola. Home from Africa, he showed no interest in work; the black market looked more lucrative. Trafficking in art let the latter-day rebel eat, drink, and dress well. His excesses didn't go unnoticed by neighbors — or the police, who charged him with "dangerousness," the crime of having too much while doing too little. A four-year sentence earned national fame for the son of the Party boss, who died before he was freed.∗

Pepé held up a pinkie to approximate his girth the day he left prison. Then he added, "One month later they put me back in jail as a political prisoner."

"What did you do?"

"I wrote some criticism on a wall."

"What did you write?"

"*Abajo Fidel*," said Pepé. Down with Fidel.

"Just once?"

"Many times."

Pepé wasn't the first Cuban to tell me he had been jailed for speaking his mind. That distinction belonged to Carlos, whom I met in Santiago. The bulky, middle-age man passed me twice before settling beside me on the bench in Céspedes Park. He didn't introduce himself. Instead, speaking with exaggerated stealth, he said, "I was in prison for two years. For political reasons."

I said nothing.

"If I live in your country, and I don't rape, rob, or assault, should I be in jail?"

"No."

"Here you can be imprisoned for anything. Or for nothing."

"So why did they arrest you?"

∗Some names in this book have been changed at the request of individual Cubans. In other cases, I decided to change names rather than endanger people critical of Castro, his policies, or the results. Roberto and Pepé are two exceptions. The sculptor's tale was no secret in his hometown. Pepé's crime was old news. He had served his sentence. Because neither man criticized the president or his system, there was no need for disguise. Insights gleaned from their stories are based on my thoughts, not their words.

"They said I criticized socialism."

"Did you?"

The fleshy fellow had been an engineer. Chatting to a couple of comrades at his factory, he asked aloud why Cuba should stay socialist when the folks who wrote the book, the Soviet Union, had dropped both hammer and sickle. A few days later the police came by his home. Next stop: prison.

"You see those two policemen," he said, pointing to a pair of officers circling the park. "They can arrest me for talking to you."

I wanted to move away.

"Once they arrested me for speaking to a Frenchman."

"You went to jail for speaking to a Frenchman?"

"No, that time they only warned me."

So why was he talking to me?

The police no longer cared about Cubans mixing with tourists. Also, the stakes were lower. Like other former political prisoners, he was banned from working for the state; his slipup became a life sentence of unemployment. With little left to lose, he saw little risk in telling his story to a foreigner. He left armed with my pen, which he promised to use to expose repression in his country.

Still in Santiago de Cuba, I met a muscular mulatto who was equally unhappy about the policing of thought. The subject arose after he told me that his father and brother lived in Miami. Why? A former political prisoner, his father had priority to emigrate.

"What did he do?"

"Nothing. My father did nothing wrong."

The indignant man glanced over his shoulder. Then he said that his father had fought alongside the rebels in the Sierra Maestra. The problem arose in 1961, when Castro declared the obvious: socialism was the goal of the Revolution. A veteran of the war that expelled the old regime, Carlos's father felt entitled to voice his concerns about the new one.

"My father fought for independence, not for socialism. So he expressed his view. A lot of men expressed their views. Fidel put them all in prison."

I said nothing.

"My father had respectable ideas. He just disagreed. Intelligent people can disagree. Right?"

I said nothing.

"Right?"

23

AT THE CHECKPOINT on the edge of Camagüey, a Yellow Man directed me to a shelter over the heads of forty Cubans. A half-hour later an old lady told me that I was in the wrong place. This was the line for a town called Florida. I joined a group under a tree, where some travelers had been waiting for transport to Sancti Spiritus for more than twelve hours.

I tried and failed to chat with the woman beside me, a curvaceous dancer from Holguín. Then I sulked for an hour. I spent the next hour wondering whether my luck had run out. The dancer turned to me. She held her nose and pointed to the air. The fumes of a dead animal were wafting over the area.

The arrival of a truck bound for Sancti Spiritus, the city Fidel Castro reached on the third day of his 1959 road trip, was a mixed blessing. People mobbed the Yellow Man. A policeman restored order. Both men looked relieved by the departure of a DeSoto loaded with thirty Cubans and one American.

I knew the drill for riding on Cuba's trucks. Standing near the front of the hold, I put one hand on a greasy oil drum and the other on the truck's rail. Other passengers tested positions and grips. These held firm when the vehicle began to roll. Within minutes the group had settled into a routine of sighing, sleeping, and watching field after field of sugarcane.

The serenity was broken by the truck's burly driver, who had a taste for sharp turns and sudden stops. The riders lost patience as serpentine maneuvers threw them against each other. People shouted for him to slow down and steer straight. In a city called

Ciego de Avila, the driver veered off the Central Road t
lunch with a friend. Later, he made a detour to deliver
age. Lost in the streets of an unfamiliar place, he needed
minutes to locate the main road. There, he resumed tossing his
human salad.

"No more trucks," I swore when, at the end of five hours, I
lowered myself out of the vehicle and onto the firm ground on
the outskirts of Sancti Spiritus.

I looked for transport to the center. Four Cubans and I shared
a horse-drawn buggy from the bus depot to Serafín Sánchez
Park. It was here, at two A.M. on January 6, 1959, that Castro told
the people of Sancti Spiritus that they were now the masters of
their destiny: "Here we don't have to ask anybody's permission
to do anything."

Eight foodless hours kept me from enjoying the calm of
cobbled streets that twisted at unpredictable angles. Peering
through the open doors and windows, I sought signs of free-
market food. None appeared until, circling back to the park, I
spotted *Paladar* on a sign hanging from a second-floor apartment. A set of marble stairs took me to the threshold of a
self-styled restaurant.

"Do you have any food?" I asked the sixty-year-old woman
who opened the door a crack.

"It's my daughter who runs the restaurant. She's out." Opening the door a bit wider, she asked, "Are you Spanish?"

"American."

She pinched her cheeks. Then she pinched mine. Satisfied
that I was real, she flung open the door. "Wash your face," she
said. "I'll make you chicken. And salad."

When she returned, I commented on the apartment. Ver-
sailles would have been an appropriate place for the marble
columns that reached the living room's dizzying ceiling. She
explained that the apartment had six bedrooms and three bath-
rooms. The extra space let them operate the restaurant, provided they paid a fee to the city.

"Do you have a room?" I asked.

"I'm sorry, my love, I can't let you stay. We have a license to sell meals. If the police find out that you are here, they will take it away."

She did offer an alternative. One of her neighbors, "a serious person with a good family," had rented rooms to foreigners, but she couldn't say whether the boardinghouse continued to operate. Strange things had been happening in Sancti Spíritus. She could walk me to the house.

Two blocks away a barefoot man opened the tall doors on a third-floor landing. Called Ariel, he confirmed that his family had rented rooms. In fact, they had made a lot of money doing so. He showed me a massive bedroom with a bathroom and a balcony overlooking the street. He continued the soft sell by showing me that the room had its own entrance. Then he said I couldn't sleep there.

"A few weeks ago we got a notice from the police. They ordered us to stop renting rooms to foreigners. If we continued, they would arrest us and give us a *multa*."

Multa, a fine, was a word that struck fear in the hearts of Cubans.

"Our friends who rent rooms also received warnings. We didn't understand. The law permits Cubans to do this. We went to the police with a copy of the law and found the official who signed the warning. He said we couldn't rent."

"Did he say why?"

"He just said no," said Ariel. "In Cuba, when the state says no, you don't ask more questions."

He had a theory about why the municipality overruled a national law. The state was getting ready to tax the earnings of the private sector. Soon, de facto innkeepers would have to hand over some of their gains. Ariel believed that the officials saw no reason to allow citizens to make money until they could claim a slice: "Here, if the government isn't making money, nobody can make money."

Ariel had another thought. His family had been told not to house visitors. His next-door neighbor hadn't been warned because she had never put up a foreigner. Still one warning away from trouble, Vilma might put me up — for a price.

The price was ten dollars a night. To that Vilma, a gaunt woman who was pushing fifty, added a list of rules. Rule One: I had to be "discrete." Translation: don't enter the front door if the police are nearby. Rule Two: if anybody asked, I was a friend visiting from America, not a tourist paying rent. Rule Three: no prostitutes — the cops followed hookers. The terms clear, two nights' rent in her pocket, Vilma vacated the two-room duplex.

She returned early the following morning, a Saturday, for fresh clothes, milk from her refrigerator, and a favor. Hoping to buy shoes with the rent money, she asked me to take her to the dollar store. True, all Cubans had access. But flashing my passport would allow her to jump the line and get first crack at the sale.

"What about the people who are waiting?" I said as we approached the one hundred–plus people pressing to enter the department store.

"They would do the same if they could," said Vilma.

The crowd at the store may have accounted for the emptiness of the square at the heart of Sancti Spiritus. Or it could have been the merciless sun, which flushed my face. Either way, the park was empty but for dozens of chairs and two busts, one of José Martí, the other of Serafín Sánchez, a hometown hero who died fighting the Spanish. Nor were there many signs of life in the rectangle of buildings with arched doorways and elongated windows.

The exception was a palatial building opposite the park's southwest corner. Broad steps led between frilly columns as thick as redwoods. Marble statues stood at the top. Fixed on a nearby wall, a plaque said: "A long process of humiliation has closed and the definitive dignity of the homeland has begun. Fidel Castro Ruz. 6–1–59. Sancti Spiritus."

"This used to be a society," said the middle-age mulatta seated inside.

"Like a club?"

"Yes, a club. A club for whites. Rich whites. If you were black, like me, you couldn't enter. Now, anybody can enter. This is a public library."

A few blocks away I found a similar vision of grandeur. An open window provided a view of columns rising from the floor of a ballroom from which marble stairs curved upward. The place held only four fogeys playing dominoes on a wooden table. Another man rocked himself in a chair near the entrance. He said that the building, like the library, had once been a society. It was still a club, a club for workers.

The folks who converted the playpens of the rich forgot one thing: fun. After two hours I had had my fill of colonial architecture. I stopped at a sign advertising sugarcane juice and an "Amazing Fact": two months earlier a man named Vladimir Ferrer had drunk fifteen six-ounce glasses of the house specialty. Beat that, said the owner, and I didn't have to pay. I stopped at two glasses.

What else was there to do on an afternoon in Sancti Spiritus? A scalding sun kept the streets empty. Indoors, people fanned themselves. I was rescued from the heat by a man who stopped me on the shady side of a street. For two pesos I could join about twenty others in his living room to watch a Mel Gibson movie.

Later, I found Vilma in the apartment. As pleased to see me as I was surprised to see her, she invited me to dine with her and a pretty twenty-year-old. Her daughter piled my plate with a mound of fish, rice, and fried platanos. The mother apologized for the simple menu. She also excused the conversation.

"All we talk about in Cuba, all we think about in Cuba, is food. Food, food, food." Vilma chewed a spoonful of rice. Then she said, "I'm dying to leave."

The assertion fit a pattern. Santiago de Cuba was the peak of Cuban contentment, and the frequency of complaints about life in Cuba increased the farther I moved west. In Bayamo locals were openly criticizing the results of the Revolution. Holguín was a hotbed of forbidden thoughts and deeds. But it wasn't until central Cuba that I heard Cubans saying, loud and clear, that they wanted out.

"I'm desperate," said a fleshy woman who lived near Pepé. She added a lengthy lecture on her hopes and dreams, which ended when she said, "There's no life in Cuba." "My love, take me with you," moaned a bony woman panhandling near the church where Castro had addressed the people of Camagüey. "I'm hungry."

Their declarations reminded me of the drummer who had housed me in Holguín. Ernesto expressed no interest in living abroad. He did, however, sum up the situation on the island: "Cuba is slowly dying of hunger. I can make extra money by teaching music. But most people have no way to make more money within our system. They are trapped. Why do you think so many Cubans flee? Why do you think thousands of Cubans have been eaten by sharks?"

Cuban flight patterns weren't news. The so-called rafters' crisis had made refugees Cuba's best-known export, after cigars. The 1994 exodus began when people began to commandeer ferries and head for Florida. Police intervention in one of the hijackings sparked a riot in Havana. Thousands of Cubans took to the streets, where they threw rocks, smashed windows, and shouted "Down with Fidel" before being beaten by laborers directed by the police. Enraged or frustrated, scheming or scared, Castro went on television and told Cubans to leave if they liked.

A handful of Habaneros tested the waters. Young men carried rafts through the streets of the capital and set sail from the Malecón in broad daylight, an act that normally led directly to jail. Incredulous bystanders told their friends and families. More people came to watch the spectacle of Cubans fleeing while the police stood by. Word spread. At the other end of the island, Cubans paddled into the American base at Guantánamo Bay. Boatless people swam to waters controlled by the U.S.

Fear kept other malcontents on the island. Every Cuban knew somebody who had reached Florida. Every Cuban also had a friend, or a neighbor, or a friend of a neighbor, who had disappeared at sea. Many refugees drowned when their rafts collapsed. Others met an uglier fate. In Havana, a college student described walking on the beach during the rafters' crisis.

One of her friends, a medical student, spotted a pulpy mass in the wet sand. It was a lung, a human lung. Farther along, the students found a piece of an arm and a liver. Other friends said they found a well-chewed corpse.

Land sharks added to the danger when, after the month-long exodus, Castro slammed the door. The police went back to arresting Cubans caught fleeing. Snitches reported neighbors plotting escapes. Fishermen reported the people who bought their boats. Imprisoned and freed, the determined ones often tried again. Resting on a stoop in Camagüey, I met a man who didn't give up after two attempts.

"Three times I tried to escape. Three times they caught me. Three times they put me in prison," sighed the middle-age mulatto. "I have very bad luck."

How bad? The self-deprecating Cuban said that he and a friend bought an inner tube during the rafters' crisis. They caught a truck to Guantánamo, where they planned to paddle to freedom. A policeman saw things differently. Temporarily unable to stop refugees, the officer confiscated the inner tube and said, "You have to swim for your freedom."

"A lot of people died in the water," said the mulatto. "I don't want to die. I want to live in the United States."

So did Jesús. "This is the worst year of my life," said the schoolteacher within minutes of our meeting on the wall of the Malecón. His assessment was easy to believe: Jesús had no job, weak eyes, and a fiancée who refused to marry him until his, or Cuba's, finances improved. But the sturdy Cuban had seen worse. Or so I judged from the story of his attempt to escape from the island.

"The rafters had been leaving for a few days. My friends and I were standing on a corner. None of us had a job. We talked about how we were tired of life in Cuba, life with no future. So we started asking the same question that everybody was asking themselves: Did we have the guts to leave? We knew that people died trying to cross to Miami. But it's funny what happens when a group of men are together. We pretended we weren't scared. So we decided to leave.

"We began to prepare. I consulted a friend on how to make a raft. We found three pieces of wood and tied them together with rope. We covered the base with rubberized cloth. But we needed more buoyancy. My friend said we could use truck tires. We bought four. One of my friends had a small motor and we bought one hundred and fifty pesos of gas for it. For insurance, we bought some cloth to use as a sail. A carpenter was selling paddles to other rafters. We bought six.

"We didn't tell anybody we were leaving. Not our friends. Not our families. We didn't want them to try to stop us. We went to the Malecón and left. The U.S. Coast Guard was looking for Cubans. They were picking up people about sixty miles from Cuba. Sometimes only forty.

"We had a good start. The engine took us about ten miles in the first two hours. Things were going well. We were happy. Then night came. There was a storm, a terrible storm with thunder and lightning. Everybody was scared. We left so quickly that we hadn't thought about dying. We used ropes and tied ourselves to the raft.

"The waves were so big. I would look up and see water fifteen feet above my head. I was sure it would crush the raft. We panicked. In fact, I'm not really sure what happened during those hours. I just remember that we started to talk about going back. Then we noticed that two of our friends were missing."

"What happened to them?" I asked.

Jesús shook his head. "I don't know," he said. "Nobody saw them fall over. They were just gone. We came back to Cuba. Nobody ever found their bodies. Maybe they drowned. Maybe they were eaten by the sharks."

Jesús's faraway look made clear the pain of revisiting the failed escape. For five minutes he simply sat on the wall along the Malecón and stared at the sea. I dared not break the silence.

"I can't take any more of this shit. I can't live a life with no future," he said. "But I can't go out there again. I'm a coward, and for that I hate myself."

There were safer ways to leave Cuba. After the rafters' crisis the United States agreed to the more orderly exit of twenty thousand Cubans a year. Others took more traditional routes out of their country. Athletes, particularly baseball players with big-league prospects, defected while playing abroad. Dancers and musicians did the same. So did doctors, engineers, and government officials sent to work abroad.

Those lacking the talent to travel took a different tack. In Havana, the sight of a slinky teenager clinging to the arm of a flabby foreigner was peculiar but not uncommon. Middle-age Europeans had what the girls needed, money. The visitors also had something many of the young ladies wanted even more, a foreign passport. Some girls wanted nothing more than to trade sex for cash. Others, however, hoped for a more permanent solution. Cubans who married foreigners were allowed to leave.

The charms of Cuban women were creating a diaspora. A friend in the capital told me that he lived one floor below a pair of sisters, one an engineer, the other a chemist, who needed a switchboard to handle the incoming calls from Spain, Italy, and other parts of Europe. Hundreds of women had already snagged foreign husbands and had long since disappeared to new homes in faraway lands. In Santiago de Cuba I hitched a ride from a man who boasted of his sister's wiles: the busty nineteen-year-old had married an American, age sixty-six, who owned a hotel in New York City.

Rare was the day when someone didn't speculate that I would take a Cuban bride. It could have happened. Near the end of my stay in Santiago de Cuba, Francisco asked permission to raise a delicate subject. His daughter, a woman I had never met, was very unhappy. She was nearly thirty and saw no future in Cuba. Miami looked like her only hope for happiness. Would I be willing, for $10,000, to marry his daughter?

Foreigners weren't the only ones who could guarantee an exit. The United States welcomed political prisoners, people Castro was happy to let leave the island, and freed dissidents could take their families to America. This freedom turned slobs such as Pepé into a catch for women wishing to leave Cuba. When I asked Pepé how he managed to marry just months after leaving prison, he revealed his pickup line: "I was a political prisoner."

After dinner with Vilma, I walked downstairs to see if Sancti Spiritus awakened on Saturday nights. I heard but couldn't see a salsa band playing on the roof of the Pearl of Cuba Hotel. At the opposite end of Serafín Sánchez Park, teenagers mingled and posed in front of the cultural center. Two men in their late twenties invited me to join them for a walk through the dim streets. They told me not to worry: robbing a foreigner wasn't worth the risk of swift retribution from the cops.

One of the laborers, Manuel, described his run-in with the police. The lanky man once belonged to an underground group that distributed religious information that the state considered counterrevolutionary. It didn't take long for the security forces to track him down. Manuel wasn't arrested but was ordered to leave Camagüey, his home. He went to Havana, where he went directly to the U.S. Interests Section to register as a victim of political persecution.

"When I went back to Camagüey a woman knocked on my door. I had known her my whole life, but there was never anything between us. She asked me to marry her. The next day another woman came to my door. She was a stranger, a doctor. She had heard I was applying to leave and asked if I would marry her. When I said no, she offered me two thousand dollars. I couldn't believe the women who came to my door. I'm just a worker. But there were engineers, lawyers, chefs, all kinds of women. They promised to have sex with me. Some offered to pay me. They would do anything to marry me."

Manuel rejected the sex. Turning down a cash offer made him even more unusual. But he had a higher priority. Having written "bachelor" on his application to emigrate, he was unwilling to let a marriage change his status and jeopardize his escape.

Crowing roosters awakened me before five the following morning. Shortly after sunrise, I heard pounding on a door in the alley behind Vilma's building. Ignored, the two men banged for ten more minutes before relocating their attempt to prolong their binge. Three more hours passed before more knocking, this time on my door, suggested that sleep wasn't in the cards this Sunday morning.

I was right. The three sharp raps were followed by the sound of a key turning the front door's lock. Feet climbed the stairs to the bedroom of the duplex. Vilma's face appeared and I relaxed, although it seemed odd that my landlady hadn't changed out of her nightgown.

She walked to the side of my bed and said, "You have to go."

"What? Why?"

"The police know you are here."

"How did they find out?"

Vilma shrugged and said, "In Cuba, they know."

A blizzard of questions swept through my head. How did the cops know where I was? Had I been spotted entering the building? Had a neighbor snitched? Once alerted to my presence, how did the police track down a woman who wasn't sleeping in her own bed? Did they confront her last night? Or this morning?

Vilma didn't want to talk. Judging by her body language — arms folded, face rigid, she stood by the bed until I rose — she just wanted me out of her apartment and her life. Twenty minutes later I was back on the road.

24

"CAN YOU HELP ME? I've had nothing to eat. Only a glass of water with sugar. I have no food. I have no socks. But I don't want money. Not from you. No, what I want is soap. I can't afford it. You can. Please give me soap. Please do me this favor." The beggar ended his monologue by cupping his outstretched hands.

Straining to escape the piercing honesty of his eyes, I feigned intense interest in the activity around Vidal Park. Couples were out for a Sunday stroll. Clusters of men talked baseball and

fanned their faces. A cyclist towed a train of carts brimming
with toddlers. I looked across the street. Too far to see from my
bench, a plaque noted that Fidel's fighters had paused here en
route to the Moncada barracks. It was also the spot where I
disembarked in Santa Clara, the next stop on Fidel's goodwill
tour.

Evicted from Vilma's apartment, I had trudged to the bus
terminal, where the stationmaster informed me that both buses
to Santa Clara were booked solid. Did I know that Sundays
were the worst day to travel in Cuba? Could I try the following
day? I couldn't. One of the half-dozen drivers loitering outside
the depot proposed a deal. For ten dollars, he, Roberto, would
take me to Santa Clara. Unable to turn back, desperate for a
way out, I agreed to pay the money and got into his battered
Ford.

The driver stopped less than fifteen minutes into the journey
down the Central Road. Two men wearing straw hats piled into
the back seat. He stopped again in a town called Placetas and
called out, "Santa Clara." Three men and two women, one
carrying a child, rushed to the car. "How much?" they asked.
Roberto looked at me. I looked at the dust-covered travelers.
"Just get in," I said.

Long faces became broad smiles. Cramped but moving, the
Cubans began to talk. One of the men complained that there
was no money. Another said there was no work. Prices — fifty
centavos for a croquette! — shocked one and all. The driver
said that gas costs were guzzling his profits. One of the women
in the back seat punctuated every gripe with "Yes sir." To have
taken their money would have been to confirm my place on the
nonstop road to Hell.

What had happened to that sense of charity? Why was I
immobilized by the beggar in Santa Clara? I had a bar of soap.
Why didn't I hand it over? Looking back, I can only guess that
the request was too small. I didn't want to accept the possibility
of a man reduced to begging for soap.

"You have a big heart, that I can see," said the beggar.

I didn't argue; I couldn't agree.

Armandito, the beggar, sighed and joined me on the sunny bench. He was thirty-six years old and worked as a mechanic. Soviet trainers had taught him to fix "socialist cars," Ladas and the like. Their departure spelled trouble. Armandito's rations dwindled during "the special period." His torn, greasy T-shirt was proof that the government had stopped providing, among other goods, clothing.

"I earn two hundred and forty pesos a month. But the state has no money, so they are only paying me half," said Armandito.

"Are you working full-time?"

"There's very little work. The state cannot afford to buy spare parts for the cars. So I don't work much."

"Isn't that fair? Less money for less work?"

"FAIR! How am I supposed to live? I have a little boy. Next week is his seventh birthday. He wants roller skates. How can I take care of him if they don't pay me?"

Armandito had another option. The depopulation of rural regions had put the government in a bind: it needed men to help with the harvest. Armandito could get his money if he went east to pick coffee or cut cane. If he refused, he would receive a fraction of his pay. Revisiting his choices quieted the mechanic. He changed the subject.

"Do you think communism is dead?" he asked. "Communism is dead in the Soviet Union. It's dead in Germany. Do you think it's dead in Cuba?"

Hungry people. Citizens ranting about shortages. A herd of Cubans dreaming of life anyplace else. Yes, it would have been fair to say that communism was dead. But I didn't voice my thought. The stranger might be a snitch. Recalling the rash of black markets and the summary imprisonment of Pepé, I said there were many signs that communism was alive and well.

"Clearly," said Armandito. "Can I have your socks?"

Armandito insisted on treating a visitor to an orange "infusion." The cost was ten centavos, a fraction of a penny. We walked to a state-run café, where the beggar relished sharing what little he had. My humiliation deepened as he spent ten minutes advising me on areas to avoid while seeking a place to stay.

"Cubans are good," he said. "But there are some bad ones."

This observation diverted Armandito to the topic of bad Cubans. His father had been a fervent communist, a man trusted by the Party. Like his son, the father was a mechanic. In the 1980s his skills and loyalty earned him a trip to East Germany, where higher wages let him send money home. The Berlin Wall crumbled. So did his father's belief in the Party. He never returned to Cuba.

Armandito didn't fault his namesake for enjoying money. He applauded a man lucky enough to miss Cuba's darkest days. But something about his father bothered him. How could he leave Cuba? How, for that matter, could any Cuban live anywhere but Cuba?

"Here I have my grandmother. And my mother. She's dead, but as long as I'm near her, I feel her in my heart. Santa Clara is my home. Cuba is my country. Cubans are my people. No, I would never leave all of the things I love."

It would be wrong to say that the flood of rafters who fled in 1994, and the trickle that followed in later years, represented the mainstream of Cuban feeling. The flight of withered grannies and tiny tots made for sensational stories in the western press. But they were the exceptions. Most of the recent refugees were men in their twenties who acted on a flash-fried mix of frustration, fantasy, and impulse. Eleven million people stayed put.

Cubans made no secret of their visceral love for the island. Questioning, even hating, communism didn't keep them from counting their blessings. Their sun was strong, their women were hot. Olympic triumphs had established tiny Cuba as a sports power. Cuban musicians were geniuses. Could one doubt it? They pointed to the success of defectors playing baseball or singing salsa in America. In Havana's Revolution Square, I watched a friend's eyes go misty at the sight of a Cuban flag.

"This island is blessed," said an aging woman who worked at

ᴇrnest Hemingway's estate on the edge of the capital. "We have no volcanos, no wild animals, no poisonous snakes. We have mines. Anything can grow here. I grow garlic in the dirt on my roof. In what other country could I do that?"

There was another reason most Cubans stayed at home. Communism *was* a flop. The loss of the Soviet subsidy revealed Castro's failure to build a socialist wonderland. What he had built, however, was a safety net. Despite cutbacks, the state continued to provide hospitals (without medicine), schools (without books), and a subsistence diet (without meat). Cubans knew that theirs was the only country in the world where a person could do nothing, absolutely nothing, and not starve to death. Blanketed by security, many were afraid of the real world.

"I could have left when everybody was swimming to the American base in Guantánamo," said the man who fed me coconuts near El Cobre. "People think the U.S. is so great, that life is so easy. But it's not like that. I know that people there have to work very hard. If I stay here I don't have to work."

In Santiago de Cuba I spoke to a sailor who spent his shore leave selling pork sandwiches and fruit frappes. The stocky mulatto listed Spain, Canada, and South Africa as the highlights of more than twenty years at sea. Had he ever considered jumping ship?

"Of course," he said. "Every sailor thinks about it."

"Why didn't you?"

"Here in Cuba I have my family, my friends, and a certain level of life. It's not much. But I have learned to cope. In your country it's not difficult to find food. Or clothes. The problem is work. You have to find a job. Am I right? If you lose your job you can lose your home. I don't want that kind of adventure. In Cuba I feel safe."

Safe also described the home I found in Santa Clara. A cabbie on the edge of the park knew a couple who rented their spare room, and he earned commissions for bringing them tenants. Near a church, across from a school, the two-story building sat on a quiet street several blocks from the central park. The owner assured me that he operated with the blessing of the police. So, for twelve dollars a night, a middle-age engineer named Joel gave me a room with a television and a double bed flanked by reading lamps.

I preferred the TV in the living room. Seated in front of the screen, Joel invited me to watch a baseball game. He briefed me on the teams, Santiago de Cuba and Villa Clara, the province containing Santa Clara. He added that several of the players for Santa Clara also played on Cuba's national team. The second baseman was particularly dangerous; he had hit three home runs the previous night. He also told me about players who had defected to the U.S. during overseas tours. Fidel, said Joel, put a positive spin on the defections: Cuban players had Major League talent.

"I would like to go too," he said.

"To live?"

"To visit."

The government allowed Cubans to travel under certain conditions. One was that they receive an invitation from a relative or friend who lived overseas. Another was that foreigners cover the costs. The unwritten rule was that old people were free to go abroad. Younger Cubans, particularly doctors, economists, and others whose skills were needed on the island, were less likely to receive permission to cruise for pleasure.

"My family has a medical clinic in Miami," said Joel. "I could work there for three months and earn a lot of money. Because I would live with my aunt I could save. I don't want luxuries. Just enough to eat. And a color television."

Ernesto, who had housed me in Holguín, harbored a similar dream. The musician said that his preference was to teach music. But he would do anything, *anything,* if given the chance to work in America. He wanted to be ready when his time came. One afternoon I overheard him rehearsing his lines, in English: "I am a musician. Do you have a job? When will you dismiss that guy?"

When the game ended, Joel opened a folder. The four pieces of coarse brown paper were Cuba's exit forms, which demanded details such as his work history and military record. A white sheet from Cuba's diplomats in the Swiss Embassy in Washington, D.C., provided background on his hosts. He asked my help in filling out other forms in English.

He also asked another question: "Do you know somebody who works in the U.S. Interests Section in Havana?"

I explained that Americans avoided the de facto embassy.

"Maybe you have a relative who can help me?"

I don't think Joel believed me when I said no. His skepticism was understandable. Cuba was a country where everybody had a friend or a cousin or a friend of a cousin who could help to clear obstacles. *Sociolismo* was a way of life. Having never left the island, Joel had probably never met a man as poorly connected as I.

Relaxing came naturally in tidy, sleepy Santa Clara. So did wandering, which took me into the public library. On the eastern edge of Vidal Park, the building was hard to miss. Giant columns supported the roof of a building formidable enough to serve as a central bank. I climbed a marble staircase. At the top, a squat, middle-age woman led me to stacks of books in the later stages of disintegration. Eager to please a visitor from America, she found the English-language collection: a work by Thornton Wilder and a copy of *Vanity Fair,* the book.

She apologized for the shortage. Years had passed since the library had had money to buy new books. Would I settle for a valentine? We walked to a desk where the librarian and a colleague had been cutting hearts from red paper. Each one had a slit in which the women inserted a blue paper on which they had copied poems appropriate for the next day, February 14. The librarian kissed my cheek.

She led me through an office that had housed the head of the province during the Spanish rule. We stopped on a balcony overlooking the park. This, she said, is the place Fidel Castro stood to address the people on January 6, 1959. Looking across the street reminded her of another hero, Leoncio Vidal, who was killed fighting the Spanish in Santa Clara.

"You should read the history of the war. It's a beautiful story of brave men," she said. "The Spanish had the best weapons in Europe. The Mambises had only machetes. But it was the Spanish who were scared."

"Cubans used to be brave," said a man in a white shirt who had quietly joined us on the balcony. "But that was before."

"What about Fidel?" I said.

"Intelligent. Crazy. But not brave. Not anymore."

"And Che?"

"Che was brave. But he was an Argentine."

Cuba's romance with Che Guevara knew no bounds. His face was on the three-peso coin and a building overlooking Revolution Square in Havana. Outside the capital, hundreds of billboards and walls bore the stone-faced likeness of the long-haired soldier-scholar. The paintings were often accompanied by his most famous words, "Ever onward to victory," or inspirations, such as "Voluntary work is the school that creates conscience." Other displays called him "the Model Revolutionary."

In the capital a group of boys had two questions for an American. Did I have a car? And did I like Che? The mention of his name sobered the beer barons in Holguín. "Ernesto was a good man," said Rubén. "We miss him."

Santa Clara was the place to excavate Che's legend. It was here that the Argentine ended his march through the mountains of central Cuba's southern coast at the head of a column of guerrillas. Che's capture of a city just 270 kilometers from Havana told Batista that the war was lost. The strongman packed and left within two days.

A right turn out the door of the library and another right onto a street called Independencia took me to the scene of the battle that doomed the dictator.

A string of brown boxcars was the mainstay of the monument. Opposite, propped on a concrete pedestal, was a yellow bulldozer. A plaque linked the two. The bulldozer had been used to destroy the railroad tracks behind the boxcars. Unable to move, a train bringing arms and men from Havana became a sitting duck for 18 of Che's guerrillas, who used rifles and

Molotov cocktails to overwhelm 408 soldiers armed with bazookas, cannons, and more.

The guard smiled, so I asked how Che's band had beaten the bigger force.

"Three reasons. One was surprise. Two, Batista's soldiers surrendered quickly because they were fighting only for money. Three, the rebels were fighting for a belief."

Idealism, even more than heroism, explained the Cubans' affection for Che Guevara. Cubans viewed rebels as patriots who risked their lives for the love of their country. Did an Argentine rate less respect? No, more. Schoolboys and pensioners agreed that Che was a breed apart. He had no personal stake in the Revolution. His motives were purer. Cubans deified Che because he fought for the principle that the people should rule themselves.

The temple to the hero stood more than a mile west of the center of the city. Alone in a broad concrete space surrounded by floodlights, I looked toward the sort of multitiered stand where dignitaries inspected soldiers on parade. On a towering pedestal stood an enormous statue of Che wearing fatigues wrinkled from experience. His head was cocked, as if looking for danger. In case he found it, his right hand held a machine gun.

To the left of the statue, a bas-relief mural described the road to glory. One scene featured Che kneeling over a map while Castro showed him the route to take. Other carvings showed Che leading a column of soldiers. The sculptor had also etched the train wreck that spelled victory. Photos of the legend, as well as personal paraphernalia, filled a museum beneath the monument.

A wall beside the entrance bore Castro's thoughts on his comrade, who died while trying to foment a revolution in Bolivia: "Che wasn't just a man of insuperable action. Che was a man of profound thought, of visionary intelligence, a man of profound culture. That is to say, that in his person were united a man of ideas and a man of action."

The epitaph didn't fully fit Che's eventual departure from

Cuba. After the war, Castro gave Che several jobs in the new government, including Minister of Industry and President of the Central Bank. Some Cubans said that governing bored the revolutionary, who sought new wars to wage. In October 1965 Castro produced an undated letter in which Che, who had vanished, said just that.

There was another view. Suspicious Cubans felt that Che had been squeezed out. Privately, they said that Castro was jealous of Che's popularity. It's possible that they disagreed on policies. So some Cubans shook their heads while speculating that their leader had expelled a hero who became a rival.

Speculation also surrounded the death of another hero, Camilo Cienfuegos. I first heard about Camilo in Santiago de Cuba, where the son of a government photographer showed me a stack of old pictures, aerial shots. One showed a stretch of the Cuban coast. Another was of an expanse of water as seen through the window of a helicopter. A third showed an airplane on the ground.

"This is one of the airplanes that looked for Camilo," said the photographer's son.

He explained that Camilo had been one of Castro's top commanders. He and Che held Havana while the Liberty Caravan made its way west. He was the man ordered to take command of Camagüey from Huber Matos, the rebel officer who questioned Castro's politics. Camilo balked before agreeing to do the dirty work. The job done, he boarded a plane to Havana. Search parties on the ground and in the air never found a trace of the man or the aircraft.

"What happened to it?" I asked.

"Nobody knows," said the photographer's son. "But we know."

Joel was seated in front of the television when I returned from my tour. On the screen was a tanned, middle-age man seated behind a desk. His thick black mustache hid the movements of his lips, which were reading the news. Then Fidel Castro filled the screen. He was in full battle gear: green hat, black boots, olive greens, and a fat black belt around his growing girth.

Fidel was addressing the workers at a sugar plant. The first to meet its production goal, the plant had won a visit from the president. The leader extolled the virtues of the group standing before him: "We are interested, above all, that you understand the importance of the task you have achieved, of all that you do in this country . . ."

I lost track of the words. As before, I was taken by Fidel's style. His brown eyes were fired with feeling. He modulated his voice from a ponderous rasp to an earth-shaking bellow. His head shook and his beard quivered. Then he went completely still. A thought formed. He stressed a point by jabbing his arm in the air. He shook his fist. This was about sugar?

"*Es loco*" slipped out of my mouth.

Joel giggled.

"He's crazy," I repeated.

Joel left the room, presumably to compose himself: laughing at the president was risky. Thoughts of a second eviction crossed my mind when I overheard Joel telling his wife about my remark. Would she tolerate blasphemy under her roof? I heard a woman splitting her sides with laughter. Joel burst out again. I imagined the couple doubled over on the floor of their bedroom.

"I want to show you something," said Joel. "Something Cubans do."

He walked to the television and twisted the volume knob counterclockwise. Killing the sound left us with the image of Fidel shaking, quaking, gesticulating. Neither Joel nor I would have been surprised to see him begin to foam at the mouth. Without the sound, there was no way to see the dictator as anything but a nut.

"What did you think the first time you saw him?" I asked Joel, who had been in Vidal Park the day the Liberty Caravan came to town.

"I thought he was a very important man, a hero. And I thought he must be very powerful to defeat the army of Batista."

I nodded.

"Everybody was so happy, talking about a better future," Joel said. "But the people expected too much. They expected an immediate change in their lives. When nothing changed, they were disappointed."

"Change takes time."

"Of course. But we had other doubts. The Revolution was executing Batista's officers. Many of them, especially the police, were terrible men, men who had tortured and killed people. But they also executed some good men."

I said nothing.

"It didn't seem right," said Joel.

25

MY ROAD MAP put Cienfuegos about sixty kilometers south-west of Santa Clara. My guidebook said that the coastal city featured Cuba's longest boulevard, a statue of José Martí, and a nuclear power plant. Why was I going there?

I remembered the trail of Fidel Castro. Having tried and failed to find him in Havana, I had substituted a metaphoric meeting. Following his footsteps from Las Coloradas, where he landed, to the Sierra Maestra, where he plotted the war against Batista, seemed a sensible way to get a sense of the man and his motives. Traveling from Santiago de Cuba to Havana would help me understand the movement that defined the man.

My plan had worked. Past miseries described by Santiagueros taught me how Castro captured a country. Cubans who had met the man attested to his magnetism and motives. Elsewhere in the east, testimonials to better living conditions explained the ongoing loyalty to the architect of their salvation. His war on poverty made me a Fidel fan. That hadn't changed.

What had changed as I moved west was my view that Castro knew what was best for his country. Cutbacks in state-spon-sored medicine, power, and food proved that the safety net was sagging. People were turning to crime. Workers called in sick and surfed the black market. Sitting by the road among Cubans stranded by the system, I could see that communism had failed. Could Fidel?

Few Cubans linked El Máximo to their misery. "Fidel is a good man," said the very people showing me their country's decay. The real culprits, they said, were the other bigwigs. Popular opinion had it that self-serving rascals had circled themselves so tightly around Fidel that he couldn't see their misery. Had he been blinkered?

Maybe there wasn't an answer. If there was, it wasn't in Cienfuegos, where Castro had stopped the day before the Liberty Caravan rolled into the capital. The answer could only lie in Havana. And I wanted to cut to the chase. I wanted to get to the end of the road and get back to the business that had brought me to Cuba. I wanted to find Fidel. Now.

Obligation tempered intuition. I had been through every town visited by Fidel Castro up to and including Santa Clara. It seemed silly to let impatience stop me short. I mustered enthusiasm by recalling past surprises. The reason to travel was that I didn't know what I didn't know.

Mimicking Fidel was my first mistake en route to Cienfuegos. He treated his visit to the southern port as a quick detour from the Central Road. He left Santa Clara, gave a speech at city hall, and headed for Havana. I too planned to see Cienfuegos in a day. Up at dawn, I expected to be back at Joel's by dark.

Santa Clara's early risers built my confidence. Walking west, I was swamped by unsolicited greetings: "What's up?" "Friend." "Brother." When I paused to confirm that the dirt street led to the main road, a woman in a nightgown served me coffee. She and others all said the same thing: *"Recto. Recto."*

Ten minutes of "straight ahead, straight ahead," took me to the Autopista, the superhighway with a missing link between Sancti Spiritus and Santiago de Cuba. I walked two hundred yards east before a crew of workers directed me to the west. About one kilometer down the empty stretch I came to a junction. According to Joel, the southbound offshoot from the highway was the loading zone for Cienfuegos. My second mistake was already made.

I shouldn't have broken my no-trucks pledge. But memories of the ride from Camagüey to Sancti Spiritus were mellowing. Four calf-cramping, skin-searing hours at the mercy of a derelict driver had become a victory parade through the Cuban heartland. I recalled the wind in my hair, not the bugs in my mouth.

The familiarity of the scene at the junction affirmed my decision to seek a truck. The only structures in sight were two snack stands. One was selling ham sandwiches. The other offered coffee and chunks of sugar mixed with peanuts. There was no shelter. Nor had the state built benches on which to wait. There were, however, thirty or so locals standing beside the road to Cienfuegos at seven A.M.

"¿El último?" I asked.

Nobody responded.

"¿EL ÚLTIMO?"

Heads turned. Nobody answered.

Something was wrong. Cubans were religious about their queuing system. The last in line always identified himself. Three months in Cuba, and I had never once seen the system fail. I had never so much as considered the implications of a breakdown. Nor had I wondered what might cause Cubans to ignore the rules and standards created to help them survive the rough patch in their history.

"There's no Yellow Man," said a man sitting on a duffel bag.

"Where is he?"

"In Cuba, you never know."

"How will we know who boards first?"

"By our consciences."

An hour later no Yellow Man had showed up. Another thirty travelers had joined the group beside the road. Not that anybody missed the man authorized to stop trucks and load passengers. No vehicles had passed.

At eight-fifteen, the day's first truck came into view. It rattled past the waiting area but stopped about a quarter-mile down the road. People who were paying attention grabbed their bags and ran for the ride. Others reacted too slowly. By the time I saw the opening, forty locals had hit their stride. As eighty buttocks were about to reach their goal, the driver hit the accelerator. The truck pulled away. Standing in the cargo bay, four workers laughed as the sprinters grabbed stones to hurl at the men who had duped them.

That's when I made the morning's third and biggest mistake: I didn't leave. I should have seen the future. A Yellow Man would have held the truck. A Yellow Man would have organized boarding. But the designated hitchhiker had taken the day off, and without an enforcer, travelers were ignoring the rules of the road.

Vehicles began to appear, but at the infuriating pace of drops from a faulty faucet. The first two trucks were packed with passengers. A jeep with state license plates stopped. One of the four men inside pointed to the prettiest woman in our midst, who jumped at the chance to be sandwiched into the center of the back seat. At nine A.M., I found myself fantasizing about flying home and preparing my tax return.

At ten o'clock an empty truck stopped up the road from a group that had bulged to at least eighty. This time I was ready. I began to run even though dozens of Cubans were closer to the green jalopy. Fitter than the underfed people, I passed about half of the pack. Twenty Cubans, mostly men, beat me to a vehicle that could easily carry thirty.

The first to board was a mustached man in a tank top. He grabbed the side of the wooden cargo bin and used the top of the rear tire to propel his legs over the rim. One of his flying feet clipped the head of the man waiting his turn on the tire. Others didn't bother with the step. Men who could get a grip on the truck struggled to swing their legs to the edge of the hold.

People heaved bags to pals who had made it aboard. Men pulled on the arms of women who had made it to the front of a crowd three bodies deep. Somebody shouted, "Order. Order." Nobody listened. The chaos multiplied as more Cubans grabbed for the truck, which began to resemble the last helicopter out of Saigon.

I don't know why I joined the mob. Maybe it was the habit of going with the flow. I came to my senses when a suitcase dropped on my shoulder. A heel connected with my temple. I backed away.

I watched the wrestling from the sidelines. I wasn't going to get on that truck. In fact, I wasn't going to get on any truck bound for Cienfuegos. Not because there wouldn't be others. I suddenly realized that the Cubans had no choice but to grapple for places. I could afford not to fight.

"I used to go to Varadero every year. Not just me, the whole family. My wife and daughter. My brother and his family. Sometimes the family of his sister-in-law. The group changed every year. But we were always eighteen or twenty people, all sleeping on the floor of one hotel room. We didn't have the money for another room."

Francisco had paused midway through his recollection of the old days. When he continued, he gushed about the beach resort. He remembered flawless sand. He remembered nightclubs, drinking, and dancing. The 1980s, he said, were good times in Cuba and great times in Varadero. Crowded? Yes. Worth the trouble? Francisco reckoned Varadero was Cuba's most beautiful spot.

"Beach" sounded like "heaven" as I walked away from the junction. Muddled, my mind turned to distancing my body from a scene that upset my vision of Cuba as a society that showed admirable calm despite considerable pressure. The snapshot of the ugly underside would require a rethinking of the big picture later, when my temple wasn't throbbing and I was surrounded by sand.

At the bus terminal a skinny watchman said that I had missed the nonstop to Varadero, which left at eight A.M. He told me not to feel bad: it had sold out the previous week. But maybe he could help: his buddy kept the waiting list. Tickets to the resort cost eight pesos. For, say, two dollars, he could swing me a spot at the top of the waiting list for the next day's departure.

But I wanted to leave today. And I wanted to leave in comfort, a realization that dawned on me the moment my eyes landed on a vehicle parked outside the depot. The sides gleamed creamy yellow, the top jet black. Shining chrome covered the bumper and the hubcaps. Inside, red seats matched the steering wheel. Except for the plastic Jesus on the dashboard, the Fairlane looked as if it had just rolled off Ford's assembly line.

The owner agreed that his vehicle was a gem. We spoke about how he had babied the car with fresh paint and parts cannibalized from American and Soviet wrecks. More important to its longevity was careful driving. He avoided long trips and stayed away from rough roads, such as the Central Road to Varadero. He added another reason for not wanting to chauffeur me to the resort: "The police don't permit me to drive foreigners."

"You can't or nobody can?"

"Nobody. The government wants tourists to take its taxis. If the police find you in my car they will fine me. Fifteen hundred pesos! And they will take my car! I'm sorry."

The apologetic car owner had an idea, however. Other drivers were looking for fares. They were his friends. Some might be willing to risk a trip with a foreigner. Walking with me to the far side of the terminal, he introduced me to a man leaning against a four-door car that might once have been brown. I didn't like the looks of the Moskvitch, Russia's answer to the Pinto.

Less appealing were the looks of the driver. Shy of thirty, he wore a gold-colored bracelet and black leather boots. The slick accessories went with a styled mane of black hair that reached the base of his neck. Groomed à la *Saturday Night Fever,* the pockmarks that dented his tapered white cheeks made Gonzalo look like a mobster from *Miami Vice.*

Gonzalo was willing to drive me to Varadero. His only condition was that, if we were stopped, I wouldn't tell the police about his fee, twenty-five dollars. A little steep? The driver reckoned (rightly) that he deserved compensation for the extra risk. I agreed to his first request but not his second, which was to be paid in advance. Seated in the front, I couldn't help thinking that Gonzalo looked just the type to rob and roll a customer.

An equally worrisome man slid into the back seat as Gonzalo turned on the ignition. The bony fifty-year-old didn't say a word but looked dead ahead through the mirrored lens of his sunglasses. I scanned the Central Road and wondered where he, or they, would make a move.

"He's here for protection," said Gonzalo.

"From what?"

"Thieves."

I asked how they robbed a moving vehicle.

"They offer to pay for a ride. Once they are inside they put a knife to your throat. They take all of your money and leave."

"This has happened to you?"

"Me? No. I have a weapon."

Gonzalo pulled a truncheon from beneath his seat. When he added that his buddy was also armed, the man in the back withdrew a thin metal cable and wrapped the ends around his hands. Reaching over my seat, he showed how he would garrote a thief. The safety demonstration continued when the scrawny enforcer leaned down to grab something under my seat. Sitting up, he held a machete, its edge silvery from a recent sharpening.

I relaxed when the arms show ended. Maybe I wasn't going to be picked clean and left for dead. Maybe I had misread the tough guys. Maybe they were teddy bears in disguise.

I asked about the car. The Moskvitch, said Gonzalo, had been a prize from the state. The right to buy it was his reward for good work. Trained as a journalist, he had worked for his province's newspaper, a daily that began to skip editions due to the shortage of newsprint during "the special period." He covered local news, international, sports . . . whatever the boss wanted.

What about the content? I asked. How did Cuban editors control the content of the newspaper?

Gonzalo outlined the basics of Cuban journalism: "Everything about Cuba is good. Everything about the United States is bad. If something goes wrong in Cuba, it's the fault of the United States.

"For example, I would be assigned to the harvest. I knew that my job was to find stories about sugar. I also knew that I couldn't say anything negative. If I did, the bosses would criticize me. If they criticized me too many times, I wouldn't be writing about cane. I would be cutting it."

"Have you ever cut cane?" I asked.

"Cane is for niggers."

The driver acknowledged the irony of providing cars to "stimulate" workers. Owning wheels took Gonzalo away from his job. He bragged about charging for rides long before the state allowed Cubans to taxi each other. If caught, the reporter would lose his job and be sent to cut cane.

"Why do you take the chance?"

"I like to drink. I like to dance. I like to fuck whores. This is the only way I can make enough money to have a good time."

His libido led the cocky driver to leave his job altogether, a risky move since the police frowned on people whose identity cards showed no current employment. Was he worried? Gonzalo laughed; everybody was quitting the state sector. Jerking his thumb backward, he asked whether I knew what the man riding shotgun used to do for a living. I didn't. He had been a professor at a university. He taught Marxism and Leninism.

Outside the car, towering stalks of sugarcane blanketed vast patches of the flat land around the Central Road. Areas not covered had recently been cut by one of the combines I saw churning through the manmade jungle. The machines were followed by tractors pulling the V-shaped trailers into which workers — who were, in fact, all black — heaved the cut cane. Steam-powered trains carried the stalks the final distance to processing plants whose tin roofs and brick smokestacks looked like castles across the sea of green.

"Have you fucked any Cuban whores?" asked Gonzalo.

"Whores? No. I *have* met a few nice girls."

"There are no nice girls in Cuba. Only whores."

I thought about speaking my mind. I thought about telling Gonzalo that he was the kind of greaseball who had to pay women to suffer his company. Then I thought about Karl Marx and the sickle in the back seat. I held my tongue.

"Were any of them niggers? Did you fuck any niggers?"

The racist banter ended when Gonzalo saw a commercial opportunity. Standing by the road outside a town called Colón was a hard-bodied man wearing a gold watch. The driver appeared not to notice that he was black. He noticed only the dollar bills the hitchhiker was waving at the car. The new passenger handed two bucks to Gonzalo. I slipped the notes from his hand — "I'm paying for this car," I said — and passed the money back to the hitchhiker, Pablo.

Pablo wasn't a racist. He *was* a tireless talker.

"Varadero is where you find the best of Cuba," he said. "You're going to see the best food, the best music, the best beach. You are going to enjoy yourself in Varadero."

26

VARADERO LOOKED LIKELY to live up to its hype as Cuba's wonderland. We crossed a four-lane bridge over a glistening lagoon. I saw a marina filled with speedboats and yachts. Behind the tidy docks stood a community of white villas. A brilliant sun illuminated the entire playground as well as the checkpoint at the middle of the crossing. Three cops glared at every car.

Gonzalo left me at the home of Enrique. A spry man whose face had been tanned and lined by nearly sixty years of sunshine, he had seen a lot during his years in Varadero. After showing me to the spare bedroom, he poured two glasses of rum and talked about the old days. The sleepy beach began to take off when, in the 1930s, the du Pont family built an estate complete with a golf course and landing strip. Their millionaire pals followed. So did Al Capone. A wave of hotel construction in the 1950s lured Enrique's father, a shopkeeper.

"Back then there were only Americans. They came from Miami in the morning. The flight was only twenty-four minutes. They enjoyed themselves at the beach, spent the afternoon relaxing, and went home the same night."

The fun ended in 1959. The Revolution scared off the Americans, whose property was nationalized. Castro proclaimed "the people's full right to enjoy all beaches," and Cubans flocked to the skinny spit of sand. They were joined by Soviet and other Eastern bloc advisers and technicians in Cuba. Canadians also frequented Varadero, one of the few places they wouldn't be mistaken for Americans.

Europeans discovered Cuba before the collapse of communism. But the trickle turned to a geyser in the early 1990s when Castro learned what Batista had known: tourism meant big bucks. That, said Enrique, marked the start of a boom that was bringing tens of thousands of tourists every year. Many came from South America. Italians and Germans were more prominent. Above all, said the wiry storyteller, Varadero was the place for Spaniards.

"The Spanish have retaken Cuba," said Enrique. "This time without Christopher Columbus, without Diego Velázquez, and without firing a shot."

Spain chose well. Just four blocks from Enrique's home, or any other point on the island, the sea was a rainbow of blues: aqua at the water's edge, electric a little farther out, and navy toward the horizon. More remarkable was the sand heating the bare soles of my feet. Soft as powdered sugar, the white grains formed an undulating ribbon flawed only by the litter of human bodies.

Strewn on rented chairs and towels, the visitors looked like tanners anyplace in Europe. Young men wore swimsuits that could double as slingshots. Older men alternately sucked in and patted growing guts. Their wives tugged at bikini bottoms tired of covering flabby fannies. Young women thin enough to ignore their bottoms didn't wear tops.

The Euroflesh attracted pests. Cuban girls awakened sleeping beauties to offer to braid hair or massage bodies. More welcome were offers from minstrels. Moving alone or in groups, musicians asked a dollar or two for concerts. Sunbathers sat up when a five-man, two-horn band began to blast salsa. Seated under the trees behind the beach, Cuban workers enjoyed the show but kept their distance. Uniformed policemen saw to that.

Guards in beachwear minded the seaside entrances of a row of hotels that extended for miles. Where the hotels ran out, the planners had taken over. Parked at distant intervals from one another, idle cranes were poised to build the next generation of traps for tourists. Turning into what seemed to be the grandest of the hotels, run by a Spanish outfit called Meliá, I found a place unlike any other in Cuba. It was a palace of glossy floors and glassy elevators. A fountain cooled an airy atrium. The toilets had seats.

What I didn't see at the hotel were Cubans. I saw tourists in buses and taxis. More intrepid sorts were riding motor scooters down First Avenue, Varadero's main street. Some Cubans manned the shops in a plaza opposite a hotel. Others sold trinkets from kiosks along the strip. But they were the exceptions in a place with few Cubans and no propaganda. Varadero didn't feel like Cuba.

That's how the Party wanted it. Many visitors to the capital made the 140-kilometer pilgrimage to the famous beach. A third of the island's visitors spent their whole holiday in Varadero. Some never left the island.

I met a crew of young Canadians on the covered terrace of a snack bar called El Rápido. A sunburned man, Lee, filled me in on the world outside Cuba. Dallas had beaten Pittsburgh in the Super Bowl. Magic Johnson had returned to basketball. Then he asked a question: "What's it like out there?"

Two of the Canadians, Casey and Tiffany, *had* left the island for an afternoon. The experience had raised a gnawing question. "Who's that guy in the beret?" asked Casey.

"Che," I said. "Che Guevara."

"He was some sort of freedom fighter, right?"

"Right."

"Didn't he get whacked in the 1960s?"

The government protected its franchise by drafting special rules. Pablo the hitchhiker had reminded me that Cubans could swap homes with people in other parts of the country. Except in Varadero. Private restaurants, legal everyplace else, were also banned. Nor were Cubans supposed to rent rooms to foreigners. The state wanted to keep tourists in hotels, dining rooms, and any other place where they might drop some dough.

Still, times were good for the people of Varadero. Hotels meant steady jobs for many of the town's ten thousand residents. The state gave workers just a fraction of the money the hotels paid for their labor. But tips from work as a chambermaid or waiter dwarfed their wages. Hotel workers were also fed. The virtual absence of theft and violence was the surest sign that Varadero's residents were a fairly happy bunch.

Their happiness wasn't lost on the rest of Cuba. People came from all parts of the island to seek their fortune at the beach resort. Take Pablo. His college education couldn't explain his fancy duds. A regular salary simply couldn't cover the cost of his patent leather shoes. Or his designer jeans. Or his earring.

I asked how he supported his flamboyant look.

"I have a business," said Pablo.

"What kind of business."

"Cigars.

"Legal or illegal?"

"There is nothing legal in Varadero."

Cigars weren't the only game in town. I hadn't walked my first block on First Avenue when a teenager jumped up from his spot in the shade of a tree. He greeted me with a warm grin and a whispered question: "Do you want cigars?

"I don't smoke."

"How about lobster? I know a *paladar* with lobster. Cheap."

"I'm not hungry."

"Maybe later?"

The nineteen-year-old tugged me into the shade he shared with a younger boy. He told me that his mother lived in Santiago de Cuba, where she earned very little money. His wife, who was four months pregnant, earned nothing. That left him the family's main breadwinner. Hearing that the bucks flew fastest in Varadero, he traveled across the island to earn commissions from selling cigars and taking tourists to *paladares*. Or he just asked for money.

"Can you give me a dollar?" said the teenager. "A T-shirt?"

"What time is the game on television tonight?" was my way of saying no.

The hustler's pal came to life at the sound of a baseball fan. Just thirteen, he had also come to Varadero to make a buck. His older brother played for Santiago de Cuba. He had pitched the final innings of the previous night's 13–3 loss to Villa Clara.

"We'll get two tickets, at the Cuban price. I'll show you everything. We'll have a lot of food. Pork. Do you like pork? And not for money. Just for friendship." The boy pounded his right fist over his left to show how tight we would be.

"What about your money problems?"

"In Santiago de Cuba, friendship is more important than money."

"And in Varadero?"

"In Varadero . . . the Struggle."

The boys from Santiago de Cuba couldn't play the biggest game in town. The main event belonged to Cuban girls. And foreign men.

The men began to emerge late in the afternoon. A pair of burly, balding Germans looked like kids at a carnival as they bustled down the steps of the Hotel Cuatro Palmas. An overwhelming cologne marked a droopy-faced man as Italian. Alone and in pairs, Europeans continued to appear in the course of the next hour. Theirs was an odd demographic: few were younger than forty-five; none wore a wedding band; all looked ready for action.

The home team was ready too. A mob of more than a hundred girls milled on the sidewalk opposite the hotel. The make-up of the so-called *jineteras* — Spanish for "jockeys," Cuban for "prostitutes" — was as skewed as the opposition's. Every Cuban in sight was black. There were dozens of mulattas, some as light as *café con leche*, their hair twisted into delicate braids. Others had skin as dark as teak, a shade that they called "original" to indicate its similarity to colors found in Africa. Most of the girls looked less than a year out of high school. A few were still years away from considering college.

Fresh lipstick was the common thread. The rest of the battle gear varied according to taste and talent. A lot of the *jineteras* didn't let the hour, five o'clock, stop them from wearing black gowns and silver heels. Other girls dressed more aggressively. Tiny tops exposed flat stomachs and caverns of cleavage. Leg men could feast on the indiscretions of short shorts and miniskirts. Then there were the "nice girls," teenagers who patrolled the plaza in bright blouses and clean bluejeans. They, like other Cubans, were making the best of a bad situation.

A man who walked the one-sided gauntlet along First Avenue could count on a dozen playful glances. Requests for a cigarette, a light, or the time were common icebreakers. Silent types simply reached out and touched the arms of men with less experience at the Varadero two-step. Guys like me pretended to be interested in nothing more than fresh air. I was a vegetarian at Cuba's biggest meat market.

Pairs formed quickly. Two girls in Lycra shorts needed no more than two minutes to charm a couple of middle-age Italians. A Spaniard strolled hand-in-hand with a girl who wanted him to consider the perfume bottles and designer dresses in the windows of shops. Less than half an hour out of the blocks, the two Germans both had mulattas on their laps. But what came next?

The old-timers showed the way. On the patio of the shopping

mall's bar I saw six men seated around a table with graying hair, spotting skin, and tummies bulged enough to demand a C-section. Three were German, two Spanish, one a Brit. Each held cards in one hand. That left a hand free to alternate between lifting a can of beer and stroking the nearest stretch of skin.

The card sharks each had a private kibitzer. One had two. Sitting by their men, the girls' eyes wandered from the cards to passersby to cans of beer. A beet-red man shielded his jelly belly from further ultraviolet abuse by letting a girl in a swimsuit splay across his front. (Don't block the cards, honey.) Keen to earn their keep and go to the game's bonus rounds — dinner, disco, a nightcap — the girls stroked their benefactors' shoulders, thigh, or ego.

They were sex tourists, men who spanned the globe in search of notches for their expanding belts. Rio de Janeiro was a popular if pricey place to sow oats. Bangkok was cheaper, though its plague of AIDS gave men the willies. Cuba, which incarcerated people with the virus, offered safer sex. But price was what made Cuba the hottest stop on the circuit. "This country has the world's cheapest prostitutes" was a common, if dark, Cuban boast.

The influx bred a dilemma. Prostitution topped the list when Castro vowed to eradicate the trappings of imperialism. Nearly forty years later he had changed his mind about money. El Commandante and his lieutenants were openly asking foreign firms to help the country develop mines, factories, and hotels. The Party hoped to rake in three billion tourist dollars by the year 2000.

Jineteras were a magnet for money. In Varadero, girls who landed foreigners headed straight for the bar in the shopping plaza. The stores were stocked to suit the tastes of young black women, not old white men. Next came dinner in a hotel or one of the government's restaurants. The girls then steered their clients into discos. There was only one thing the girls did that didn't help to fill Fidel's coffers.

The state maintained the appearance of segregating locals from foreigners. Unescorted Cubans weren't allowed to enter hotels. Ladies with escorts were limited to the lobby and other public areas. Security staffs stopped couples from boarding hotel elevators. But Varadero's police ignored the mating game. I didn't see a single cop during the hours I spent watching it.

Government greed was one explanation. Pragmatism was another. Enrique had a daughter, Elena, who told me that her hometown hadn't always been a cesspool of sin. She had grown up in a resort that was busy, clean, and under the thumb of the law. No more.

"The police can't control the *jineteras*. If they arrest one hundred, there are two hundred more ready to come to Varadero and take their places. But women have their needs. Women want clothing, shoes, a little jewelry. Looking pretty makes women feel good. They want to fix their hair and paint their nails."

Fair enough, was my response. Everybody wants stuff. But not everybody gets it by turning fifty-dollar tricks.

"Look at me," she snapped. "I am over thirty years old. I don't want to start looking old. Because we can earn dollars by renting the apartment I can buy makeup. And face cream. Not every woman can do that." Recognizing the rising volume of her voice, she paused. Her face relaxed and she looked at me with a gaze that said, You just don't get it. Elena let loose a melancholic sigh and quietly repeated her mantra: "Women have their needs."

Acknowledging need wasn't the same as applauding prostitution; she bit her lip. Then Elena admitted to pain every time she saw a *jinetera*. Sure, Cubans liked sex. But no woman with the freedom to choose would sleep with the overweight, overage slobs flocking to the island. So upsetting was the sight of girls as young as thirteen loitering along First Avenue that she had begun to avoid Varadero's main drag.

Vilma, whose home I had rented in Sancti Spiritus, summed up the situation like this: "The *jineteras* are a national disgrace."

Neither woman blamed the girls. Cubans rarely turned their guns on individuals doing what they could to survive. The fault, they said, was with a system that had impoverished the country.

The fault was with the men who drove the people to desperation.

The angst and anger never reached the sex surfers, most of whom never laid eyes on the propaganda posters, ration books, and trappings of daily life on the island. Theirs was a tunneled vision of Cuba. Was I any better?

Abstinence made me a freak. Girls who smiled during my first and second laps of the shopping plaza looked puzzled when I passed their perches for the third and fourth time. An athletic teenager asked what was wrong. Didn't I like girls? Didn't I want to enjoy my time in Varadero?

A twenty-something was more persistent. Dressed in a low-slung gown, the mulatta grabbed my arm and, in rapid succession, asked where I came from, where I was going, and whom I was with. Clipped answers — America, home, and nobody — failed to convey my lack of interest. The girl knew one direction (forward) and one speed (fast).

"Do you want a girlfriend?"

"Cuban girls don't like me."

"Liar!"

"It's true," I protested. "I won't give them money."

"You're hard," said the mulatta. She meant "cheap."

27

I TRIED TO PINPOINT the oddness of the men walking my way. There was nothing unusual about three well-fed fellows heading down First Avenue. Their clothing, slacks and short-sleeve shirts, were par for the course. Three thick mustaches were one hint. A better tip was the accent I heard when they passed me on the dim sidewalk. They were Cubans. What were highly styled Cuban men doing in Varadero?

I turned for another look. The men had also turned. Showing no interest in a tourist, they were inspecting two wiry Cubans walking ahead of me. The pair looked back but kept walking. So did I. The mustached men lost interest and continued.

"Police?" I asked the two guys.

"Police," said the taller and gaunter of the youths.

"What are they looking for?"

"Crooks."

In a town filled with vice, the three-man squad was eyeballing the only honest men I met in the resort. Javier, who had spoken to me, and Fernando were construction workers. Natives of Santa Clara, the pair had spent a combined ten years sweating under Varadero's sun. "We build the hotels," said Javier. "And when we finish we can't go in."

I liked the workers. They took to me when I told them about my travels in trucks, wagons, and anything else that moved in Cuba. They gaped at a foreigner who traveled courtesy of the Yellow Men. Then they doubled over with laughter. Once calm, Javier invited me to join them at El Rápido.

Outsiders occupied just one of the dozens of plastic tables beneath the covered patio. The rest were either vacant or filled by young Cubans, few of whom could afford the snacks that the state sold for dollars. I bought three cans of beer. The workers protested a gesture they couldn't reciprocate.

"If you had the money, would you buy me a beer?" I asked.

"You're Cubanized," said Javier.

The talkative builder told me about his day. He and Fernando punched in at nine A.M. and worked until six P.M. Had they been tired, they would have stayed "home" in their rented room. ("Cuba isn't like the United States," said Javier. "Here work is like a sport. You do it when you feel like it.") Come quitting time, they put in two hours for a local who paid them to build a room in which he planned to house tourists. If caught, they would be fined and banned from Varadero.

"Is anybody not doing something illegal here?"

"Varadero has become an ugly place," said Javier. "It's pure prostitutes. And not just girls. There are also homosexuals because that's what a lot of foreign men want. And there are pimps. They exploit and beat up the girls. But so do the police, like the men we saw. They arrest girls who won't give them money and sex. The place is one big garbage can."

A steady flow of young women began to fill the space beside the snack stand and beneath the fluorescent lights. A few came with foreign men, big spenders who treated their dates to a hot dog and a beer. Most, however, arrived with a girlfriend or two. The mating dance at the shopping plaza was over. The time had come to rest their feet. Sagging smiles suggested that some girls had given up fishing for the night. For others, El Rápido was a rest stop before dangling their live bait at a disco.

I recognized a woman who played another game. Seated on the passenger side of a Lada, the angelic mulatta had leaned from the window to ask a favor. She extended a twenty-dollar bill and asked for change. Few locals could break a big note, so my inclination was to help. But something felt wrong. As with the undercover cops, I sensed but couldn't identify the oddity. Discomfort led me to compare her twenty-dollar bill to one of my own. The difference was minor. But her cash was counterfeit.

The mulatta blushed when she saw me at El Rápido. She hadn't known the money was funny. We took a longer look at a bank note she said was a "gift" from a tourist. Our conversation was overheard by a boy who made her an offer. For a commission he would get change for the phony twenty. Elated by the mulatta's acceptance, he grabbed the twenty and raced into the night.

Another counterfeit caught my eye. The long blond hair of the woman ambling onto the patio had to be fake. Why? This was Varadero, a place free of single foreign women. But if the blonde came from Cuba, an island of dark-haired people, her golden cascade couldn't be natural. And what about her lightly toasted skin? Green eyes and a skirt that flowed to her ankles left me thinking she was European. Maybe German.

Another offer distracted me from the blonde. A small man wearing jeans and a T-shirt made a point of catching my eye as he walked past the table. Succeeding, he put a forefinger to the side of one nostril and sniffed slightly with the other. Had I just been offered cocaine? I turned for a second look. So had the sniffer, who repeated the gesture.

Rum, not coke, was the vice of choice at El Rápido. Two teenage boys lurked at the end nearest First Avenue. When foreign men entered, the hustlers made their pitch: "Rum, Cuban rum. Havana Club. The best in Cuba." Two other boys made similar offers on the sidewalk. They were the salesmen. The supplier was the small man with the short afro who had joined Javier and Fernando.

Félix pulled a bottle of the rum from his backpack. The main label said HAVANA CLUB and FOUNDED IN 1878. A smaller tag said AGED 7 YEARS. I asked whether the contents were really Havana Club or a knockoff. Félix removed the bottle's cap and offered me a swig. The rum was the real deal, smooth enough to tingle rather than burn the throat. But where did he get it?

Like the construction workers and the prostitutes, Félix was an out-of-towner. He lived in Matanzas, a city roughly thirty kilometers southwest of Varadero, and worked in the Havana Club distillery. He went to work carrying four empty bottles, which he concealed beneath clothes selected for their bagginess. Every day he filled the containers and walked out the door with four liters of top-grade rum. What about getting caught?

Félix wasn't worried. Tapping two fingers to the opposite shoulder, he said that his father was one of the bosses at the distillery. Leaving next to Dad meant freedom from body searches, which were rare. In fact Dad, who had access to rum intended for export, also had a knack for slipping out with an extra bottle or two.

But Félix was the kingpin of the family's business, and it was he who came to Varadero, the easiest place to sell the day's haul. He charged five bucks a bottle, less than half the retail price. Salesmen, such as the boy in high-tops who brought a Spaniard to our table, were paid a dollar a bottle. The sale reduced the stock to three bottles. An Argentine whom Félix had arranged to meet cut the stash to two. I bought one for our table.

Years had passed since the construction workers last tasted

Havana Club. The good stuff turned Javier melancholy. He joined the dozens of locals who had noted soberly that Cubans no longer got the best of Cuba. Not the rum. Not the hotels. Not the women. The laborer hummed as a wandering guitarist strummed "Guantanamera." Minutes passed before anybody spoke.

"Look at those beautiful girls," said Javier. "One is from Guantánamo, the other is from Camagüey. But do they want to go home with me, a Cuban? No. They want to go home with a tourist like you."

"She's Cuban?" I said, indicating the blonde.

Javier was right. The fine-featured blonde, Nuria, confirmed that her home was Camagüey. Weakened by her looks, I melted as she told me a story that began in a hotel in her hometown. Three years of service got her a summary dismissal from a boss who gave her job to a friend. That had been six months ago. Two weeks ago she came to stay with a friend who lived in Varadero. "For vacation," she said. "To relax." She planned to return home in about a week.

Was Nuria a hooker? If not, why was she stroking the back of my hand? I couldn't shake the ugly thought about the beautiful woman who was searching my eyes, and I found myself questioning our conversation. Was she as warm as she seemed, or was it an act? She said she loved my eyes. She said she liked me. Unaccustomed to facile compliments, I suspected a hidden agenda.

Or did I have it all wrong? Maybe Nuria was on vacation. This *was* Cuba's best beach. Her lodgings were free. The stroking — the woman's hand had moved from my hand to my thigh — could also be explained. Cuban women weren't shy.

I stepped back from my debate and saw a bigger problem. Cuba's crime wave made possible my travels and my fun. Cabbies broke the law when they carried me. Bootleggers crossed the line by selling me beer and rum. Black marketeers had shown me society's innards. Indoctrinated to the dark side, it was hard not to expand on the dubious wisdom of Gonzalo, who had said that all Cuban girls were whores. Varadero made it hard to believe that the same shouldn't be said of all Cubans. But was Nuria a whore?

"Maybe we'll become friends," said the golden girl.

"Maybe."

"Maybe we'll get married."

"Maybe."

"Maybe you'll take me home with you."

"Home in America or home in Varadero?"

"Whichever."

Same scene, next night.

I arrived from watching sunburned men and sunsplashed girls pair off like animals on the ark. Two Spaniards came into the snack stand and began plying a pair of teenage girls with hot dogs and Cokes. Handfuls of other Cubans occupied a fraction of the tables on the concrete floor beside the snack bar. The locals who weren't talking watched El Rápido's counter staff, who served customers at a rate of three every ten minutes.

Javier and Fernando were already seated on the patio. So was Félix. But the normally animate bunch was quiet. They came to life, barely, when I put four cans of beer on the empty table. The laborers grumbled about fatigue and food. The bootlegger was tired too. He couldn't remember the last time he had slept as many as five hours at a stretch. All three men griped about the cold.

The temperature in Varadero had plummeted. The drop caught the Cubans off guard. To a northerner, Cuba's midwinter air felt like a spring breeze. Locals saw the onset of the ice age. Goosebumps covered the arms of men who weren't wearing, and may not have owned, long-sleeve shirts.

The girls were even less happy; short sleeves and skimpy skirts were their stock-in-trade. One by one and in pairs, *jineteras* scurried into El Rápido, their high heels clicking from quickened steps. Groans — "The cold!" — filled the air. Two girls in minidresses, one black and one red, spotted and joined Javier. Neither looked keen to give up their proximity to warm-blooded bodies.

"This is a bad night for the girls," said the girl in black.

"The cold?" I asked.

"The police."

A crackdown was under way. All over Varadero — in the shopping plaza, in front of the hotels, and up and down First Avenue — the cops were stopping unaccompanied Cubans and demanding identity booklets. Those whose IDs showed that they had neither homes nor jobs in Varadero were arrested on the spot. The girl pointed to a passing bus of the type used for importing tourists. The police, she said, had filled the vehicle with friends and associates being expelled from the resort.

"This is a bad night for the girls," she repeated.

I felt sorry for her. Like her fellow hustlers, both men and women, she came from a poor family. Tales of riches had lured her from Santiago de Cuba. She didn't mind the men — the foreign men, that is. They bought her dinner, took her dancing, and told tales about life outside Cuba. The problem was Cuba's men in blue. The police treated the *jineteras* like a public well; they dipped in at will. Having given in to extortion, she resented the roundup.

"What happened?" I asked. "Why tonight?"

"Fidel is coming."

"Excuse me?"

"Fidel is coming to Varadero. Whenever Fidel comes here, or goes anywhere, the police become very hard. They arrest anybody they don't like."

"Who said he's coming?"

"Everybody knows it."

Another goosebumped girl confirmed the assertions of her associate. The police were indeed carting away *jineteras* by the truckload. When asked, some of the cops had said that the cleanup was inspired by an imminent visit from Castro, who had recently railed against the plague of "pirates" infecting the island. Rumor had it that he was going to dedicate a new hotel. I got similar buzz from two other teenage girls who bustled into the shelter.

I believed them. My earlier attempts to meet the man had

taught me not to expect banner headlines announcing his movements. Later efforts taught me the value of rumor in a country
that doctored its news. Years of reading between the Party lines
had turned Cubans into expert sleuths. Ears ever to the ground,
they recognized the sound of possibility. Probability was determined by comparing today's gossip with the history of tips,
some realized, others not.

Javier was skeptical. He ran down the list of hotels under
construction. None, he said, was ready for inauguration. Indeed, the cranes visible down the shore and the work-as-sport
attitude of the workers combined to suggest that the structures
I saw were years from completion. But had I seen them all?
Maybe not.

A policeman appeared in front of El Rápido, which was
quickly filling with shapely women who treated it as their base.
The officer respected the boundary: he didn't pass the wooden
fence separating the terrace from the sidewalk. He did collar a
bone-chilled girl who, just yards from the divide, probably
thought she was home free. Instead she was asked for identification and loaded into a military truck. I looked at Javier.

"Maybe he is coming," shrugged the worker.

I couldn't sleep. At dawn I bounced out of bed and shaved. I
went to a hotel for breakfast. To a buffet of cold eggs, cold
waffles, and cold bacon I added toast, which I burned on my
own.

"Did you hear that Fidel is coming today?" I asked a waiter.

"No."

"Do you think he is?"

"He was just here four days ago."

"How do you know?"

"It's easy to find out afterward, but very difficult before."

"So it's possible that he's coming back."

"It's possible."

What to do? Choose a hotel lobby and wait for the man to
pass? Take my chances on a construction site? What if I picked
the wrong one? Waiting by the road presented a similar risk, for

the resort had two main roads. First Avenue ran up the center of town. Four blocks away, South Highway skirted the side opposite the beach. I needed to cover both bases.

I knew where to go. The roads met at the spot where Gonzalo had entered Varadero. The steel bridge I had hiked across was the only way onto the resort. Whichever road he chose, whichever hotel he hit, Fidel had to use that bridge. The chokepoint is where I would wait.

Javier, whom I met on my way to the stakeout, agreed that the plan made sense. He also gave me a tip: look for three black Mercedes-Benzes, the cars that Castro used to travel in and around the capital. Worried that I couldn't identify a Mercedes, the construction worker joined me.

"Aren't you going to work?" I asked.

"I'll go later."

We walked to the end of First Avenue. At nine o'clock we settled in a shady spot with a view of both the bridge and the lagoon it traversed. Our seats also had a view of the marina. Behind gleaming yachts stood rows of white villas whose luxury contrasted with the decay across the channel. The possibility that three official cars might cross the bridge raised an old question: What would I ask Castro?

I imagined a preface in which I distinguished myself from other Americans. My disdain for communism was matched by my dislike of Jesse Helms. I didn't want to talk about the embargo. Nor was I interested in Soviet missiles or Kennedy's assassination. I hoped that my travels on his island and in his footsteps would impress the president. Then I would ask my first question: Did he know?

Did Fidel Castro know what was going on in his own country? Did he know what was happening to his own people? Or were the people right? Was he being blinded by yes-men? Say his eyes were open. Say Fidel did grasp the sorry state of Cuba. What did he plan to do about the unraveling of his life's work? True, there had been changes, but not enough. Were more reforms in store?

I entertained two more possibilities. Assume my earlier ques-

hadn't landed me in the dungeon. And assume Fidel found
an amusing observer of life on his island. The thing I really
wanted to say to him was this: consider history.

As things stood, Castro would be remembered as a revolutionary who toppled a dictator, put his country on its feet, then
ruined his work because he was too proud, stubborn, or ignorant to change his ways. There was an alternative. Change now,
I would say, and be remembered as a pragmatic leader, a man
who helped his people by soaking the Soviets and then, when
that well ran dry, was astute enough to shift gears.

I heard helicopters. Looking up I saw a military chopper,
complete with missile launchers. A few minutes later another
helicopter passed the spot where Javier and I had been sitting,
mostly in silence, for well over an hour. Protection for the
president, was my thought.

Javier shot down my optimism. The helicopters, he said,
were military. They were not the advance team of a presidential
motorcade. Many countries had turned swords into plough-
shares since the end of the Cold War. Cubans did so by taking
tourists for joy rides in Soviet helicopters.

"How much longer will you be in Cuba?" asked Javier.

Roughly three weeks remained on my visa.

"Let's go to Camagüey, to my house there. We'll go out,
meet my friends, go to parties. I want to show you that Cubans
know how to live."

"What about your job?"

"I'll take a vacation."

The vacation never happened. A policeman approached the
spot where Javier and I were waiting. A gesture brought the
laborer to his feet. The officer motioned for me to keep my
distance. He wanted to be alone with the Cuban.

The men argued after the lawman checked Javier's identification. The laborer said that his job on the island entitled him
to be in Varadero. The cop agreed. He didn't even order the
shirker back to work. What he wanted, however, was for the
Cuban to keep his distance from tourists. I last saw Javier walking up First Avenue in the hands of the police.

I left shortly thereafter. El Máximo hadn't shown up. Meltdown was a possibility were I to spend another hour under the sun. Walking across the bridge from Varadero, I denied defeat. I would find Fidel in Havana, the Liberty Caravan's last stop.

28

YELLOW MEN, watchful cops, stranded Cubans.

Beat-up trucks, rust-bucket cars, makeshift buses.

Unfinished overpasses, empty eateries, fading slogans.

The snapshots flashing through the windshield of the 1940s Pontiac reminded me how much I had learned along Cuba's Central Road. Santiago de Cuba was grateful. Holguín was crooked. Varadero defied description. I also thought about my last attempt to see Fidel. Nearly a month had passed between his no-show at the film festival and my departure for Santiago de Cuba. I had spent the time sightseeing in the capital.

An Italian provided a fresh angle for meeting the dictator. Castro's political rallies were legendary. For decades Cubans had gathered to cheer loudly, wave banners, and listen hard to their leader's speeches, which could run five hours or longer. Some of the rallies were held regularly. One was on July 26, the day the rebels attacked Moncada. May Day was another. Two other annual speeches were just around the corner: New Year's Day marked the anniversary of the Revolution, and January 8 was the day Fidel and the Liberty Caravan rolled into Havana.

I thought back to my first visit to the site of the January 1 speech, Revolution Square. To a pedestrian approaching from Vedado, a tapered tower was the first sign of the square. A guidebook provided details: white marble, 142 meters high, five bucks to ride the elevator to the top. To these I added my own thought: Was the architect lynched for creating an eyesore? If not, the builder may have been paroled for designing the statue at the base of the four-sided obelisk, which sat on a grassy knoll.

Hewn from seventeen meters of white rock was a likeness of José Martí, seated and lost in thought.

Che kept an eye on José. On the opposite side of Revolution Square, the face of an office block bore a giant line drawing of the Argentine who became Castro's right hand and Cuba's conscience.* Nine stories high, the bars of black metal outlined the trademark beard and beret. If Martí was the thinker, Guevara was the dreamer. Beneath a rendering that captured the rebel looking into the distance were the words HASTA LA VICTORIA SIEMPRE. Ever onward to victory.

Between Cuba's demigods lay a space long enough for drag races. The rectangular expanse took me back to nightmares in which I found myself naked but unable to hide. It was a concrete wasteland whose only features were shafts of wood bristling with gramophone-shaped loudspeakers. The slightest breeze sent scraps of paper skittering like tumbleweeds. Chilled by the emptiness, I walked around the edge of the square.

A whistle blasted. I spotted a lone policeman previously obscured by one of the poles. His quarry was a man who had made a mistake. The zone was forbidden as well as forbidding. Head lowered, the lone cyclist slowly pedaled toward the spot where the cop stood, authoritatively rigid, clearly prepared to lay down the law. Months later, I remembered making a quick exit.

I also remembered my second visit to Revolution Square, on New Year's Day. *Granma* hadn't mentioned that Fidel was set to speak. Nor had the television. Some friends said that the silence meant there would be no talk or that the speech might be given in Santiago de Cuba. Others didn't rule out the possibility. Cubans had long since given up forecasting El Máximo's next move.

Unusually quiet streets were the first sign that something was wrong that morning. Stepping out my front door, I looked across the street and, for the first time since my arrival in Cuba,

---

*The fact that Che signed hundreds of execution orders didn't affect his goodness in the eyes of Cubans.

didn't see the coffee lady. The guys who sold produce had also taken the day off. I walked a block before seeing a soul. A beer-bellied man in orange shorts and blue high-top sneakers wished me a happy new year as he added a bucket of refuse to the overflowing Dumpster on the corner.

Three more blocks passed before I saw two bleached blondes idling at a normally busy intersection. One wandered into the becalmed boulevard to look for a ride. Her partner wiped sweat from her forehead and tugged at her purple shorts. The pair was still waiting when I turned up the avenue called Paseo.

At the crest, trees obscured the view of Revolution Square. Walking down the six-lane ramp, I looked to the right where a wall was painted with WE WILL CONQUER! and 37 AND WE'RE NOT STOPPING, the Revolution's slogan for the coming year. I passed the National Theater. Missing letters — T, e, l, and u — the low concrete billboard said " atro Naciona de C ba." At the bottom I turned left into the epicenter of Cuban communism.

The square was dressed for a party. Banners hung from the roof of an office building on the far side. A massive red and black cloth with "36" in the center reminded me of Third Reich newsreels. More banners reached down three floors from the roof of another building. A blue flag belonged to Cuba's union of high schoolers. A red one flew the colors of the federation of university students. A third bore the motto of the Young Communists Union: STUDY. WORK. GUN. The only thing missing was people. Revolution Square was empty on New Year's Day.

A week later Fidel failed to appear for another annual speech, normally delivered at Liberty City, where he ended his road trip in 1959.

Inexplicable at the time, the failures of my second and third attempts to close in on Fidel made more sense as the Pontiac reached the outskirts of the capital. No longer squeamish about speaking the dictator's name in private, I told the fifty-year-old driver, Ramón, about my visit to Revolution Square.

"You didn't see Fidel, did you?" said Ramón.

"No."

"He doesn't speak in public anymore."

"Never?"

"Not like before," said Ramón. "Fidel is intelligent. He knows that this is a very bad time for Cubans. He knows that the people are angry. When people were happy, he gave speeches all the time. Now nobody wants to listen to him."

"Isn't it embarrassing to cancel an event that happens every year?"

"It would be more embarrassing if Fidel spoke and nobody came."

For decades Castro had no trouble drawing Cubans to his speeches. The people loved their leader. They, and the Party, were also suspicious of folks who skipped the mass rallies. Snitches reported anyone caught playing hooky. People lost their jobs, a threat that boosted attendance until employment became less lucrative than hustling. The carrot rotting, the stick bending, the Party rolled out a secret weapon: salsa.

"When there is a speech, by Fidel or his brother Raúl, they put on a salsa orchestra," said Ramón. "That way they know people will come."

"So what happened this year?"

"Maybe they couldn't find a band."

The driver offered another example of the state's duplicity. He stopped the car to show me a recent edition of *Granma*. A page-one article quoted an official in Havana. Inside, a separate story cited the same official on the other side of the island, a discovery Ramón took as an insult to his intelligence. Did I know how Cubans requested *Granma*? "Twenty centavos of lies, please."

They also mistrusted the official version of foreign affairs. In Camagüey a worker divulged his theory that the top brass knew the likely fallout from the collapse of the Soviet bloc long before the people began to feel the effects. Angola, the site of one of Cuba's overseas adventures, was presented as a glowing example of Cuba's devotion to international fellowship. Veterans

I met said the death toll had been underreported. A rugged mulatto refused to describe his five years in Africa. He simply shook his head and mumbled, "It was an ugly war."

Harder to hide were fibs about the U.S. For years the only unfiltered facts entering the isolated island came from Radio Martí, a U.S.-backed station that broadcast its own share of distortions. The flow of reliable facts about life in America increased when Cuban emigrants began returning to visit relatives, who admired the visitors' clothes and cash. They lapped up tales of the good life, evidence that contradicted the grim portrait painted by the local press.

"Tell me this," demanded Holguín's beer baron. "If America is so bad, why does every Cuban want to go there?"

The gap between Party-say and Party-do was most obvious in Holguín. In the center of town on a Sunday morning, I heard hymns coming from a church at one end of a shady park. I followed the singing through the doors and into a cavern whose pews couldn't accommodate the congregation. A white-robed priest began a sermon that mesmerized the packed house. I thought of Fidel Castro's bad rap. Infamous for squelching religion, the state appeared to have changed its mind.

Sounds from the park outside the church changed my mind. Maybe thirty yards from the entrance I found a band. Not a guitarist. Not a pianist. At nine A.M. on a Sunday morning a thirty-piece band was playing brassy tunes such as "When the Saints Come Marching In" for a handful of listeners. My outrage grew when I spotted the trumpeter. It was my host, Ernesto.

"The communists have to say they are allowing religion because they get help from religious groups in the U.S.," said Ernesto's father, whom I asked to confirm the link between the loud music and the church service. "So now people can go to church. And look what the communists do! There are two churches in the center of Holguín. They put music groups outside both of them every Sunday."

"It's not our fault," said Ernesto. "The state tells us where to play and when. They pay my salary. I have no choice."

The driver and I also swapped stories about Cubans' growing sense that the state was cheating them. Ramón brought up fraud in the markets. The so-called Agros were supposed to give farmers a place to sell their produce at free market prices. In fact, the driver moaned, many of the vendors weren't farmers at all. They were middlemen, the beast reviled by Marxist-Leninists. Where did they get their produce? Ramón said they bought food from the state, which earned a profit by selling to the rich instead of giving to the poor.

I rehashed stories about the government's reselling goods received as aid. The woman who housed me in Sancti Spiritus said that a lot of aid went to the dollar stores; she had bought bags of rice labeled AID FOR CUBA. The beggar who badgered me in Santa Clara said the same about medicine: doctors who got hold of pharmaceuticals were as likely to sell them in the street as dispense them in the hospitals. People said that computers earmarked for Cuba's health system wound up on the black market. True or false, the fact was that Cubans felt ripped off by their leaders.

"I'm going to teach you something," fumed Ramón.

He turned off the highway into the maze of streets on the rim of Havana's bay. Piles of scrap metal lined the two-lane street. Stacked five high, the rusted shells of cars and buses called to mind the movies. It was the set of an apocalypse in which human beings turned into animals in a place reduced to a shell of its former self.

"This is what has become of Cubans," he moaned, pointing to the people poking through the rubble. "It's a disaster."

"All countries have poor people."

My refusal to rubber-stamp the criticism drove Ramón to seek more evidence. He turned down a narrow street, pointed to a crumbling building, and said, "Look at that. You think people can live in there?"

We passed the facade of a building whose innards had collapsed. The problem, said Ramón, an engineer, was simple. No investment. Years had passed since the state had put any money into the housing stock. Some buildings hadn't been touched since Batista skipped town. Structures were collapsing at a rate of about three hundred a year.

I noted that the government had no money.

The engineer counterattacked. He noted that Cuba's resources hadn't changed since the last regime. There was still nickel to mine and sugar to refine. The island was no less attractive to tourists. No, he said, the problem was the management. Havana, and the rest of Cuba, had gone to pot because the Party had mismanaged its natural riches.

Ahead, two cars and a truck were making a slow serpentine. Closing in, we saw that a concrete tower had toppled. I saw a street littered with rocks bigger than bowling balls. Ramón saw red. He demanded, "Do you see *this* in a normal country?"

A pothole airlifted from Sarajevo took his mind off his country's disintegration. Ramón eased the Plymouth into the crater. Another driver gently entered the other side of the hole. The two shared a laugh about the state of the city. At the corner Ramón sighted a chunky woman in white spandex.

"¡Oye, niña!" he shouted. Hey, baby!

The woman turned into an open doorway.

"Thank God we have Cuban girls," he said. "If we could sell them we would be millionaires."

"But they are for sale."

My crack put Ramón back in his funk.

The Cubans' low spirits dragged me down. The extended view of the inside of local life darkened my vision of the outside. Stretches of street that I once admired as lucky leftovers from the colonial past became sad symbols of the communist present.

Take the Malecón. Walking the familiar curve from the Hotel Nacional to Old Havana, I chose the sidewalk opposite the sea. Unsightly from afar, cracking plaster became a health hazard. Who knew when a chunk might drop? The same could be said of the rickety beams supporting ceilings over sidewalks that stank of urine. Open doors offered unfettered views of dark, dank hallways. Men and women looked out through the bars of unshuttered windows. A boy who was swatting a playmate with a strip of inner tube took a breather to pose a question.

"Do you have any gum?"

"No."

"Money?"

"No."

The boy resumed the beating. I changed course, walking a few blocks inland to a street called Neptuno. Halfway down the first block I stopped at a tower of rubble. Mostly chunks of concrete and mortar, the chest-high heap included rusted cans and a tangle of iron rods. Protruding from the bottom were the battered innards of an upright piano. Similar piles, and long ridges of rubble, turned the area into an obstacle course. Nearby, a gutted building reminded me of photos of Dresden.

Later, I stopped to examine the Dumpster near my apartment. Piled high on the sides, pink shopping bags stuffed with refuse obscured most of a steel container overflowing with waste. Banana peels and orange rinds were scattered across a mountain of brown mulch and yellowed newspapers. An unwashed scavenger stirred the contents with a short plank. He exhumed a torn shoe and tipped onto the sidewalk the foul contents of a shopping bag, which became a carrier for his treasures.

Still, I found myself more hopeful than the Cubans. Reforms were under way. Free markets for food had become a part of life. The right to hold dollars had made a big difference to people with relatives abroad as well as those with the means or the brains to wheedle dough from tourists. Decades of communism hadn't dimmed their ability to think in terms of profits. Pressed, Cubans would admit that life was getting ever so slightly better. Blackouts were no longer daily; buses did run; everybody had gained a few pounds since the low point of the post-Soviet period.

There was another sign of an upswing. For centuries Cubans had celebrated Carnival at the end of the sugarcane harvest in mid-July. The three-week blowout was later moved to February.

In 1990, the party was taken off the calendar: the state had no money to spare for fancy floats and frilly costumes. A rumor that spread when I was in Santiago de Cuba had become fact by the time I reached the capital. Carnival was back!

I saw another benefit to its return. His failure to deliver two annual speeches taught me that Fidel no longer appeared like clockwork. On the other hand, a celebration that he had personally authorized seemed the ideal moment for him to see and be seen by the masses. I headed toward Carnival, hopeful of finally catching a glimpse of the man.

Shortly after dark I rang the bell of the Old Havana building where José, whom I had met during my first stint in the capital, lived with his in-laws. At the crest of two flights of marble stairs I found my tubby friend waiting at the door of an airy apartment. Inside, his wife was watching music videos.

Carnival didn't interest José's wife. She had a higher priority, *Mujeres de Arena,* or *The Sand Women.* The decision was understandable. All across the island Cubans dropped everything to watch the Brazilian soap opera. People without televisions gathered in the living rooms of those who had them. Keen to damp social unrest, the government scheduled blackouts before or after the eight P.M. screenings. But could TV be a better option than the return of Havana's favorite party?

"Yes" appeared to be the answer when José and I reached the parade route. Bleachers lined one side of Paseo. Across the floodlit boulevard was the Inglaterra, a nineteenth-century hotel whose twentieth-century guests filled tables alongside the street. Everyone looked more hassled than happy. People jockeyed for seats. Once settled, they grumbled. The air was cold. The parade was late.

The wail of sirens marked the start, and a phalanx of cops on motorcycles rolled our way. Puppets from a children's TV show followed them. Next came a handful of horsemen. Dressed in period clothing, the men were actors from a Cuban soap opera in which brave Mambises routed cowardly Spaniards on a weekly basis.

The music began when a bulky red tractor pulled a band down the street. Sitting on a platform, the group blasted salsa through speakers that turned music into noise. The distortion didn't appear to faze the dancers hired to follow the float. One group was dressed in Arab costumes. Another bunch wore yellow with black polka dots. Behind them came more troupes, none showing any sign of annoyance at the soot spewing from the exhaust pipes of the tractors.

"It's not like before," said José as we walked along the Malecón after the parade. "Before there were beautiful floats and costumes. The people used to dance in the streets. Tonight nobody was dancing. What's Cuba if people aren't dancing?"

I asked about Fidel. Why hadn't he come to Carnival?

"He's afraid of the people," said José.

"That they'll hurt him?"

"That they won't welcome him."

José thought that he knew that Cubans were beginning to point the finger at the man who had accepted credit and adoration during the good times. He agreed with Ramón that the perception of his sinking popularity was behind the cancellation of annual speeches. These days Castro appeared only at "controlled events," occasions where a captive audience of Party hacks or cowed workers was sure to cheer.

"But Fidel is a Cuban," I said. "Won't he want to dance and celebrate?"

José's answer had two parts.

Part one: the people were hoarding, not celebrating. José pointed to a long line of people waiting to fill plastic bags with discounted sandwiches. Two longer lines stretching from a vat on the sidewalk were for the crude, watery beer that the state rolled out and sold cheaply on special occasions. José said that the lines reminded Cubans of daily life, not fun.

Part two was shorter: "Fidel doesn't dance."

29

"Where does President Clinton live?" demanded José.

"The White House."

"What about the president of France?"

"I think it's called the Elysée Palace."

"And the president of England. Where does he live?"

"The prime minister lives at Number Ten Downing Street."

"What about Cuba's president?"

José folded his brawny arms across a yellow T-shirt too small to disguise a growing gut. Waiting for my answer, he stroked brown hair too short to comb and placed his palms behind his neck. Elbows butterflied, he leaned back and smirked.

"Nobody knows," cried José. "Nobody knows where Fidel Castro lives. Cuba is the *only* country in the world where the people don't know where the president lives!"

The vocal criticism sent my eyes skittering across the vicinity. Shaded by striped umbrellas, the other plastic tables at the café were empty. So was the space in front of us, a patch of asphalt where taxis and buses dumped tourists. There were potential eavesdroppers in the mottled apartment building on the far side of the parking lot. Dazed by boredom, the handful of day-dreamers leaning out of the gallery of elongated windows were well out of earshot. Nearby stood a chocolate-colored man whose hard shoulders tapered dramatically to a narrow waist.

"Carlos," José called out. "Do you know where Fidel lives?"

The human sculpture knew more than he indicated by his upturned palms and theatrical shrug. No, he couldn't give us Castro's address. He could, and did, repeat the rumor that the leader had thirty or more homes on the island. The property portfolio was more a security measure than a perk. "Many people who would like to kill" — a tap of fingers to imaginary epaulets — "so he has to sleep in a different place every night" was Carlos's interpretation of an excess that conflicted with communist asceticism.

Carlos had a point. The CIA had long since called off its not-so-secret efforts to bump off Fidel Castro. Others, however, picked up where the agency left off. Cuban emigrants in Miami and elsewhere made no secret of their urge to reclaim control of their homeland. A magnate called Mas Canosa openly expressed his desire to topple and replace Castro. Keeping enemies off balance kept him on the move.

My efforts elicited more curiosity than sympathy from Maria, an anesthesiologist. Although our relationship had nothing to do with medicine, it had everything to do with killing pain. The thirtyish woman had been alone since the day her husband decided not to return from an overseas assignment. Because he wouldn't return, she couldn't get a divorce. She, like myself, was on the prowl for relief.

The doctor looked angelic the night we met at a film festival party. Drawn into a tight bun, her golden hair glowed like a halo around the caramel contours of her face. Manicured eyebrows formed gentle crescents over brown eyes that glimmered above high cheekbones. Her lips were painted gold, the same color as the fine chains that hung from her neck to the top of a deep cleavage. Maria defined warmth and redefined beauty.

She fretted about our differences. She listened to Michael Bolton, Whitney Houston, and Barry Manilow. I didn't. She worried that a Cuban woman wouldn't know how to make love to an American man. She did. She liked to spend afternoons indoors. Evening meetings were my preference.

The gap we never bridged was the question of Fidel Castro. Maria saw more madness than method the first time I explained my interest in meeting him. My departure for Santiago de Cuba mystified her. "You will be very uncomfortable" were her parting words. Maria hadn't solved the puzzle by the time I returned to Havana.

"Why do you want to meet that man?" she asked.

"It's hard to explain."

"So you admire him?"

"No . . . Maybe . . . I want to see what he's like."

"He's evil."

"What do you mean, evil?"

"Look at what he has done to us."

I mentioned what I had learned in the past months. Wa__ _
she grateful that her rent was capped at one tenth of household
incomes? Would she even be alive without Fidel, whose pro-
grams had decreased infant mortality from 60 to 9 per 1,000 live
births? And what about education? Had she paid so much as
a peso for her schooling, from kindergarten through medical
school?

"Are you a communist?" asked Maria.

"Communists aren't the only ones who know statistics."

"I have my doubts." She softened her tone and said, "If you
do meet him, be careful. He's intelligent. Very intelligent."

"So?"

"If you meet him he will convince you to become a communist. He has that power over people." She tugged on one of her
hoop earrings and said, "Christopher, I don't want you to get
hurt."

Maria kissed my forehead and walked to the kitchen. I
turned on the television. A snowstorm of specks congealed into
a familiar image: Fidel filled my screen. Flaccid flesh hung from
a pale but weathered face. A dust of gray peppered his scraggly
beard. He pressed his index fingers together and to his lips.
Turning thoughts into words, he paused, unconcerned that
a full auditorium might grow impatient. Ready to speak, he
raised his eyebrows and spread his arms like a bear preparing to
hug the group.

"Without socialism," he said, "all of this would not be possible."

El Máximo rambled. He touched on the importance of steel
and the evils of capitalism. How he made the transition to
sugarcane productivity I'll never know. Nor did I catch the rele-
vance of references to José Martí and Antonio Maceo, a general
during Cuba's wars with Spain. It's possible that I was distracted
by the speaker's emphatic gesticulations and comically trilled *r*s.

"You are *not* going to watch this," snapped Maria. She extinguished the picture with a sharp twist of the television knob. A

quiet spell followed. She ended the tension when she said, "There are some things you can't understand."

"About Fidel Castro?"

"About Cuba. Cubans have two faces, one public face and one private face. The public face is for lying. We have to say we like Fidel and that we think his policies are working. If we don't, we have problems. They can hurt you at school. They can destroy your job. That doesn't mean that we're stupid. That doesn't mean that Cubans don't know what's going on in their own country."

She cited the Union of Young Communists. It was possible that youngsters who joined truly believed in the organization's ideals. It was impossible to imagine that members as old as thirty couldn't see the economic bellyflop produced by the state's adherence to defunct theories. Youngsters signed up anyway. In a country where everybody watched everybody, contriving an excuse could be tricky. A refusal to join, she said, could dim the prospects of the brightest student and the ablest worker.

"We have no choice. We have to pretend we like Fidel Castro."

The job of monitoring the charade fell to the CDR, the Committee for the Defense of the Revolution, the hybrid of block association and Spanish Inquisition. But the evil eye was going blind. Chewing Chiclets or wearing Nikes no longer brought reprimands from Big Brother. Starred and striped clothing wasn't a one-way ticket to jail. Once banned as a symbol of imperialist waste and Catholic authority, Christmas trees were all the rage.

Official easing only partly explained the outbreak of activities once deemed counterrevolutionary. There was no mistaking the scent that wafted into Joel's Santa Clara home late one afternoon. It was coffee, roasting not brewing. When I asked about the neighbor's brazen use of a controlled product, Joel confirmed that there was a time when the CDR would have had the police at the door within an hour. That time had passed.

"Nobody reports anymore," he said. "Everybody is doing something illegal, even the people in charge of the CDR. And everybody knows what his neighbors are doing. If you report him, he reports you."

Some of the motions of defending the Revolution were unavoidable. Screaming "Fuck Fidel!" was still a no-no. So were direct criticisms of the Party's policies. And Cubans were still expected to take turns on guard duty. Tapped by the CDR to patrol the neighborhood for an evening, nobody said no.

Mario was no different. Participating in the fraud infuriated my twenty-five-year-old neighbor. Not participating frightened the unemployed engineer, who couldn't afford fresh obstacles to entering the work force. Moaning about the three-hour shift, he leapt at my offer to keep him company.

Defending the Revolution required no more than a clipboard. The attached sheet named the zone and the number of the CDR. Mario added his name and that of the neighbor also assigned to the watch. He didn't write my name. Including an American might land him in hot water. The civil defense system was for catching, not entertaining, suspicious outsiders.

The duty sheet named the four stops on the patrol. Listed in a column on the left were bodega, medical clinic, kindergarten, and butcher shop. To the right were boxes for the hourly checks of each location as well as spaces in which watchmen were to describe anything odd. What might be odd? Mario took a limited view.

"In Havana, robbery is now normal," he said. "My house has been robbed three times in the last year."

"What if we see a robbery?"

"We write down that we saw a robbery. Then we call the police. But they won't come. They never do. Last week my neighbor saw two black men with machetes. They began to fight. When he saw them cut each other's heads he called the police. Do you know when the police came? One hour later! Do you know what they did? They touched the blood on the ground and said, 'It appears that this is the scene of a crime.' Appears! No wonder those assholes never catch anybody."

Round one began at ten P.M. Weeds grew in the gaping cracks of the dimly lit sidewalk that led us to the bodega. Though it looked impenetrable, the steel gate hadn't kept burglars from raiding the bodega five nights before. Seeing no trouble, Mario wrote down the time, 10:10, and moved on. At the clinic, he wrote that the door was closed but not the grate. All was quiet at the kindergarten and the butcher's.

I pointed out the open door of a hospital. "Not my problem," said Mario. I asked about the pharmacy. "Not my problem." When I noted a third potential disturbance, a ragged man digging through a Dumpster, Mario stopped in his tracks and said, "I'm responsible for four places. Anything else is not my problem." He smirked. "Anyway, in Cuba there are no homeless people. Fidel says so."

With half an hour to kill until round two of the circuit, we sat in front of the butcher's. Mario noted the irony of guarding a meat store that offered no meat. He used the recent crash of an overcrowded bus as further proof of Cuban incompetence. Just as he ran out of sarcasm he saw something genuinely odd, a white Lada driving the wrong way on a one-way street. The car swerved to a stop, and the driver opened the door and spilled onto the pavement. Stumbling to his feet, he peed on the car's door and drove away.

"A drunk Cuban," said Mario. "Nothing unusual."

"What if somebody yelled, 'Down with Fidel'?"

"That's their problem. Mine is to report on these four places."

At eleven o'clock we began another lap. Shuffling at a rate of five minutes per block took very little energy. Mario used his surplus to slam the state. He pointed out a shoeless man shivering in a filthy T-shirt and said that beggars were once unheard of in the capital. The police used to collect and carry the poor and the sick to central evaluation facilities. These days, more and more beggars had to fend for themselves.

"There has never been such a terrible time for Cuba," said Mario.

"It's a new year," I said.

"This year will be the same as last year and the year before and the year before."

"Maybe this is the year things get better."

"We used to think that way. We used to say that maybe this will be the year that things change, that we will be able to live like humans. Then the year passes and nothing happens. Cubans have stopped hoping."

Mario's neighbor, our fellow watchman, asked for a ten-peso note. I handed over a soiled brown paper. The front depicted a hero called Maximo Gomez. The reverse showed Fidel Castro's back as he raised an arm to make a point to a crowd in Revolution Square. The neighbor pointed to his opposite hand, which rested on the small of his back.

"Fidel's making promises," he said, "but you can see he's crossing his fingers."

At midnight we left for our third and final lap of the area. Ten minutes later Mario filled in the remainder of the log: 12:30 — Bodega; 12:35 — Clinic; 12:40 — Kindergarten; 12:45 — Butcher Shop. He handed the clipboard to his neighbor, who agreed to pass the log on to the CDR's chief watchdogs, the so-called Vigilance, the following day. Thinking again, Mario added a last note to the sheet: "The rest of the night was normal."

30

"THERE IS ONLY ONE WAY to know where the president is," said Diego. "When you see a lot of police, Fidel is nearby."

A useful tip?

Three policemen were patrolling Revolution Square the day I decided to inspect Castro's office. The cops eyeballed pedestrians wandering across the lot. The sharp blast of a whistle reminded me that bicycles weren't allowed. The officers converged on a man pedaling across the concrete. One checked his identification. The others skewered him with the kind of stern look normally reserved for hanging judges.

On the rise overlooking the square stood a lone soldier. Behind him, out of sight, was the Palace of the Revolution. Christened the Ministry of Justice in the year before Batista's ouster, it was to have been the scene of the film festival's bash. The rest of the year the place served as the headquarters of Cuba's Communist Party.

I saw the palace from a street running perpendicular to the square. The long, low building was no more impressive than a polytechnic. More noteworthy was the taut soldier guarding the foot of a drive that curved up the knoll. Lowering my head didn't keep me from spotting two more men wearing fatigues and carrying machine guns. Across the street stood four more commandos in maroon berets. How many more would emerge to tackle an American who sprinted up the hill?

Aggressive acts weren't all that sprung police traps. Diego told of driving with his uncle on an empty road on Havana's outskirts. A policeman stationed on the shoulder flagged down their car. They produced their identity booklets and followed directions, which included vacating the car, handing over the keys, and squatting in a shallow ditch beside the road. The policeman gestured for them to stay put. Three black Mercedes-Benzes hummed past. No longer in the path of Fidel Castro, Diego and his uncle were set free.

Another friend described a longer detention. Driving in an unfamiliar section of the capital, Juan waited at a stoplight. When the light turned green, he stayed put to wait for a signal for a left turn. Two red lights later he moved on but was immediately stopped by four men, two wearing uniforms. For half an hour they questioned him: Where was he from? Why was he here? Another thirty minutes passed before his release. The enforcers never explained their purpose. Only later did Juan learn that he had paused too long in front of Fidel's home for the night.

"What if they hadn't believed your story?" I asked.

Juan shuddered. Cuba's secret police weren't running a hospitality tent. Beatings were common. Cubans who didn't confess to crimes they might not have committed were tortured.

Kept in windowless cells, they were awakened at irregular intervals. Meals served in odd sequences deepened their disorientation. Shuffling prisoners between cold and hot cells sapped strength and will. The guilty cracked. So did the innocent.

There were other versions of life at Villa Marista, a Jesuit school converted into Cuba's best-known police station. Carlos, José's buddy, said that his father was an interrogator. Dad said that the secret police used a gorilla. Its teeth and fingernails removed, the ape was put in a dark room with the prisoners. The animal's heavy breathing was enough to make most captives talk.

"People are silent when they arrive," said Carlos. "When they leave it's impossible to shut them up."

I mentioned these unusual tactics to a history professor I met before leaving Havana. Rafael always told it straight. So I believed him when he said that he hadn't heard the gorilla story. And I believed his variation on the hearsay. He had heard that the animal was a reptile, that the police left prisoners in a dark room with a toothless crocodile.

"Terrifying, but not fatal," said Rafael.

"Do you think it's true?"

"Something happens there. I don't know what. And I don't want to find out," he said. "What's important is that Cubans *believe* the stories are true."

"You don't understand the fear in this country."

Seated on the stiff sofa in my apartment, Maria stirred the contents of her handbag. To the top rose a pack of cigarettes and a book of matches. Relaxed by a long drag, she continued.

"When Batista was in power, people whispered. They were afraid. If you said the wrong thing to the wrong person, the police might find out. It's no different now. Talking is still very dangerous. They can take away everything. They can put you in jail."

Maria echoed remarks I had heard elsewhere. In Santiago de Cuba, Francisco ranted about a neighbor who inquired about the fruit growing in his back yard. Where I saw friendliness he saw nosiness. My friend said that the woman had seen his garden hundreds of times. What she wanted to see was me. Having spotted a foreigner next door, she wanted to know more.

Pepé lodged a similar complaint in Holguín. "Here you can live near somebody for years and not know what *type* of person they are," he said. "Anybody can be a spy."

He gave me an example. Two months earlier an acquaintance of his son's had dropped by. He sat in a rocker and accepted a cup of tea. The scene was purely social until the man began mouthing off. "I'm going north," he said, a phrase that meant "I'm heading for Florida." The family listened, nodded, but didn't join in. The following week Pepé spotted the acquaintance when, passing the Ministry of the Interior, he saw the man filling his gas tank at the state's pump.

"The police send people who pretend they are counterrevolutionaries. When you join them, they denounce you," said Pepé. "This is the fear we live with."

Maria nodded knowingly when I told her the story. After placing a second cigarette in her lips she asked what I thought would happen were she to walk into the street and denounce the government.

"I would be put in jail," she said. "Maybe not today. Or tomorrow. But they would come to my home or the hospital. Cuba looks calm. But they watch. They listen."

She told me how her husband had once been called to his boss's office. The supervisor said that he had been visited by two men from the secret police. They said that the husband had spoken to a woman who worked for a human rights organization. Did he know her? No. Shown a picture, he did recognize a woman who parked her car in the same lot as his Lada. Their regular exchange of greetings and pleasantries had been reported.

The doctor took her own medicine by avoiding acts that might be misconstrued. When I proposed a stroll along the Malecón she proposed we stay home, alone. When I wanted to go to the market she wanted to make coffee. Frustrated by our confinement, I recognized the irony of protesting long afternoons in the embrace of a lovely woman. I also saw that Maria was the only Cuban afraid to be seen with me. Was I missing something?

"You don't understand Cuba," she said. "This is a very tense society."

State surveillance was part of the reason for the tension. Hunger was another part, as I learned while delivering a letter from America to a woman called Carmen. My first glimpse of the thirty-year-old was through the sliver of a door cracked open just enough to examine a stranger. Ruthless brown eyes sized me up. When I introduced myself, her right hand pushed open the door while her left grabbed for the neck of a snarling dog. Carmen dragged the animal to another room.

Her exit left me alone with an old woman and an even older man. Both were as thin and hard as the wooden chairs in which they sat. Pale, puckered skin hung from the bones of their arms. Shins protruded like stilts below the hem of faded clothing. The lack of flesh turned their wrinkled faces into fields of angles. Neither spoke, although the woman did bob her head after an unsuccessful attempt to lift her hand.

"What do you think of Cuba?" Carmen asked on her return, twisting her long black hair into a ponytail.

"I like the people."

"Cubans are good people," she said, "but hungry."

"One pound of yucca used to cost seventy centavos," cried the old woman, Carmen's mother. "Now it's ten pesos. Ten pesos for one pound of yucca!"

"These are bad times," said Carmen.

"We only get this much oil for one month," said her mother, holding a bony index finger an inch above her thumb. "Have you ever tried to cook without oil?"

Carmen allowed that the worst was behind them. Food had been even more scarce in 1993. Some days her only meal was *sopa de gallo*, rooster soup. Meatless, the concoction's main ingredient was water, which was mixed with sugar when there was nothing else to eat. She raised a pinkie to show me how skinny she had been. Having regained five of the twenty pounds she lost following the fall of the Soviet Union, she showed no optimism about the other fifteen. Rations had increased. But she deprived herself rather than her parents and five-year-old son. Saved from starvation, Carmen was still hungry.

"Can't you buy food at the markets?"

"With what?" cried Carmen. Sweeping her hand across the decrepit room, she shrieked, "Does it look like we have any money?"

Her problem was her job. She worked in a dance school, where there was nothing to steal and resell. Until she found another angle, the family would have to survive on her earnings and her parents' pensions. About five hundred pesos a month, the total was a fraction of what they needed to buy food at the markets, which, like a string of other government decisions, hadn't improved her life.

"Thirty-seven years of this shit," she said, turning to indicate the world outside her window. "Thirty-seven years of Fidel Castro and we're still hungry."

Carmen's candor caught me off guard. I was accustomed to hearing griping about shortages of food, power, and transport. Sarcasm and black humor were replacing baseball as the national pastime. But nobody had dared criticize Castro by name — at least not in my presence. I asked how she dared knock him.

"Everybody criticizes him. We didn't used to. But now we agree."

"Agree on what?"

"That he's bad. BAD!"

My eyes fell on Carmen's parents. The skeletal couple had nodded off. Would ten dollars' worth of food help their revival? What about twenty? I had two ten-dollar notes in my wallet. How could I withhold an amount that, while small to me, would mean a lot to them? I folded the money into a small bundle and passed it to Carmen. I can't remember what I said.

I can, however, remember Carmen's reaction. She didn't shout "Hallelujah!" She didn't even say thanks. She slid the money out of my fingers and into the breast pocket of her sleeveless blouse. Once free, her hand reached for mine. She lifted my fingers to her face and looked at me while kissing my palm. Her eyes didn't move as she placed my hand on the pocket. The heft of her breast surprised me, as did the length of time she pressed my hand against it.

"I have a girlfriend," I said.

"Thank you," she said, releasing but not removing my palm. "Can't you do something?"

"No. Only *he* can do something."

Mrs. Guerra stopped charging me for her oversugared coffee. Kind though she was, captivating though she may have found me, there was no overlooking the reason for my freebies. Deterred by the long lines at the state money exchanges, accustomed to mixing with black marketeers, I had begun buying pesos on the street. The hustlers who haunted commercial areas looked unreliable, so the pudgy granny became my banker.

Brief chats followed our deals. We talked about her sister in Miami and about the cold snap that had forced her to wear a sweater for the first time in years. A deep breath usually marked the end of our conversation. We watched the street and hoped for distraction. The passing of a Toyota elicited a comment on Cuba's rich. A neighbor stopped to discuss the proposed income tax.

Another neighbor, a woman of sixty whose dark hair flopped around her ears, brought more gossip. A few days earlier, a resident of my building had come home to an empty apartment. Gone were the television, the stereo, and the refrigerator whose acquisition had taken years of wheeling and dealing. The burglars took every stick of furniture and every stitch of clothing for the family of three. From the bathroom they removed the towels, soap, and a half-bottle of shampoo.

"The shampoo," gasped Mrs. Guerra.

"Do you think it's true?" I asked.

The women gave me a look I confused with disdain. What they felt, however, was pity. Their hearts bled for a man unable to see the obvious.

"Can't you see what is happening in this country?" said the neighbor, Celia.

"What do you mean?"

"For a long time everybody was poor. We suffered, but we suffered together. Cuba felt like a place of equals, a society," said Boris, who gurgled with joy the day I returned to his apartment. "Now some people have money and others don't have any. It's destroying society. Cuba is in crisis."

The assertion didn't jibe with the view from our seats in front of the apartment. Neighbors paused for friendly chats. The produce sellers awaited customers for their green oranges. The freckled woman who lectured me on ration books was sitting in the shade beside a girlfriend. This was a crisis?

"Cuba looks tranquil on the outside," said Celia. "The crisis is inside."

She pointed to my building. "Look at that. It hasn't been painted for thirty years." Farther down the block she indicated a home whose face was riddled with fissures. "This place is falling apart and *they*" — two taps to imaginary shoulderboards — "don't care."

Keen to prove her point, Celia took hold of my elbow and led me down the block to a two-story home set back from the sidewalk. A marble staircase led to a front door carved from dark, heavy wood. Inside, I found a living room beneath towering ceilings. Molded columns supported the roof over the terrace to the left. To the right, a chandelier hung above the dining room's antique table and chairs. Oil portraits in ornate frames hung from the walls.

Where I saw style, Celia saw deterioration. She was angry at her inability to maintain a decent home. The feeling ignited criticism of the faded paint, the fissured walls, and a ceiling from which a slab of plaster hung like a bat. The sound of running water drew me to the bathroom's open door. Why was the porcelain tub full? Never certain when, or for how long, the water supply would be cut, the family kept a reserve.

Celia was no less critical of the state of her mother, a wrinkled but sturdy woman who emerged with wet hands from the kitchen. "My mother has headaches. But we can't get aspirin. She also has kidney problems. But there's no medicine for them. She's a disaster. And my husband is a doctor. Imagine, he's a doctor and he can't get medicine. What kind of country has doctors but no medicine? Only Cuba."

Celia looked at the fist that had formed for her oratorical flourish. She opened her hand to stroke her hair. Showing me to a sofa, she excused herself and left to make coffee. Her mother stayed behind but didn't speak. She nodded repeatedly and widened her green eyes, as if confirming all that her daughter had said and would say.

"You want to learn something about this country? About this government?" said Celia as she returned carrying a tray with two china cups, a pot of coffee, and a sugar bowl.

She threw her ration book onto the coffee table. She showed me the empty lines that represented unfilled rations. The necessities that had arrived weren't enough. Like Carmen, Celia moaned that she lacked the money to buy what she needed on the free market.

"But do you think *they* eat like us?" she asked. "This is supposed to be a society without classes. It's not. Fidel Castro and his friends are a special class. They have food, cars, clothes. They travel abroad. They live like kings. Kings!"

The old woman scurried to comfort her daughter, whose spitting rage turned to tears. The mother wrapped an arm around her shoulders, stroked her forehead, and led her to the kitchen. She returned alone.

"Celia says more than she ought to," she said.

I wanted to leave. I wanted to slide under the door and leave the women to cope. Before I could make an excuse or a move toward the exit, the middle-age mother returned.

"I met him once," said Celia. "I met Fidel Castro. My daughter and I went to visit a cousin, who's married to an official in the Party. We were walking up the stairs to their apartment. I heard footsteps and looked up."

"Fidel?"

"Fidel was right there. In front of me. He said hello, but I couldn't speak. I couldn't even breathe. I just stood there."

Celia showed me how her shoulders had clenched, how she had clutched the top of her blouse with both hands, how she had looked up, wide-eyed, as if she were staring down the barrel of a pistol. To a small woman, the man known for his size seemed enormous. But there was more. He had an aura, an invisible field of charisma, that overwhelmed her.

"There's an air around him. You cannot describe it. But you feel that you are in the presence of power."

Celia's daughter ended their standoff. Surprised but not debilitated, she managed to greet the leader, who continued past them. His presence lingered. Celia needed the better part of an hour to calm down.

"That was the only time you saw him?"

"Thank God."

"Thank God?"

"If I saw him again, I would try to strangle that man."

Celia was disgusted by the deterioration of her home, her neighborhood, and her society. She resented her inability to buy milk for her grandchildren and medicine for her mother. She also resented the men who put her down and kept her there. And there was something else.

"He killed my son," she said.

Her mother covered her ears and screamed: "Celia! Celia! Don't say that. I can't hear such things."

"Fidel Castro killed my son."

"How?"

"During 'the special period' he lost so much weight, he had no energy, he had no work. Three years with no work! What would you do? He got so depressed. We couldn't help him. We couldn't do anything for him. There was no life for him in Cuba. He couldn't see any future . . ."

Celia's face fell into her lap to muffle her sobs.

31

OBSTACLES LITTERED Vedado's westbound streets. The driver of a city bus showed no mercy for a lone cyclist. Forced onto a sidewalk, I paused to consider faded red letters that said SOCIALISM OR DEATH! Death was the choice of the dog stretched across the side of the narrow street just beyond the billboard. He didn't flinch when my front tire met his mangy fur.

The rot vanished when I crossed a steel bridge and entered a district called Miramar. Children played beneath the banyan trees that shaded a tranquil park. Nor was quiet the only oddity. There was no propaganda. Fifth Avenue, the main street, wasn't decorated by slogans such as DIGNITY NEVER DIES and LOVE IS THE BEST LAW. Split by a narrow park, the four-lane boulevard was flanked by robust trees. Freshly painted walls separated empty sidewalks and the grounds of mansions.

Cuba's magnates were long gone. The rich had been replaced by the powerful as embassies took up residence in homes worthy of Rockefellers. The yellow star on a red background identified a set of pastel buildings as Vietnamese. The Swiss worked in the mansion flying a white cross on red. I didn't recognize a flag whose center, a black star, was set on stripes of red, yellow, and green. Only a photograph of Ayatollah Khomeini saved me from mistaking Iran's embassy.

Harder to mistake was Miramar's security force. A squat concrete tower stood at every intersection along Fifth Avenue. Cops manned every post, but they looked anything but alert. Officers struggling to stay awake shuffled their feet. One had nodded off in a seat overlooking the avenue. My guess was that they were several uppers away from stopping a jaywalker. My guess was wrong.

The scream of a whistle stopped me cold. I turned and saw a uniformed youth pointing a ramrod arm at me. Hard eyes glared from the shade of his blue baseball cap. Capable muscles were evident beneath his long-sleeve shirt. When he spoke, he did so with confidence.

"Get off the bicycle."

I followed instructions.

"Your identification."

I offered my passport.

The officer balked at the sight of an American passport. But he took the dark blue booklet and looked hard at my picture. Watching him slowly riffle through the pages, I saw myself as a participant in a scene played out thousands of times every day.

Cop stops, a part of life all over Cuba, were a constant nuisance in Havana. At least once an hour I saw a policeman stop a local, demand identification, and, after several skeptical frowns, send the innocent on his way. Once a day I saw a teenager led away in handcuffs. Near Old Havana a troop of paramilitaries regularly filled a truck with suspected delinquents. Heightening resentment was the fact that the officers had been recruited from eastern Cuba. Harassed and intimidated, Habaneros felt themselves under the thumb of an occupying force.

"No bicycles on Fifth Avenue," said the cop who stopped me.

"I didn't know. Sorry."

The officer narrowed his eyes. He warned me not to get back on the bike. Colleagues farther down the avenue *would* arrest a repeat offender. The cop returned to his perch and picked up the handset of a telephone, presumably to alert others to a troublemaker. Walking, I imagined that the policemen on every corner were itching for the chance to crack down on a man who dared to remount a bicycle.

I also imagined getting a glimpse of Fidel Castro. I owed my renewed hope to my friend the history professor. A resident of Vedado, he had a sister in Siboney, a neighborhood west of the city's center. He loved his sister, but he hated visiting her.

"I've been there many times. Every time I go, or almost every time, the police stop me, look at my identification, ask me where I'm going. I've never had any trouble. But you never know. The police are so stupid. Blacks. From the east."

"Why do they stop you?"

"Because Fidel lives there."

I needed a few minutes to get the story straight. Everybody knew that the president had a home near or in Siboney. Residents of the leafy district had a more detailed read on his whereabouts. Stepped-up security in a neighborhood populated by several of the Party's hacks made their lives more miserable than usual whenever El Máximo was in residence. Only at the end of the tale, which included directions to the house, did the professor see what I might do with the information.

"Don't go there," he warned.

My ride to Siboney wasn't about meeting Fidel. Having seen the security around the Palace of the Revolution, I didn't expect to walk up the president's drive, knock on the door, and ask to borrow a cup of sugar. I did, however, expect to be able to get a sense of his neighborhood and, maybe, just maybe, a glimpse of one of his homes.

The roundabout at the end of Fifth Avenue marked the halfway point of the journey. I resumed pedaling and headed toward a long billboard whose message wished Cubans happiness in the thirty-seventh year of the Revolution. Beneath the propaganda stood two policemen and four Cuban men. One of the officers flipped through the detainees' identification booklets. The other motioned for me to join the group.

He lost interest in me during the seconds it took to extract my passport. Glancing over my shoulder, he had seen something more troublesome. He stiffened, as did his partner, and tugged on my shirt to move me even farther from the street. The civilians also went rigid.

I turned in time to see a car hum by our spot. Sleek and black, it was a Mercedes. Close behind were two more, just as sleek and just as black. The triplets disappeared to the west, toward Siboney. Moving fast, windows closed, the cars hid their passengers. Still, nobody doubted what we had seen.

I looked to my fellow prisoners for confirmation. Three were gazing at the shrinking sight of the motorcade. A fourth caught my incredulous look. He nodded once. Then he stroked a long, imaginary beard.

The back-to-back cop stops unnerved me. Weak knees were enough to send me back to my apartment. Once home, I decided that the stops were bad luck, not bad karma. I would make a second attempt to drive by the president's place.

Days later I set off at the crack of noon. Somebody had cleared the dead dog from the street in Vedado. In Miramar, I knew not to cycle down Fifth Avenue. The sign wishing Cubans a good year still loomed, but the cops were gone from the roundabout. I continued down lanes that traced the capital's shore.

Ten or so miles from home, I came to a thin river. Just before a bridge I took the left turn described by the professor and found myself on a narrow street. A pack of boys on bicycles waved as they rode in the opposite direction. In the yard of a school, children chased one another and laughed. Adults danced to salsa blasting from speakers the size of suitcases. A right turn took me onto a two-lane road.

Water towers were the most prominent structures in the open spaces beside the pavement. Trees bristled with fruit. Palms wavered in a steady wind. I passed a man laboring to move his heavy Chinese bike. Two other cyclists pedaled leisurely in the opposite direction. Their calm made me wonder whether I had taken the wrong turn. Or was there simply nothing to worry about? Were the rumors that Castro lived behind a wall of armed men false?

The thought died when I saw barbed wire rimming the fields. The lines of prickly metal weren't the only obstruction. Barriers marked DO NOT ENTER blocked the entrances to the roads between the fields on the left. I stiffened at the sight of a soldier holding an automatic rifle and wearing a rigid stare.

Suddenly aware of how foreign I looked in a tank top and shorts, I felt the involuntary clenching of my shoulders. My feet pumped harder. I wondered whether my nervousness was noted by a second soldier, a muscular man guarding a low fence with no house in sight. He held his gun chest-high and glared like a hawk tracking a mouse.

I didn't expect him to shoot — at least not without warning. I did think the men in green wouldn't hesitate to stop anybody who appeared to be sizing up the area. Though I had a strong urge to return to the main road, I had a stronger suspicion that passing a post more than once was a bad idea. Ten minutes elapsed before I dared to make a U-turn. When I did, a road on the right looked as if it might lead back to Fifth Avenue.

Where it led was directly to two more men in fatigues. The pair rose from their seats in the shade the moment they saw me. Guns in hands, they looked ready to stop me. What would they say? What would I say when asked why I was in the area? Would they believe me?

Unprompted, I swung my leg over the seat of the bike and walked toward the armed men. I needed a reason to be there and a way to get out. Both were inherent in my question: "Which way is Fifth Avenue?"

"Straight ahead," said the older of the pair.

"No problem," said his partner.

More security — three policemen and two patrol cars — en route suggested that the president wasn't around. The area didn't fit Cubans' description of the force field around Castro. Did he live around here? Maybe. Was I going to meet him? No way.

"Enemy!" shouted Diego's mother.

"¡Yanqui!" cried Diego himself.

"Blam! Blam! Blam!" spat a tot with a plastic pistol.

Diego said that there had been "an incident." The state-run radio was saying that the previous day, at the very time I was pedaling around Castro's neighborhood, two Cuban jets had shot down two civilian aircraft from the U.S. An early report said it had been an accident. Later, it was no accident. Then the word was that the Air Force didn't know the identity of the intruders. By noon the announcer was saying that the planes belonged to Brothers to the Rescue, a Florida outfit founded to save rafters at sea. All versions put the home side in the right: the intruders were in Cuban air space.

"Do you think it's true?" I asked.

"Even our government couldn't create a lie so big."

Details followed on the evening news, which I watched at the home of the professor. The dead pilots had been dubbed "pirates." Out to undermine the Revolution, they were intending to litter the Malecón with anti-Castro leaflets. The following night's broadcast featured an interview with a Cuban who had infiltrated the infiltrators. His assessment of the dead pilots? Counterrevolutionaries.

The spin made sense. What government wouldn't try to justify the most uneven fight — MiGs shooting down Cessnas — since Norman Schwarzkopf booted the Revolutionary Guard back to Baghdad? Less comprehensible were the reactions of Cubans such as José, who took me to Carnival, and his buddy Jorge.

The friends were squared off like prizefighters when I visited their hangout in Old Havana. I saw José, his arms folded, withstanding a verbal blitzkrieg. The force of his argument swelled the veins in Jorge's neck. Flecks of saliva flew from his mouth. He threw up his arms and walked a full twenty yards away from José before returning with more force than before. José was ready.

"The Americans will destroy us," he said.

"No, no, no," screamed Jorge. "You know nothing."

"If we resist, the war will be over in twenty-four hours. If we don't resist, the result will be the same."

"Who had the best army in Latin America? Who sent troops to Angola? To Nicaragua? Cuba! Maybe the Americans will win. But they will lose a lot of people."

"Bullshit! They will use bombs. They will flatten Havana."

"Americans have no balls. Cubans do. We can resist them."

"The Americans —"

"I can't listen to this shit. I'm no communist. But I'm tired of hearing that everything good comes from America. Everybody is forgetting the good in Cuba. That's what we have to fight for."

The friends also differed on the question of whether the move was wise. Jorge was fiercely nationalistic. Cuba had every right to kill the intruders. Screaming, he insisted that no country, *no country,* could allow repeated, *repeated,* invasions of its air space. Would the United States? Of course not. To allow the flyovers to continue would be a national embarrassment. Fidel had no choice but to shoot down the planes and save Cuba's reputation.

"Reputation!" shouted José. "I don't want a reputation. I want food."

José's was a more practical view. Yes, Cuba had the right to kill intruders. But one had to consider the effects of violence. Thousands of Cubans survived on cash from relatives in America. The country couldn't afford any act that might affect the remittances. It couldn't afford to set back the long-awaited end of the embargo on trade with the U.S. When the chest-thumping died, the people would find themselves prouder but hungrier.

The friends then found an issue on which they agreed completely: in Cuba, decisions were made by one man, Fidel Castro. He hadn't pulled the trigger. But he had certainly authorized the shooting.

José began to sing. The song — "Arriba de la Bola," "On Top of the Ball" — was one I heard all day every day. The refrain — *"Ahora soy el rey. Si te gusta, bien. Y si no, también"* — echoed through urban alleys and rural fields. Most Cubans just liked the music. Others identified with the bravado of the singer. A few, like José, saw the refrain as a mockery of Castro's attitude toward his people: "Now I'm the king. If you like it, fine. And if not, the same."

"How can Fidel Castro still be in power?"

The history professor didn't answer right away. He leaned back in the armchair of his airy but artless living room and

ed a snowy white beard. When he did speak, his answer
ght me off guard; I had anticipated an explanation of the
suffocating power of a heavily policed state.

"Cubans ask themselves the same question," he said. "We
may not like him, but we need him."

He linked Castro's longevity to the history of the island.
Cuba had always been under somebody's thumb. For nearly
four hundred years Spanish royalty and traders called the shots
taken by governors on the ground. The U.S., which began
wielding commercial clout in the 1800s, took charge at the turn
of the twentieth century. A senator from Connecticut "legal-
ized" decades of dominance when he backed a bill that gave
Washington the right to meddle with Cuba. The U.S. built the
base at Guantánamo Bay to cow Cubans seeking sovereignty.
Cuban leaders played along and lined their pockets.

Castro, said the professor, appeared to alter the pattern. He
removed the grips of overseas powers for a time. He tried to
eradicate the past by confiscating businesses and land owned by
foreigners. He pledged a Cuba run by and for Cubans. He also
monopolized power, a move that effectively sustained the pater-
nalism that had cheated Cubans out of the chance to determine
their own fate.

Fidel was an all-powerful father. He fed, housed, and clothed
his people. He built hospitals to keep them healthy and schools
to make them smart. Worshiped by the destitute-turned-poor,
Castro made himself the repository for a nation's self-esteem.
Soviet backing and a knack for enraging America elevated him
in the eyes of the world and his people. Cubans proudly pointed
out pictures of their president standing beside the likes of Boris
Yeltsin and Ziang Zemin.

Not that Cubans didn't recognize Castro's wild side. I remembered the man who referred to the attack on Moncada as
"the day Fidel went crazy." A painter who lived in Havana offered a similar analysis, based on the legend that Castro had
begged Khrushchev for permission to launch the missiles aimed
at America. When the dust settled after the downing of the

Cessnas, Cubans agreed that their leader had, once again, been rash.

Still, Castro remained the father to people who had never known an alternative. The professor said that his office at the Palace of the Revolution received more letters than Santa Claus did at the North Pole. In August 1994 the president drove to the scene of the riots against his rule. His presence sent an immediate calm over the crowd. A local expression summed up the national need for coddling: "Cubans take milk from the tit."

The professor told me another local saying: "Up there, God. Down here, Fidel."

"What if Fidel died tomorrow?"

"That," he said, "is a very scary thought."

Castro had named his successor. When he died, power would pass to his younger brother, who had headed the army since the Revolution. Known for his long ride on his brother's coattails, Raúl wasn't expected to be able to fill Fidel's shoes. Nobody could. Years of hogging the spotlight and eliminating rivals meant that only Fidel, a man of unquestionable moral authority and undeniable personal charisma, could hold the country together. And when the glue was gone?

"There could be a war," said the professor.

He believed what he said. He painted a picture in which Cubans based in Florida invaded or armed dissidents on the island. Another scenario involved a power struggle between rival branches of the security apparatus. The army was already at odds with the Ministry of the Interior. Who could say whether the two armed camps could coexist without Fidel?

The professor saw other sources of disorder. The moment power changed hands, the reprisals would begin. Fathers would seek revenge for sons jailed for anything from carrying dollars to chewing gum. Snitches would be the first targets. Neighbors would attack neighbors. A witch hunt for the secret police wasn't impossible.

"Fidel has been in control for so long that Cubans don't know how to act without him," said the professor. "If people could do whatever they wanted, there's no telling what would happen. It could be chaos."

"Chaos" triggered memories of Santa Clara. Experience told me to expect a long wait for a truck to Cienfuegos. I also counted on orderly boarding when transport did turn up. But the Yellow Man never came. Without an authority figure, the order defining the society of hitchhikers collapsed. People lunged for the truck and tore at one another. One man was all that kept Cubans from behaving like wolves around raw meat.

Cubans each had a way to sum up their situation. The sculptor in Camagüey ended a conversation about his rotting mural by saying, "This is a strange country." Mario, the unemployed engineer, was more blunt when we talked about Cuba's conflicting urges. He noted that people wanted Castro dead but needed him alive. Then he sighed and said, "We're fucked."

The professor put it more delicately: "Cubans are like people watching a movie about their own lives. They know there's a bad ending. They just don't know which bad ending."

"And there's nothing you can do?"

"We have to wait."

32

"A Cuban is a man with two shopping bags."

I raised an eyebrow in the direction of the husky teenager seated beside me on the stoop opposite the Hotel Capri.

The freelance philosopher adjusted his baseball cap and bowed his arms to pantomime an overburdened shopper. "In one bag is fear. In the other bag is hunger. To survive, the Cuban must balance the two bags."

Not bad, said the slight nod of my head. Not bad at all.

"Cuba is a tide that rises and falls. To survive, the Cuban must know how to stay on the boat."

I nodded again.

"Cuba is like a ball on a roulette wheel. It has to stop. But nobody knows where, and nobody knows when."

The teenager fell silent. Turning to hear another encapsulation of life on the island, I saw that he was gone. Not physically. Mentally. The bursts of insight had given way to a trance. His eyes were open but vacant. He didn't blink when the neon lights spelling SALON ROJO went dark. Nor did other sights distract him. The man checking his watch, the dog nibbling an itch, and the fisherman hawking his catch all attracted my attention. The teenager simply gazed through the intruders on the stillness.

The others on the corner shared the stupor. Like the teenager, they stared dead ahead into the night. They, like the teenager, were detached from the place and from each other. Nobody talked. But for deep sighs and occasional scratching, the Cubans might have been frozen alive.

Not that the scene was unfamiliar. Nearly four months on the island had taught me that idling was a big part of Cubans' routine. The first indication that downtime was plentiful was the dozens of people clustered on the sea wall during my first stroll along the Malecón. The unemployed and furloughed workers who packed the parks in Santiago de Cuba were just as hard to miss. Along the Central Road, travelers languishing until the arrival of transport were as common as potholes.

Activity would have surprised me more than the inertia on the steps opposite the hotel. Time and again I had wondered how Cubans got out of bed without a double dose of Prozac. Where did the hungry, hopeless people find the will to laugh? Equally mysterious was the source of the energy locals summoned when salsa began to play. The sound of music brought people to their feet. They danced for hours and, when the congas stopped, begged for more.

There was one exception to the late-night lethargy. We met when I rose from the steps and walked the fifteen paces to the neighborhood's snack stand. Clothes worn, muscles relaxed, he looked like the zombies on the steps. The difference was in his eyes. Sensitive to every movement in the vicinity, the man wearing the Chicago White Sox cap was on edge.

Ricardo called himself a hustler. Rum was his main business. He wagged a bottle labeled Havana Club and boasted that the booze was homemade. Production began with a trip to Matanzas, where workers at the Havana Club plant sold rum's most important ingredient, syrup distilled from sugarcane. Back home in Havana, he added the concentrate to water in his bathtub. The mix went into bottles, which he decorated with stolen labels and caps. Produced for two dollars, the rum sold for five.

The bootlegger had a second line. He grimaced at the word "pimp"; Ricardo preferred "middleman." Cuban girls, he said, were desperate to lay their hands on tourists' cash. Tourists were nearly as desperate to lay their hands on Cuban girls. So Ricardo helped boy meet girl, earning ten dollars every time he landed a foreigner on behalf of one of the eight girls he represented. He charged another fee for leading couples to nearby apartments whose owners rented rooms by the hour, at any hour.

"People rent their homes for sex?"

"They need money."

"I thought Vedado was a good neighborhood."

"In Cuba, nothing is as it appears."

Ricardo cut short our chat when a sedan stopped at the curb. Two local girls were bouncing in time to salsa on the car's stereo. With them was a pair of men from southern Europe. The hustler consulted the driver, who said that the passengers needed short-term accommodations. He boarded the car and disappeared into the night, though not before bequeathing to me his rum, which, because he used ingredients from Havana Club's distillery, tasted like the real thing.

I looked at the bottle. So did Rosa, the woman seated beside me. She took a gulp and began talking about her time in the capital. I wondered how I would feel in her place. Transplanted from a small town in the east, Rosa had watched her teenage sister disappear night after night, with man after man. Tonight she was with a flabby Spaniard. Where had they gone? For how long? Rosa knew only that she was staying put until her sister returned.

"Do you want a girl?" she asked.

"I have a girlfriend."

It was a lie. Several hours earlier Maria had killed our relationship. A breakup was inevitable. I had to leave Cuba; my visa expired in less than a week. She had to stay; she had a daughter, a family, and a career on her native island. Still, the ending caught me off guard.

I missed the first hint of trouble. Maria telephoned to cancel a plan to go to a nightclub. She didn't want to have dinner. She did want to talk. An hour later, the doctor was at my doorstep. Suddenly spooked by the apartment she normally refused to leave, she drove us to an open-air bar along the Malecón.

We listened to the surf sloshing into the sea wall. Then we talked about my grandmother, whose frustration with the slow arrival of an imminent death made her moan for pills that would end her life. I was surprised that Maria didn't offer to sell me a lethal dose; Cuban doctors were known to deal their drugs. The conversation skipped to suicide. Once Cuba's seventh most common cause of death, it now ranked fourth or fifth.

"People can't cope with the pressure of life in Cuba," said Maria. After a pause to focus on the sea, she continued. "I'm a doctor. In any other country I would have a good life. Am I wrong? Here I can barely live. Is that fair?"

Maria wavered between anger and gratitude. She dwelled on the unfairness of a system that turned the best and the brightest into an impoverished elite. Then she told me how she counted her blessings every time she went home to her building, which was inhabited by laborers. When her mind turned to the privileges available to people outside of Cuba, she resumed cursing her luck.

"It's a prison," she said, gesturing to the necklace of lights along the boulevard. "Beautiful, but prison."

I agreed.

"You belong there. I belong here. We don't belong together."

The words echoed in my ears. Maria's eyes welled with tears. They continued to resonate when, after we parted, I walked along the Malecón. The scent of sadness followed me to dinner, to a salsa club, and into bed. Unable to sleep I began to walk. I stopped opposite the Hotel Capri, where the company of people with heavier loads than mine provided a perverse sense of comfort.

The solace ended abruptly. A police car stopped in front of the stoop. Hailed by a uniformed officer in the front seat, I had no choice but to approach and follow orders. The cop directed me to the back seat, where I found the hustler, grinning. Chauffeured past the impassive gazes of the people gathered opposite the hotel, I scolded myself for telling Ricardo about my attempts to find Fidel.

The white Lada turned right at the end of Twenty-first Street. A left at the bottom of an incline put us on La Rampa, where we passed a dollar store on the right and the office of Cuba's airline on the left. As the driver turned left along the Malecón, I remembered the legends of Villa Marista. Was I headed toward the toothless crocodile, the clawless gorilla, or just a summary expulsion from the country?

My agitation contrasted with Ricardo's ease. The hustler-turned-informant griped about the two girls he had helped to find spare beds. "Ambitious" was how he described prostitutes who tried to cheat him out of his commission. He unwound by bragging about bedding the girl in the room next to his honeymoon suite. He topped his tale with another, this one about humping a woman an hour before his wedding.

The lawmen in the front burst out laughing. When the last snicker died, the officer in the passenger seat asked whether I was married. My answer — "No" — drew a round of praise.

"Keep your freedom," advised Ricardo.

"Wise man," said the driver.

"Marriage is like handcuffs," said the other officer.

Not handcuffed, charged with no crime, I wondered why I was cruising down the Malecón in a police car. A U-turn compounded my confusion. Now headed back to Havana's center, I asked a question of my own.

"Ricardo, are you a policeman?"

The hustler erupted into a fit of giggles. He grabbed my knee to keep from falling into my lap. How the driver kept on course I'll never know. He and his sidekick were quaking beyond control.

"This guy is the biggest delinquent in Vedado," said the driver.

"The biggest crook in Havana," said his partner. "I know. He's my cousin."

The cousin reached back and grabbed the bottle lying near the center of the rear seat. He twisted off the top and tipped rum down his throat. The driver did the same before passing the bottle back to Ricardo. I took a swig in the hope that the alcohol would improve my grip on reality.

I thought I had it straight. Ricardo wasn't a cop. I wasn't under arrest. The hustler hadn't snitched on me. He had simply returned to the stoop to pick up his rum and his American buddy, and to take both for an after-hours joy ride.

"Why are you in Cuba?" asked the cousin.

"He came to meet Fidel," answered Ricardo.

The crack ignited a fresh explosion of hysterics.

"The *Yanqui* wants to meet Fidel."

"Sure. Let's ALL go meet Fidel!"